UNION-CASTLE LINE
A Fleet History

WINCHESTER CASTLE (TH)

UNION-CASTLE LINE
A Fleet History

by
Peter Newall

Published by
Carmania Press

*This book is dedicated to all the men and women who served with
Union Steamship Company Ltd., Castle Packets Company Ltd.,
and Union-Castle Mail Steamship Company Ltd.*

Published by

Carmania Press

Unit 202, Station House, 49 Greenwich High Road, London SE10 8JL, Great Britain
http://www.anthonycooke.force9.co.uk

ISBN 0 9534291 4 8 First published 1999
British Library Cataloguing for Publication Data
A Catalogue Record of this book is available from the British Library

Artwork production by Judy and Peter Newall
Printed by The Amadeus Press, Huddersfield, Yorkshire

CONTENTS

FOREWORD

Very many years ago I was asked by the late Adlard Coles - a name then well known in shipping - to produce a small book on the Union-Castle Line. A very slim volume indeed! Now Peter Newall has produced what promises to be the definitive book on this famous company.

For the greater part of a century the mailships of the Union-Castle Line could be recognised from afar by their distinctive livery. The lavender grey was unique and made an eye-stimulating contrast to the funnel red. This had history behind it, since it had been inherited from the old Castle Line whose founder had previously been with Cunard. With hindsight, the Union-Castle story was one of periodic change, alternating between vigorous and enlightened management and something approaching complacency, this reflecting the qualities of those at the top - and that all-important factor, competition.

It was in the early 'thirties that Union-Castle first made me appreciate the importance of "hunch". After booking for a round trip of Continental ports on the GUILDFORD CASTLE I changed my mind - for no apparent reason - and re-booked to go on the next ship. So, from the deck of the GRANTULLY CASTLE I had my first sighting of a sunken passenger ship, with only her topmast and tip of funnel visible.

Although adequate for those days, the GRANTULLY CASTLE's accommodation would today seem primitive. Later I was able to get to know various of the newer ships and next the mail and cargo carrying SOUTHAMPTON CASTLE and the elegant and long-to-be-remembered WINDSOR CASTLE. On another occasion, on the shake-down trip of the then brand-new TRANSVAAL CASTLE, there was time to assess and fully appreciate all that she offered in terms of service, appointments and furnishings, all evidence of new blood at the helm. Also witnessed was a momentary lapse into smoke making (see above) - only about 30 seconds!

All power to Peter for his painstaking research and devotion to the fine detail of his subject. This book deserves to be a great success.

Laurence Dunn

INTRODUCTION

One of the goals of this book is to set the record straight.

Donald Currie was the archetypal business tycoon. He was not only a ship owner but also a major investor in South African mining. His skills at charming the powers-that-be were legendary as was his ability to gain the maximum benefit for himself. Unlike Cecil John Rhodes, Currie left nothing in his £2.5 million will to South Africa, yet his legend continues in that country as the giant who established Union-Castle Line. For most of the latter half of the 19th century, however, it was Union Line which had a far superior fleet to that run by Currie. It is hoped, therefore, that through this fleet history, a more balanced view of the relative strengths of the Castle Packets and Union Line companies will prevail.

Sir Vernon Thomson Chairman of Union-Castle from 1939 to 1953 also attempted to create a myth about his time with the company as Marischal Murray found out to his cost when preparing his beautifully written *Union-Castle Chronicle*. Murray was so frustrated with Thomson's interference that he briefly withdrew from the project. Despite this, key omissions remained including LLANDOVERY CASTLE hitting a mine during the Spanish Civil War and the grounding of WINCHESTER CASTLE off Portland Bill. The book also pays relatively little attention to the substantial cargo fleet, war managed ships and many smaller craft.

If there is a hero in the Union-Castle story, it is Owen Philipps, Lord Kylsant who brought the company into the modern era and whose contribution is often overlooked.

This fleet history has only come about because of the enormous amount of help which I have had from an international gathering of people. At the core has been a team of experts whose combined knowledge would be hard to beat. They include Fred Hawks, Brian Ingpen, Bill Laxon, Alan Mallett and Bill Schell – these gentlemen have been unstinting in their generous sharing of information, time, and constant checking of the data included in the fleet history.

I would also like to thank Laurence Dunn for his excellent foreword, unlimited use of his photographic collection and for his tuition over the years which has helped immeasurably in my understanding of ships. A special thanks to my wife Judy for her help with the design of the book and for researching and writing up the location of all the castles; John Clarkson, Denise Crous, FotoFlite, Ambrose Greenway, Tony Haslett, Robert Pabst, Ian Shiffman, Terry Toohey, The Ship Society of Southern African for the use of numerous photographs; Roy Fenton for spending much time meticulously checking the fleet list for inconsistencies; Duncan Hawes for lending me his notes on Union-Castle Line; John Landels for yard data; Kevin O'Donoghue for providing considerable information from the World War One Service List; Stuart Rankin for historical background on early Thames shipbuilding; Søren Thorsøe for fascinating information on Danish ships; Graeme Somner for background to Currie ships; Andrew Bell and Anthony Cooke for suggestions on the text and finally to Michelle Scott for much help and access to her father David Reynold's photographic collection - sadly, David, the leading expert on South African tugs died soon after the start of the project and the tug section is dedicated to the memory of this generous and enthusiastic shipping historian.

Many thanks also to: Chris Adams, Alastair Arnott, Cecil Ashdown, Declan and Ruth Barriskill, David Burrell, Ian Buxton, Stephen Card, John Clarkson, Louis Cochet, Kevin Cole, Luis Miguel Correia, Denise Crous, Robert De Lange, Charles Dragonette, Jennifer Dunn, John Dwyer, Maurizio Eliseo, Micky Forster, Brian Galer, Alan Giddings, Richard Greenwood, Rowan Hackman, Erik Hag, Bill Hultgren, Peter Jeftha, David Jenkins, Trevor Jones, Arnold Kludas, Bård Kolltveit, Jack Lancaster, Bernd Langensiepen, Martin Lindenboom, Jackie Loos, Paul Louden-Brown, Ian Mayoh, Rod Mills, John Naylon, Andrew Newall, Arturo Paniagua, Bob Pflug, Clive Powell, Stephen Rabson, , Richard Robinson, Leslie Ruecroft, Anthony Sigwart, Jimmy Smith, Clare Sorensen, Brian Spencer, Paul Tichmann, Wendy Vineall and Larry Walsh. If I have left anyone out, please accept my apologies for the oversight.

Peter Newall
Blandford Forum
Summer 1999

FLEET LIST NOTES

The (numeral) following the name of a ship indicates if the ship was the first, second etc. with that name in the fleet. If (numeral) is not given, it was the only one with that name. The ship name is followed by the material the ship was constructed of and the type of propulsion i.e. Steel, screw steam means steel hull, steamship with a single screw. The period in which the ship was in the fleet is also shown e.g. (Union 1854-1858) means that the ship was with Union Line from 1854 to 1858. Union Steamship Company Ltd. and Castle Packets Company Ltd. merged on March 8, 1900 to form the Union-Castle Mail Steamship Company Ltd. BBC = Beira Boating Company; ABC = African Boating Company; B&C = British & Commonwealth; MBCS = Messina Bros., Coles & Searle; and UC = Union-Castle.

O.N. is the official number which is allocated to a British ship when first registered. This numbering system applied throughout the British Empire and Commonwealth and remained with the ship whenever it was British Empire and Commonwealth registered. In Lloyds Register and the Mercantile Navy List, the official number for the ship is always shown in the first column. For new ships, the date of registration is when the ship was completed, prior to trials and delivery.

Wherever possible, yard numbers are given as this is a useful guide to show the sequence of ships built by a particular yard.

Tonnage and dimensions are those when completed. For British ships built prior to 1880, this information has been taken from the original registration certificate at the Public Record Office, Kew. For cargo ships, deadweight tonnage has been included wherever possible. Dimensions are length, beam and depth and are shown in feet and tenths of a foot. If the measurement is for example 259.0 feet, for the sake of space, it is shown as 259 feet.

Engines: the number of cylinders is shown next to cyl. For diesels, 2S/4S indicates 2 or 4 stroke engines, whilst SA or DA indicates single acting or double acting. Horsepower is usually shown as registered (h.p.) plus, where available, indicated horsepower (i.h.p.) for reciprocating engines, shaft horsepower (s.h.p.) for turbines and brake horsepower (b.h.p.) for diesels. The speeds shown tend to be service speeds or best averages when the engines were relatively new, and during fair weather conditions. Obtaining consistent data on speeds is always a problem but it was decided to include these (with a health warning!), as they usually are a good indicator for the non-technically minded of the relative power of the ship.

Passenger numbers can also vary considerably and where they are included they are usually when the ship was completed.

PHOTOGRAPHIC SOURCES

Every effort has been made to correctly attribute photographs used in the book. Any photograph not coded with one of the following codes is from the author's collection.

AA	The late A. Andrews Collection
AD	Alex Duncan Collection
AG	Ambrose Greenway Collection
AM	Alan Mallett Collection
BG	Brian Galer Collection
BI	Brian Ingpen Collection
BS	Bill Schell Collection
CA	Cape Archives
CP	Canadian Pacific Collection
DR	The late David Reynolds Collection
DUR	Durban Local History Museum
EL	East London Museum
FF	FotoFlite
FH	Fred Hawks Collection
HAN	Hanson Collection,
ILL	Illovo Sugar Ltd.
IS	Ian Shiffman
JC	J. & M. Clarkson Collection
JM	John Marsh Collection, SA Maritime Museum
JN	John Naylon Collection
LD	Laurence Dunn Collection
LIM	Limerick Museum
LMC	Luis Miguel Correia Collection
ML	Martin Leendertz Collection, SA Library
MP	Margaret Parkes
NOR	Norsk Sjøfartsmuseum
P&O	P&O S.N. Co., London
PN	Peter Newall
RP	Robert Pabst
SAL	South African Library
SOU	Southampton Museum
TH	Tony Haslett Collection
TT	Terry Toohey Collection
WSS	World Ship Society Collection

ARUNDEL CASTLE leaving Cape Town in the 1950s (IS)

CARNARVON CASTLE at Madeira 1958 (IS)

9

CARNARVON CASTLE at Southampton (AG)

WINCHESTER CASTLE (IS)

STIRLING CASTLE (RP)

CAPETOWN CASTLE final departure from Cape Town - August 1967 (IS)

EDINBURGH CASTLE (RP)

S.A. ORANJE (ex PRETORIA CASTLE) final sailing from Cape Town 1975 (IS)

PENDENNIS CASTLE (IS)

OCEAN QUEEN (ex PENDENNIS CASTLE) (IS)

WINDSOR CASTLE at Southampton (AG)

WINDSOR CASTLE final sailing from Cape Town September 1977 (IS)

TRANSVAAL CASTLE (IS)

S.A. VAAL (ex TRANSVAAL CASTLE) final sailing from Cape Town September 1977 (IS)

DURBAN CASTLE (IS)

BLOEMFONTEIN CASTLE (IS)

Chapter One
PASSENGER MAILSHIPS

ARUNDEL CASTLE at East Pier, Cape Town on her maiden voyage (ML)

With the Isle of Wight acting as a natural breakwater, Southampton offers a perfect shelter from the ravages of the Channel. The port also has double tides, lengthy periods of high water, and is ideally situated geographically for easy access to continental Europe, and for services to the Iberian Peninsula, the Mediterranean, and southern tracks to South America and Africa.

Southampton's role as a major seaport, however, was slow in coming mainly because of its distance from the industrial heartland of the country. With the rapid introduction of the railway network in the 1830s, however, everything changed, and in 1836 an Act of Parliament was passed which allowed the recently established Southampton Dock Company to build the first dock - the tidal Outer Dock which was completed in 1843. The turning point for the port was 1840 when the railway linking Southampton with London was opened, and the two major shipping companies, the Royal Mail Steam Packet Company and the Peninsular & Oriental Steam Navigation Company were awarded the mail contracts to the West Indies and India respectively.

When the second dock, the non-tidal Inner Dock, was completed in 1851, Southampton was ready for a period of rapid expansion. This was also the time of great advancement in engine design and companies like P. & O. were starting to move away from paddle to screw propulsion - of the 20 ships built for the company between 1850 and 1853, less than half were paddlers and the final ship of this group was not only screw-driven, but also the largest ship in the world, the 3,438 gross ton HIMALAYA. The increases in Royal Mail Steam Packet Company (awarded the mail contract to Brazil and the River Plate in 1851) and P. & O. activity meant a huge increase in the demand for coal and although P. & O. introduced its own collier, the RAJAH, in 1853 to bring coal from Cardiff to Southampton, a group of business associates led by Arthur Anderson, decided to form a separate collier company to supply the port with South Wales coal.

Arthur Anderson and the founding of Union Line

Arthur Anderson, a sixty-one year old Shetlander, had started the Peninsular & Oriental Steam Navigation Company with his partner Brodie McGhee Wilcox, and was still the managing director when he founded the Southampton Steam Shipping Company on September 28, 1853. For some reason, the concern was restyled the Union Steam Collier Company just over a week later on October 7, 1853.

The new company announced plans to build five colliers which would be in constant use between Southampton and Cardiff, each undertaking two voyages per month. Although these vessels were built on the Thames, the first ship UNION was ordered from Charles Lungley, Rotherhithe, whilst the next two, BRITON and SAXON, came from across the river, at Poplar, from the Samuda Brothers. Probably influenced by the design of the north-east coast collier, the JOHN BOWES of 1852, the first three Union ships had their engines aft - this arrangement with all hatches forward of the engine room provided the ideal solution for the loading of a bulk cargo such as coal. The reasons for dividing the order between the two yards is unclear, and may have been because they were both relatively new, and the company wished to limit the risk of placing the entire order with an untried yard. In the event, Charles Lungley became the prime contractor for Union until 1865.

UNION was completed in June 1854 and immediately went into service on her intended route between Cardiff and Southampton. By now, however, the Crimean War was three months old, and Southampton had become the premier port for troops and supplies. Many of the P. & O. and Royal Mail Steam Packet Company ships had also been chartered to carry men and horses to the Black Sea, and the principal raison d'être for the formation of the Union Steam Collier Company had suddenly disappeared. With a depleted fleet, P. & O. was unable to serve the Southampton-Constantinople-Smyrna mail and cargo route, and the three new Union vessels were chartered to operate the service. This did not last long, however, and by the end of the year they were all on charter as transport ships.

Because of the change in operation, the design of the next pair of ships was altered. Not only did NORMAN and DANE have engines amidships, they were also given more powerful engines built by Day, Summers & Company. It is likely that almost all the Lungley-built ships were taken to Southampton, where Day, Summers fitted the engines at their Northam Iron Works. In 1856, George Lungley, the brother of Charles, took over Rubie's yard, which was next to Day, Summers, and thus Union had two Southampton facilities, which could service their vessels. An extra ship, CELT was also ordered in 1855 and, although she was similar to NORMAN and DANE, she had a vertical engine instead of a horizontal one.

After the signing of the Treaty of Paris in February 1856, the Crimean War ended, and the three-year-old Union company had six new ships and no work. Whilst an attempt was made to sell the Samuda pair, the rest of the fleet, apart from DANE, was laid up until the decision was made to start a new monthly cargo and passenger service to Brazil from Southampton in direct competition with the Royal Mail Steam Packet Company. NORMAN inaugurated the new route on September 23, 1856 when she set sail for Rio de Janeiro, but after only six months, the port of departure was switched from Southampton to Liverpool, with DANE taking the first sailing on March 21, 1857. In the meantime, BRITON and SAXON were chartered out or used as feeder ships for the South American route - the latter was also used on an experimental service between Liverpool and Hamburg. In keeping with these new challenges, it was decided to reform the enterprise into a limited liability company, under the newly enacted Limited Liability Act, and with coal no longer the business, the company was registered as the Union Steamship Company Limited on December 5, 1856.

The 1857 Cape mail contract

The Liverpool-Brazil service was not a success, and CELT took the final sailing in May 1857. A few months later, however, the British Admiralty asked for tenders for the mail contract to the Cape Colony. This was the third attempt at establishing a regular mail service to Southern Africa since 1851 - the first two by the General Screw Steamship Company and the Lindsay Line ended in the commercial failure of the operators. The new five-year contract, which carried an annual subsidy of £33,000, stipulated a monthly service terminating at Table Bay or Simon's Bay (Simon's Town), on the eastern side of the Cape Peninsula. Mails would be embarked at Devonport (Plymouth) in steamships of not less than 530 tons, with the passage in either direction taking no more than 42 days. Calls at St.Helena and Ascension were also to be made on the homeward journey.

On September 4, 1857 the Union Steamship Company was awarded the Cape mail contract, and eleven days later, DANE left Southampton with fifty bags of mail, six passengers, £5,000 in specie (coins) and a "moderate" cargo. After a voyage of 44 days, this tiny ship anchored in Table Bay on October 29, virtually unnoticed among a large fleet of ships - this was the time of the Indian Mutiny, and most were carrying stores for India. This arrival was the start of a regular mail and passenger service between Britain and South Africa, which would continue virtually unabated for the next 120 years.

Since only the engines amidships vessels were suitable for the new service, the company had to rely initially on chartered ships to meet the monthly sailings - these included BOSPHORUS, which had initiated the first Cape mail contract in 1851, and PHOEBE, which was later bought as a stopgap until the arrival of new purpose-built mailships. Another nearly new, second-hand steamer ATHENS, was also purchased from Alexander Denny, the Dumbarton shipyard. Because Board of Trade regulations made it very difficult to change the name of a ship, most of the second-hand vessels purchased by Union kept their original names.

A major rebuilding programme was set in motion, which would result in six new mailships being built between 1860 and 1866. In September 1860, the first of these was completed. Built by Charles Lungley, with engines by Day, Summers, CAMBRIAN was not only the first purpose-built Cape mailship, but also the first Union ship over 1,000 tons gross. BRITON followed the next year also from the Lungley yard, achieving great publicity at the time because she was built according to Lungley's "unsinkable plan."

In March 1863, Union was awarded a new seven-year mail contract which reduced not only the subsidy, but also the passage time, from 42 to 38 days. Within months, two new record breakers appeared on the scene, SAXON and ROMAN, and their arrival consolidated Union's position as the premier operator on the South African run.

The new ships also freed up the smaller vessels in the fleet for coastal feeder duties, and in February 1863, NORMAN inaugurated the Intercolonial Service from Cape Town to Algoa Bay (Port Elizabeth) and Port Natal (Durban), with occasional calls at East London - this was extended to Mauritius in 1864 (See Chapter Four Coasters & Feederships). In February 1864, the England-South Africa mail service terminal was moved to Algoa Bay, much to the delight of the citizens of the Eastern Cape who had been campaigning long and hard for a direct link.

By the mid-1860s, the outlook for Union seemed very positive, despite the tragic loss of ATHENS in 1865. The company sought to double the sailings between England and the Cape, and the capital was increased to £260,000 through the issue of new shares. Two new mail ships were ordered from the Lungley yard - NORSEMAN and CELT, the latter being the last Union ship to be built on the Thames, after the bankruptcy of Charles Lungley. The mail contract was renegotiated with the British Postmaster General and was extended until 1876. As a result, a new twice-monthly service with voyage times not longer than 37 days commenced in January 1868. Sadly, a month later the chairman and founder of the company, Arthur Anderson died and his place was taken by Sir Benjamin Phillips, brother-in-law of one of the original shareholders.

Enter Donald Currie

1868 was the start of a major depression in the Cape, and many were also concerned about the impact on the Cape trade of the Suez Canal, due to be opened in 1869. The *Star of Africa* diamond, which had been found in the Northern Cape in March 1869, and was subsequently sold for a staggering £11,000, changed everything. With the outbreak of diamond fever, Southern Africa would never be the same again, with mining equipment and people pouring into the Cape Colony. Needless to say, shipping companies had a field day, with a number of new lines emerging, and the failure of one of these allowed the wolf through the door - the ambitious Donald Currie, who would eventually swallow up Union Line.

A London broker, George Payne, with many contacts in South Africa, was determined to break Union Line's near monopoly on the South African run. Despite an initial failure with chartered ships, he established the Cape and Natal Steam Navigation Company in 1871, which offered a monthly sailing from London to the Cape via Dartmouth, Devon. Using chartered tonnage until their new Clyde-built ships were completed, Cape and Natal had an immediate impact on Union Line, which was forced to lower its first class fares. A series of mishaps brought about the closure of the line in March 1872, but before this happened, George Payne made a valiant final bid to keep the business afloat by chartering two new North Sea traders GOTHLAND and ICELAND from the Leith, Hull and Hamburg Steam Packet Company which was controlled by Donald Currie and his brother James. Soon after these vessels were on their way, George Payne informed Donald Currie that he was unable to meet the costs of the charter. Currie recognised that this might be the opportunity he needed for diversifying his interests away from the highly competitive markets of India and the Far East and, encouraged by shippers to South Africa, he took over the venture. Messrs. Payne and Company were appointed as loading brokers in London and the first sailing of his Colonial Mail Line commenced on February 23, 1872 with WILLIAM MILLER which had been bought earlier that month from the defunct Oriental Screw Collier Company.

Born at Greenock in 1825, Donald Currie joined the British and North American Steam Navigation Company (Cunard Line) at the age of seventeen and remained with them until the formation of his own operation, Donald Currie & Company at Liverpool in 1862. In the same year, his brother James became the manager of the Leith,

Hull and Hamburg Steam Packet Company in which Donald took a shareholding. The involvement of the Currie brothers certainly revitalised the Leith company, and within a short period of time a sizeable fleet of small ships was operating across the North Sea to Stettin, Copenhagen and Christiansund. In 1866, an associate company, the Liverpool and Hamburg Steamship Company, was established and, judging by the registration documents, both companies appeared initially to use the same pool of vessels, which is why the North Sea ships used on the South African run are referred in this book as "Currie family" ships.

Not content with the success of the North Sea business, the insatiable Donald Currie started a sailing ship operation between Liverpool and Calcutta in 1863. His first ship was STIRLING CASTLE and within five years, nine new "Currie Castles" were built for the trade. The financing of Currie's vessels (and probably most of his businesses) was always complicated, with various different shareholders. He also had a close involvement with Scottish ship builders, Robert Napier & Sons, John Elder & Co. (which later became Fairfield) and in particular, Barclay, Curle & Co.

One of the shareholders in the sailing ship fleet was the South Wales mine-owner John Nixon who continued to be associated with Currie for the rest of the century. This alliance also gave Currie the opportunity to carry Welsh coal to Calcutta. This type of coal was, of course, the preferred choice for ship owners who were now moving away from sail to steam, especially after the success of Alfred Holt's experiment with compound engines in 1864. It was ironic, therefore, that Currie was involved in a trade which would ultimately see the end of sail. With the opening of the Suez Canal in 1869, the Far East business was changed completely and there were now many more competitors, both in Britain and in Europe. Decisions were certainly very difficult for a small operator like Currie, but in December 1870 he took the plunge and ordered two steamers for the London-Calcutta service (Currie had moved his business from Liverpool to London in 1865). These were over 2,300 tons gross and came from Barclay, Curle. Soon after, two slightly larger vessels were ordered from Robert Napier & Sons.

By the time DOVER CASTLE was completed in April 1872, the City Line of George Smith and Sons already had four similar sized steam vessels operating to Calcutta, with more in the pipeline. It is perhaps for this reason, that Currie chartered his first two ships, DOVER CASTLE and EDINBURGH CASTLE for a year to the Pacific Steam Navigation Company for their Liverpool-South America service. This turned out to be a disastrous move as DOVER CASTLE was lost on her maiden voyage. As luck would have it, however, the new service between London and the Cape, provided Currie with the ideal lifeline and by 1873 the three remaining sisters were running between London and South Africa.

The new Currie mail service offered twice monthly sailings from London, via Dartmouth, with schedules deliberately designed to show up the relative slowness of the official Union Line service which in reality, was due to the inadequacies of the mail contract rather than the engine power of the Union ships. Leaving England three days before Union, the Currie ship would usually arrive at Cape Town ten days before the Union contract steamer. The mail was also cheaper, with the "private" mail starting at 4 pence compared with the shilling cost of the official mail. The efficiency of the Currie operation also meant that for the first time the Cape had a "private" mail service, which was not only cheap, but also fast and reliable.

In the meantime, Union Line, which had already started reconstruction of its fleet in 1869 to meet the new schedule, was spurred on by the increased competition. The company again issued extra shares to increase the capital so that the tonnage of the fleet would effectively be more than doubled by 1873, with the purchase of second-hand ships and new-buildings. The plan also called for three of the 1860s mail ships to be lengthened and given poop decks but in the end, only ROMAN and CELT were stretched, whilst SAXON was rebuilt with a new poop - all three had their horizontal engines replaced with Maudslay inverted compound engines. The remaining three Thames-built vessels were sold. The new ships were a mixed bag and, although they included some fine vessels, there appeared to be no consistency in the company purchases. It was almost as if, without the direction of Arthur Anderson, the company had lost its way.

The 1876 joint mail contract

Union Line also realised that their monopoly of the Cape mail service was seriously under threat and with four years still to run on the existing contract, they put forward a proposal to the Postmaster General in January 1872. This submission included a fortnightly service, with voyage times reduced from 37 to 30 days from January 1873. They also requested the right to operate a third "extra" mail steamer each month and most controversially, they expected the existing mail contract to be extended by a further three and a half years beyond 1876, which would have effectively ensure their monopoly for the rest of the decade. Later that month, the Postmaster-General wrote to the Treasury recommending that their offer be accepted.

Meanwhile, negotiations had been taking place over the Cape-Zanzibar mail contract (See Chapter Four Coasters & Feederships) and in June 1872 a joint Union Line and British India Steam Navigation Company bid was placed on the table. This proposal was, however, conditional on the England-Cape mail contract being extended until 1880. Confident about the outcome, Union placed orders for new ships and at the end of October the Treasury confirmed the contract. Unfortunately, with typical Imperial insensitivity, no one in Whitehall had involved the Cape colonists, especially since the Cape was to be granted Responsible Government in December of that year. Needless to say, the citizens of the Cape and their first Prime Minister, Sir John Molteno, were outraged.

For Donald Currie, this was yet another answer to his prayers. After his initial success, the Cape experienced another sharp contraction in trade, which seriously affected his delicately financed operation. An attempt to increase freight rates with Union Line had been rebuffed and he even had discussions with the British India Steam Navigation Company to sell his ships. Now, Currie went into overdrive and the government was soon besieged by protests from merchants and aggrieved Cape citizens. It is often forgotten that although Currie started on the Cape mail service in 1872, his sailing ships had been operating to India via the Cape since 1863, and thus he already had strong links with the colony. He was also careful to nurture anyone of influence and in the case of Sir John Molteno, he looked after his son Percy when he studied in England - Percy also, later married Currie's daughter Elizabeth.

Overwhelmed, the Treasury retreated and the agreed contract was withdrawn. For Union Line this was a major embarrassment. The subsidy for the Zanzibar mail service was substantially increased, but the company had incurred considerable expense in new ships for their western mail operation and in 1874, for the first time ever, Union did not pay a dividend. Currie, on the other hand, was awarded a bonus of £150 per day by the Cape Government for each day his ships undercut the mail contract passage time of 26 days. He was also given a greater share of the postal revenue. These generous concessions ensured that by the time the next mail contract was negotiated, Donald Currie would remain a viable alternative to Union Line.

Still smarting over the debacle of the Zanzibar contract, Whitehall left much of the detail for the 1876 mail contract to the Cape legislature who naturally created the maximum benefit for the Cape Colony. After lengthy negotiations, the new seven-year contract was signed in October 1876. The mail contract was to be shared by Union Line and Donald Currie, on the condition that they did not merge. The service was to be weekly, with the voyage time reduced to 26 days and although there were now no subsidies, all mail revenue (the minimum postal charge was halved to 6 pence) would be retained by the shipping line and speed premiums earned for passage less than the contract time. The Cape emigration contract was also to be shared between the two companies.

Because of the uncertain economic climate, Currie had not built any new ships since 1872. In fact, although the first CASTLE-named steamer, WALMER CASTLE, arrived at the Cape in October 1872, Currie had operated the service with a combination of charters, Currie family ships and his three Indian steamers. In 1875 he ordered his first purpose-built Cape mailship DUNROBIN CASTLE, the first of five ships of just under 3,000 gross tons completed between 1876 and 1877. On November 10, 1877, the Castle Packets Company, which had been a private partnership since 1873, was incorporated as an unlimited company. With Donald Currie holding less than a third of the shares, among the other principal shareholders were his brother James, the mine-owner John Nixon, the shipbuilder John Napier and a "gentleman out of business," Thomas Brassey who later became Lord Brassey.

With a reduction in their annual mail contract sailings from 36 to 26, Union used up some of the surplus capacity with extra sailings, and the first of the "intermediate" routes the Southampton-Port Elizabeth direct service, was inaugurated by SYRIA in November 1876. Currie also had "extra" steamers built with the first two, TAYMOUTH CASTLE and DUART CASTLE, arriving in 1877 and 1879 respectively (see Chapter Two Intermediates and Extras).

New generation of modern mailships

Although they shared the England-Cape mail contract, the rivalry between the two companies intensified after !876 and for the next quarter of a century each tried to outdo the other with improved ships. Whilst Donald Currie undoubtedly had the upper hand for self publicity, Union always won the day for the quality of vessels placed on the route, starting with GERMAN in 1877, the first of a new generation of fast, modern mailships. Between 1877 and 1883, Union built ten new liners which were able to undertake the voyage to the Cape in 21 days, with far superior passenger accommodation to that provided on the Castle ships. Operationally, however, these years were a disaster for Union Line with the loss of AMERICAN and TEUTON in 1880 and 1881 respectively. The sinking of TEUTON was a particularly bitter pill for the company, as it was not only the biggest maritime loss in South Africa, but also the large number of lives lost was a result of the captain's negligence. Great extra expense was thus incurred in the chartering of numerous vessels to cover for the lost tonnage, and because most of the new buildings were seriously behind schedule due to strikes at the shipyards. In September 1882, further trouble arose when the Chairman of Union Line, Sir Benjamin Phillips, now ill and in his 70s, announced that the board had decided to change the port of arrival and departure from Southampton to London so that they could compete head to head with Castle Packets. Only one director had voted against the change, the deputy chairman Alfred Giles, who had been on the board of Union since 1857. The public outcry against this move was overwhelming and in March 1883, the entire board resigned except for Alfred Giles who became the new chairman.

Donald Currie also had to rely on chartered vessels in the early years of the joint mail contract to replace the WINDSOR CASTLE which had been wrecked in 1876, and whilst his new ships were being built - a number of these charters came from the Leith operator, Seater, White and Company (See Chapter Seven Sail, Currie family & chartered ships). His response to the new Union ships was, however, one of caution and in 1879 he took advantage of low prices to build KINFAUNS CASTLE and GRANTULLY CASTLE, the former being one of the first ocean-going ships built of steel. These were followed by a similarly sized pair, GARTH CASTLE and DRUMMOND CASTLE which were completed in 1881, shortly before Currie converted the Castle Packets Company into a new limited company, the Castle Packets Company Limited which was registered on July 15, 1881. The new capital from the flotation allowed him to purchase the unique four masted PEMBROKE CASTLE, which was bought on the stocks, and to place an order for three 4,250 gross ton "flyers" which were completed in 1883 - these were HAWARDEN CASTLE, NORHAM CASTLE and ROSLIN CASTLE. He also managed to ensure that the new shareholders picked up the bill for the final payments of GARTH CASTLE and DRUMMOND CASTLE. 1883 also saw the sale of four of the sailing vessels to the Dundee jute carrier Charles Barrie and the completion of Currie's last sailing ship CLUNY CASTLE.

The five year mail contract of 1883 was more restrictive for the joint operators, with a further reduction in the passage time to 21½ days (22½ days if calls were made at St Helena or Ascension), penalties for voyages longer than 23 days and a fixed subsidy of £25,000 per annum in place of a share of the postal revenues. In September that year, led by Currie, the first South African Shipping Conference was also formed with the seven main shipping companies agreeing mutually acceptable freight rates. Three years later, the Conference introduced the "Deferred Rebate", a loyalty bonus system for shippers who used Conference vessels. Thus, in fourteen years Donald Currie had turned from poacher to gamekeeper. The rebel had also become part of the establishment with a knighthood and the obligatory estate in the Highlands.

In 1883, freight rates started to tumble because of a global recession which had a serious impact on South African trade and neither Union Line nor Castle Packets were able to provide a dividend for their shareholders the following year. Ships were laid up or chartered as government transports, whilst Union started a short-lived Liverpool-Baltimore service. Recovery from the recession was slow and neither Castle nor Union built any new mailships until 1890 and 1891 respectively. The conversion of mailship engines from compound to the more efficient triple expansion system, however, was started by Union soon after the arrival of their coaster AFRICAN in 1886, the first ship in the fleet built with this new type of engine. Castle followed this technology a little later.

Gold was found on the Witwatersrand in the Transvaal in 1886 and as with the discovery of diamonds some twenty years earlier, the result had a tremendous impact on both the trade and the political environment of Southern Africa. With the rapid economic expansion in the subsequent gold rush, it is surprising how long South Africans had to wait for decent harbour facilities to be built at the key seaports. Cape Town had the only dock for ocean-going ships, whilst at Durban, Port Elizabeth and East London, goods had to be offloaded into barges from the mailships. This unsatisfactory situation was a major constraint for the two mailship operators and even at Cape Town, the dimensions of the 1870-built Alfred Dock severely restricted the size of mailships - in November 1881, Union Line reported that they had a "tempting offer to build a ship of 5,000 tons, but from the bar afforded by the Cape Town dock, they were obliged to decline it." By 1889, work on a new outer harbour at Cape Town recommenced after a six-year break because of the depression, and although it would take another ten years before the Victoria Basin was complete, the 600-foot Loch Jetty was finished in 1893. Meanwhile, at Southampton, the deep water Empress Dock was open for business in July 1890.

The battle for supremacy in the 1890s

The new harbour works meant larger mailships and in 1890 battle recommenced with the completion of Castle Packet's DUNOTTAR CASTLE by Fairfield on the Clyde. Although the largest liner built for the South African run, this two funnelled ship was surprisingly old fashioned - essentially a larger version of the HAWARDEN CASTLE class but with three masts, she was only single screwed. She did, however, reduce the Cape mail run records in both directions, although her triumph was short-lived with Union's introduction of the magnificent Denny-built SCOT onto the route in 1891. The first twin screw Cape liner and the largest Union ship to date, SCOT was an outstanding vessel and her March 1893 Southampton-Cape Town record of 14 days 18 hours 57 minutes remained unbroken until the arrival of the STIRLING CASTLE in 1936. Despite lengthening in 1896, which considerably enhanced her appearance, she remained a failure because of her high operating cost, and limited cargo capacity. By now, Union were working closely with the Belfast shipbuilders

Harland and Wolff and their Managing Director, William Pirrie, who had successfully introduced the highly profitable "G" class intermediate ships for Union. The result of this collaboration was the 1894 NORMAN which was a smaller version of Harland's elegant White Star Atlantic liners. NORMAN also started off a series of two funnelled liners, the next being the beautifully balanced three masted BRITON in 1897, the first mailship over 10,000 gross tons, and the 12,000 ton SAXON and CELT (completed after the merger as WALMER CASTLE).

Castle meanwhile, struggled to keep up with Union, whilst Donald Currie continued to build outdated type ships. The 1894 TANTALLON CASTLE and 1896 DUNVEGAN CASTLE were simply enlarged, single funnelled versions of DUNOTTAR CASTLE, each driven by a single screw. In the closing years of the century, Currie at last ordered his first twin screw mailships, the Clyde-built KINFAUNS CASTLE and KILDONAN CASTLE which were poor copies of BRITON with their long forecastle incorporating the foremast, and tall funnels bearing the distinctive Castle Line rim-tops. The major problem for Currie was that he was unwilling to widen the share base of his company because this potentially could mean a loss of control, and as a result, he relied mainly on bank loans for his new ships. Union, on the other hand, throughout the history of the company, tended to go back to the shareholders whenever they needed to increase the capital.

The Union-Castle merger

Unable to compete effectively, Castle might have been consigned to the history books had it not been for the insistence by the Cape Government that the 1900 mail contract would only be awarded to a single company. Union and Castle both declined to submit tenders. The Cape Government was forced to climb down and allowed the two lines to continue to share the contract, but with one significant change - for the first time, the clause forbidding an amalgamation of the two companies was omitted. Currie, once again, seized the initiative and came to an agreement with Sir Francis Evans, Chairman of Union Line after the death of Sir Alfred Giles in 1895, that the two companies would merge. The proposal put forward to the shareholders of both companies was that Castle Packets would take over the fleet and assets of Union Line and that Donald Currie and Company would remain the managers. As an added incentive, the shareholders of Union Line were given £350,000 in 4½ percent debenture stock paid for by Castle Packets - considering the cost of building new ships, this was a small price to snuff out the competition. Donald Currie was still a household name and shareholders probably felt that their investment was more secure under his direction than that of a lesser known Union Line director. The amalgamation was thus agreed, and the new company, the Union-Castle Mail Steamship Company Limited was formally registered on March 8, 1900.

Despite having a new board of directors, including Sir Francis Evans, the seventy-five year old Donald Currie continue to run the show as before i.e. seldom attending board meetings, making decisions without consulting his fellow directors, and acting as if he owned the company which he did not - at the formation of Union-Castle, he only held a quarter of the company share capital.

The Anglo-Boer War, which had broken out in October 1899, was a time of great opportunity for the new company with many of the ships chartered by the British Government as transports. The Union-Castle owned African Boating Company (see Chapter Five Tugs & Tenders) also had the major contract for landing troops and supplies at Durban and freighters were built in anticipation of the post-war boom. The end of the war, however, resulted in a major slump, and this, combined with a rates war with Robert Houston, meant that many ships were laid up. The relative weakness of the Castle ships was soon apparent during the inevitable clear-out of the fleet in the next decade, with only a third of the Castle ships built in the 1890s still in service with Union-Castle at the outbreak of World War I, compared with around two thirds of the equivalent Union ships.

Although the company now divided the orders for new mailships between Harland and Wolf, Belfast and Fairfield on the Clyde, the design of these liners followed the pattern set by NORMAN in 1894. ARMADALE CASTLE and KENILWORTH CASTLE, sisters of WALMER CASTLE were completed in 1903 and 1904 respectively, whilst the final pair EDINBURGH CASTLE and BALMORAL CASTLE appeared in 1910 – these were also the last built under the Currie management, with the death of Donald Currie on April 13, 1909. The leadership of the company passed to Currie's son in law, Frederick Mirrielees, and one of his first tasks was to discuss with the South African authorities the new mail contract which was due to start in 1910.

Royal Mail take-over

The formation of the Union of South Africa on May 31, 1910 was a turning point for South Africa and for the Union-Castle Line. At last, South Africans were able to throw off the constraints of colonial rule and decide their own future. Self government also generated a new-found confidence, and one of the early acts of parliament was the Post Office Act of 1911 which specifically forbade the shipping company which held the mail contract to operate the "Rebate System". The directors of Donald Currie and Company, however, insensitive to the needs of the newly independent South Africans, obstinately stuck to their belief in this shipping "ring" which on the one hand stabilised rates, whilst on the other, seriously limited competition. For the 1912 contract (extended by two years because of the establishment of the Union), Union-Castle, therefore, refused to tender and it looked as if there would be no way out without the capitulation of one of the parties.

In the meantime, a pair of predators was on the horizon in the form of Sir Owen Philipps, chairman of the Royal Mail Steam Packet Company, and his business partner, Lord Pirrie, the head of Harland and Wolff. Together, these two had recently made a series of major acquisitions, including Elder Dempster & Co. Ltd., which resulted in their controlling the largest shipping concern in Britain. In December 1911, they announced that they would be offering £32.10s. for every £10 ordinary Union-Castle Mail Steamship Company Limited share, conditional on Donald Currie and Company relinquishing their management of the company. The offer was accepted, and on April 18,1912, only three years and five days after the death of Donald Currie, the new chairman of the company, Sir Owen Philipps, took charge. Two weeks later, he left for South Africa to sort out the mail contract.

The new ten-year contract, which came into effect in October 1912, abolished rebates and included a number of significant cargo agreements, including the provision of cold storage chambers on the mail and intermediate ships for the expanding fruit industry. Union Line and Castle Line had been in at the start of the fruit exports in the early 1890s, when the Molteno family, whose interests included fruit farming, initiated the first shipments to Britain, one result of which had been an enormous growth in fruit farming under the aegis of Cecil Rhodes and the Rhodes Fruit Farms.

The 1912 agreement also stipulated a passage time of 16 days and 15 hours, and six new mailships of not less than 15,000 tons each were to be built - the first two (AMROTH, later ARUNDEL CASTLE and WINDSOR CASTLE) were ordered in 1913, with the orders for the next pair being confirmed in July 1916 (these were later cancelled in 1920 and 1921).

The outbreak of war inevitably meant that all expansion plans had to be put on hold, whilst most of the fleet were requisitioned for war duties. Although the company lost a number of ships during the 1914-1918 conflict, all the mailships survived intact, which was a mixed blessing for the company because they were now stuck with ten old-fashioned two funnelled mailships. To make matters worse, it was decided that the construction of the two new mailships, which had been delayed because of the war, would recommence using the original 1913 design. Although ARUNDEL CASTLE and WINDSOR CASTLE were the largest Cape liners built so far, they were coal-fired, with totally outdated profiles for the early 1920s - the last four funnelled liners ever to be constructed. The uptakes for the four stacks

(one was a dummy) created immense problems for the layout of the public rooms, which were never resolved, even after their 1937 rebuilding.

Despite this backward-looking lapse, the strong association with Harland and Wolff, who were keen proponents of the motorship, led to the next mailship, the 1926 CARNARVON CASTLE (originally ordered as a steamship), being diesel powered. This ship and her slightly larger sisters, WINCHESTER CASTLE and WARWICK CASTLE, with their low modern motorship funnels, finally heralded Union-Castle's break with the past, and the start of a new era for the company. In 1928, a lucrative new freight contract was signed with an agreement for a significant increase in the amount of refrigerated space available on the mailships - the earlier ships were modified to increase capacity to over 140,000 cubic feet, whilst the new motorships were completed with over 200,000 cubic feet.

The collapse of the Kylsant empire

Owen Philipps, now Lord Kylsant, continued to expand the Royal Mail Group, despite the death of Lord Pirrie in 1924, and in 1927, he acquired the Oceanic Steam Navigation Company, better known as the White Star Line. The timing of the White Star purchase, however, was extremely bad as this coincided with the start of a global downturn in trade, which would lead ultimately to the Wall Street Crash and the onset of the Great Depression. By 1929, the group controlled a sixth of Britain's merchant shipping tonnage, and was seen in Britain as a "business of national importance". In July 1930, when it was apparent that the company was in serious financial difficulties, the British Government stepped in to avoid a collapse of the entire group. Unravelling the complex structure of the company meant that it was not until the end of 1937 that dealing in Union-Castle shares could start again. For Lord Kylsant, the shame of the failure of his hard earned enterprise, was compounded by being sentenced to a year in jail for falsifying a company prospectus, a charge which could have easily been dropped in the light of the fact that his efforts had in fact modernised much of Britain's merchant marine service.

Robertson Gibb took over as chairman of Union-Castle in 1932 and in the same year he appointed Sir Vernon Thomson as deputy chairman. Already over sixty, Gibb joined Union Line in 1883. Thomson had been with Owen Philipps, Lord Kylsant since 1897, and was also chairman of King Line. As joint managing directors of Union-Castle they oversaw one of the most crucial changes in the history of the line.

The Great Depression created financial problems for most major shipping lines in the early 1930s, and for Union-Castle the disentanglement from the rest of the Kylsant empire was a serious constraint. Added to this was increased competition from other operators including non-British lines. In 1933, to the complete surprise of Union-Castle, the South African and Italian Governments announced that the newly-formed Italia Line would be providing a five year subsidised passenger service between the Union and Italy. The two ships chosen for this operation were GIULIO CESARE and DUILIO. The arrival of these two crack Italian liners in 1934 had a profound impact on the South Africa-Europe route as they showed up the inadequacies of the Union-Castle mail service for both comfort and speed. Offering 11 days from Cape Town to Gibraltar, whilst the Union Castle ships took 17 days to Southampton, and with a Friday afternoon departure time from Cape Town 30 minutes after the Union-Castle northbound sailing at 1600, the Italians were easily able to catch the coal-fired opposition who were soon left in their wake.

At the end of 1936 a second attack came from an old competitor, the Deutsche Ost-Afrika-Linie, when the first of two new passenger liners, the PRETORIA, set off from Southampton on her maiden voyage. Driven by steam turbines, PRETORIA and her sister WINDHUK were only two knots slower than Union-Castle's fastest motorships, which is why their clever 15-day sailing schedule included a departure from Southampton the day before the mailship, with both ships arriving in Cape Town the same day.

The 1930s rebuilding programme

Although a new ten-year freight contract had been agreed in 1933 which resulted in the order for two mailships STIRLING CASTLE and ATHLONE CASTLE in 1934, the mail contract had continued on an ad hoc basis, subject to twelve months' notice. The speed of the Italian ships no doubt impressed the authorities to such an extent that when in 1937, the South African Government awarded a ten-year mail contract to Union-Castle, it stipulated that from 1938, the weekly mail service between Southampton and Cape Town be reduced by a full 3 days to 14 days. To meet this obligation it would be necessary to overhaul the mailship fleet completely, and between 1937 and 1938 five of the mailships constructed between 1921 and 1931 were sent back to the builders for major work to bring them up to the required speed.

The STIRLING CASTLE and ATHLONE CASTLE entered service in 1936 and were followed by a larger version, CAPETOWN CASTLE in 1938. In terms of overall impact, this handsome trio were arguably the finest mailships ever placed on the Cape mail run. Not only were they the most powerful British motorships of their day, the public rooms in first class broke away from the period style of the earlier mailships. In September 1936, STIRLING CASTLE shattered SCOT's 43-year-old southbound record and she and her sister were the last mailships whose length was restricted by the dimensions of the Victoria Basin in Cape Town. With the construction of the new dock (later called the Duncan Dock) well underway, the CAPETOWN CASTLE was the first mailship over 700 feet between perpendiculars and the first CASTLE liner named after a South African location rather than a British castle (Union Line in fact had two mailships with South African place names, DURBAN and PRETORIA).

With the reconstruction programme now complete, EDINBURGH CASTLE, the last of the pre World War I mailships was withdrawn from service in January 1939. In April, Robertson Gibb retired and was replaced as chairman by Sir Vernon Thomson, but a few months later war was declared with Germany and soon all the mailships were requisitioned as troopships. Sir Vernon, in the meantime, was appointed Controller of Shipping, a position he held until April 1946.

Post-war reconstruction and Cayzer ownership

At the end of the war, the need to repatriate thousands of troops from all over the world meant that the resumption of the mail service was a slow process. A new ten-year mail contract starting in January 1947 was negotiated and ROXBURGH CASTLE took the first post-war sailing on January 2, 1947, followed a week later by CAPETOWN CASTLE, the first passenger mailship departure. Between 1947 and 1949 reconditioning of the three oldest liners was further delayed as they were used to carry emigrants to South Africa, a scheme later cancelled by Daniel Malan's Afrikaner-led Nationalist Party, which won power in the South African elections of May 1948.

Two new mailships, PRETORIA CASTLE and EDINBURGH CASTLE, were ordered to replace WARWICK CASTLE and WINDSOR CASTLE which had been torpedoed in 1942 and 1943 respectively. Whilst Orient Line developed the style of their ships after the war, the dictatorial Thomson, now almost seventy, kept Union-Castle in a pre-war time warp, and when PRETORIA CASTLE and EDINBURGH CASTLE arrived in 1948, they were essentially slightly larger versions of CAPETOWN CASTLE but with bigger funnels and steam turbines instead of diesels. As is often the case with strong willed leaders who are reluctant to delegate, should they die in harness, as was the case with Sir Vernon in 1953, they leave a vacuum and the company is suddenly exposed. Such was the case two years later when in October 1955 a merger between Clan Line Steamers Ltd. and Union-Castle was announced.

The Cayzer family, which owned Clan Line, operators of cargo services to South Africa since 1881, had had its eye on Union-Castle for some time. In 1935, during the Kylsant crisis, they offered to buy the company - a bid which was successfully resisted by Vernon Thomson who did not wish to see the company "once more in the

hands of a single concern." A second attempt in 1944 met with a similar rebuff. Ironically, because of his lack of foresight in preparing the way for a successor, Thomson allowed his company to be taken over by the Cayzers in January 1956 after a vociferous battle led by the ship-owner Jack Billmeir and other Union-Castle shareholders. The British and Commonwealth Shipping Company Ltd. was formed to acquire Union-Castle and its subsidiaries (Bullard King and King Line) plus Clan Line and its various component companies.

Soon after the acquisition of Union-Castle the new owners announced that they planned to reduce the mail passage time from 13½ to 11½ days and to achieve this, the design for PENDENNIS CASTLE, which was being built at Harland and Wolff, would be modified and two larger mailships would be built by Cammell Laird at Birkenhead and John Brown on the Clyde - the WINDSOR CASTLE and TRANSVAAL CASTLE.

Originally designed as a repeat of the PRETORIA CASTLE and EDINBURGH CASTLE, PENDENNIS CASTLE was lengthened on the stocks by sixteen feet to incorporate Denny-Brown stabilisers and alterations made to the forward part of her hull. The latter, combined with modifications to the engine design, significantly increased her operating speed. Her interior layout was also changed and she was given partial air-conditioning. The planned launch in December 1957, however, was postponed because of a strike at the yard and the result of this embarrassment was the end of shipbuilding for Union-Castle by the Belfast firm after sixty-four years of close association.

The largest ever South African mailship, the 37,640 gross ton WINDSOR CASTLE, was completed in 1960 and she was followed in 1962 by a smaller, one-class version, the TRANSVAAL CASTLE, the last passenger mailship to be built. In February 1963 the South African Government agreed to the accelerated mail service, which would include two new cargo only mailships SOUTHAMPTON CASTLE and GOOD HOPE CASTLE. This meant the end of the pre-war liners, whilst PRETORIA CASTLE and EDINBURGH CASTLE had to be modified. The faster mail service was inaugurated by WINDSOR CASTLE in July 1965 and at the end of that year the South African Marine Corporation (Safmarine) bought PRETORIA CASTLE and TRANSVAAL CASTLE. Renamed S.A. ORANJE and S.A.VAAL they continued on the mail run in conjunction with the Union-Castle ships and in 1969 were transferred to the South African flag.

The end of the line

The arrival of the wide-bodied Boeing 747 at the beginning of the 1970s heralded the end of liner travel across the world and the start of mass cheap air travel, whilst the rise in fuel prices after the 1973 Arab-Israeli war saw further increases in sea fares. It was containerisation, however, which was the final blow for the South African passenger mail service. In March 1974 the South African Conference lines announced plans to containerise the South Africa-Europe trade and in 1977 the first of Safmarine's *Big Whites*, the large containership S.A.HELDERBERG entered service.

Without cargo the passenger mailships were no longer viable and on November 15, 1976, British and Commonwealth and Safmarine announced that with the introduction of cargo only containerships in September 1977 the passenger mail service would cease.

WINDSOR CASTLE took the final Union-Castle passenger mailship sailing from Cape Town on September 6, 1977 - 120 years and two days after the Union Line was awarded the first mail contract to the Cape. The mail service finally ended just over a month later with the arrival of SOUTHAMPTON CASTLE at Southampton on October 20, although the Union-Castle name continued to be used in conjunction with cargo ships in the British and Commonwealth fleet until 1984.

FIRST UNION SHIPS

The first three Union Line ships were engines-aft colliers. These were followed by a series with engines amidships. It appears that almost all the Lungley-built ships were taken to Southampton for engines to be fitted by Day, Summers & Co.

UNION (1) Iron screw steamer (Union 1854-1858)
O.N. 25117
Builders: Charles Lungley & Co., Rotherhithe, London
Tonnage: 310 gross 201 net
Dimensions: 157.5 x 21 x 14.1 feet
Engines: 2-cyl. direct-acting by Day, Summers & Co., Southampton 40 h.p. 227 i.h.p. 6.5 knots **Trials**: 7.1 knots

1854: Launched: April 29. Registered: June 16. Maiden voyage Cardiff–Southampton with coal. July: used on P. & O. Southampton-Constantinople-Smyrna service. Later that year was chartered to British Government for Crimean War duty as transport ship. **1856**: January: returned to Southampton and appears to have been laid up until October 23 when placed on Southampton–Brazil service. **1857**: April: arrived from Brazil with 3,700 bags of coffee. Later that year used to carry coal from Cardiff-Southampton for Union ships. **1858**: November: sold to Peninsular & Oriental S.N. Co, London - employed on Mauritius-Réunion service and later as a supply ship for Ashrafi and Daedalus lighthouses in the Gulf of Suez and Red Sea. **1863**: February: sold to Dent & Co. Hong Kong. **1865**: Sold to Choshu-han, Japan, renamed OTSUJU MARU. **1866**: Bought by Satsuma-han (Prince of Satsuma), Kagoshima - renamed SAKURAJIMA MARU. **1871**: Sold to Odaya & Co., Shimonoseki. **1872**: Sold to D. R. Spedding, Shanghai, reverted to UNION. **1873**: January: arrived in Shanghai from Nagasaki under U.S. flag with Spedding as captain. May: sold to A. Murray, Shanghai who, after repair work at the Pootung Foundry & Engineering Works, resold her to Tong King Sing (in charge of China Merchants Steam Navigation Co.). Renamed YUNGNING. **1878**: Purchased by China Merchants Steam Navigation Co., Shanghai. **1887**: After extensive repairs in which she was probably given a 2-cyl.compound engine (200 i.h.p.) by S. C. Farnham & Co., Shanghai - renamed HAE CHANG. **1894**: February: reduced to a floating pontoon on the Yangtze.

BRITON (1) Iron screw steamer (Union 1854-1857)
O.N. 12787
Builders: Samuda Brothers, Poplar, London
Tonnage: 491 gross 407 net
Dimensions: 162.5 x 23.2 x 16.9 feet
Engines: Not recorded but possibly the same as SAXON (1)

1854: Registered: September 26. Used initially on P. & O. Southampton-Constantinople-Smyrna service, and later chartered to British Government for Crimean War duty as transport ship. **1856**: February 27: C. S. & C. C. Hanson, Constantinople were given power of attorney to sell BRITON and SAXON within 6 months. With the end of the Crimean War, she was laid up with CELT at Constantinople between May and September. November: arrived in London. **1857**: January 11: during voyage from London to Seville with wheat, foundered off Ushant, when heavy seas overwhelmed the vessel during a gale. All 22 crew were rescued by a small Jersey schooner WAVE QUEEN and taken to Jersey.

SAXON (1) Iron screw steamer (Union 1854-1858)
O.N. 594
Builders: Samuda Brothers, Poplar, London
Tonnage: 395 gross 335 net
Dimensions: 162 x 23.5 x 15.7 feet
Engines: Single cyl. 40 h.p. 6.5 knots

1854: Registered: October 10. Placed on P. & O. Southampton-Constantinople-Smyrna service. **1855**: chartered to British Government for Crimean War duty as Transport No. 212. **1856**: February 27: C. S.

& C. C. Hanson, Constantinople were given power of attorney to sell BRITON and SAXON within 6 months. April: with the end of the Crimean War, she arrived back at Southampton. **1857**: Used as feedership for Union's Southampton-Brazil service. January: arrived at Southampton from Le Havre with 40 tons of French goods for Brazil to be transhipped onto NORMAN. May: whilst being used on experimental route between Liverpool and Hamburg, with a cargo of grain, spirits and general, her shaft broke and her screw was lost - she was later repaired at Southampton. **1858**: March: sold to Bremer, Bennett, & Bremer, London. **1884**: March: given new boilers and 2-cyl. compound engine by J. Stewart & Sons, London. **1895**: September: sold to John Bannatyne & Sons Ltd., Limerick. **1896**: December: renamed GARRYOWEN and later converted into grain elevator based at Limerick. **1922**: October: sold to T. O'Sullivan of Tarbert, Co. Kerry for scrap – register closed **1923**: January 5: the locally based LOOP HEAD (550/1906) collided with her at Limerick. She was later taken to Tarbert (near the mouth of the Shannon) for demolition. The scrap metal from her hull was apparently loaded in the Belfast owned schooner SUSANNA which foundered August 18 off Clew Bay bound for Glasgow.

NORMAN (1) Iron screw steamer (Union 1854-1864)
O.N. 13978
Builders: Charles Lungley & Co., Rotherhithe, London
Tonnage: 561 gross 465 net
Dimensions: 171 x 24.7 x 16.8 feet
Engines: 2-cyl. horizontal trunk direct-acting by Day, Summers & Co., Southampton 60 h.p. 7 knots
Passengers: Few saloon

1854: Registered: November 24. Chartered to British Government for Crimean War duty as Transport No. 155. **1856**: July: with the end of the Crimean War, she arrived back at Southampton. September 23: inaugurated unsuccessful Southampton-Brazil passenger and cargo service. **1857**: May 5: arrived at Southampton at the end of second Brazil voyage with cargo of coffee. November: placed on Southampton-Cape Town mail service. Arrived Cape Town: December 24. **1863**: February: inaugurated Cape-Natal coastal service. **1864**: May: sold to George Lungley, Southampton, brother of Charles. **1866**: August: sold to G. Y. Mercer, Southampton. It is likely that this sale may be linked to the collapse of George Lungley's Thames shipyard in April, as George Lungley was declared bankrupt in 1867. **1867**: March: sold to Bremer, Bennett, & Bremer, London who bought SAXON in 1858 - name unchanged. **1881**: June 10: stranded 2½ miles north of Seaham Harbour whilst on a voyage from Danzig to Stockton with a cargo of wheat. Crew saved and vessel declared constructive total loss.

DANE (1) Iron screw steamer (Union 1855-1865)
O.N. 12994
Builders: Charles Lungley & Co., Rotherhithe, London
Tonnage: 530 gross 421 net
Dimensions: 177.2 x 24.6 x 16.7 feet
Engines: Not recorded but possibly 2-cyl. horizontal trunk direct-acting by Day, Summers & Co., Southampton 60 h.p. 7 knots
Passengers: Few saloon

1855: Registered: March 16. Chartered to French Government for Crimean War work. **1856**: August: final voyage to Turkey from Dunkirk. Arrived at Liverpool in November. **1857**: March 21: first ship on the Liverpool-Brazil passenger/cargo service. September 15: inaugurated Southampton-Cape Town mail service with six passengers, specie and cargo. October 29: arrived Cape Town. **1863**: Transferred to Cape-Natal coastal service. **1865**: Used briefly on Cape-Mauritius mail service before being replaced by the new MAURITIUS. November 28: left Simon's Town on Admiralty charter to Zanzibar. December 1: approaching Port Elizabeth, was wrecked on Thunderbolt Reef off Cape Recife - no loss of life.

The engines-aft GARRYOWEN (ex SAXON) as a grain elevator at Limerick (LM1983:25)

DANE (LD)

CELT (1) Iron screw steamer (Union 1856-1862)
O.N. 25147
Builders: Charles Lungley & Co., Rotherhithe, London
Tonnage: 551 gross 427 net
Dimensions: 179.4 x 25.4 x 17.2 feet
Engines: 2-cyl. simple 95 h.p. 7 knots
Passengers: Few saloon

1855: Registered: September 28. Like the earlier ships, was also used on Crimean War service. **1856:** With the end of the Crimean War, she was laid up at Constantinople between April and September with BRITON (1). December: placed on Southampton-Brazil route. December 24: left Southampton for Brazil but returned five days later with engine trouble. December 31: sailed again but forced to return January 1 after springing a leak. Eventually set off at third attempt January 10. **1857:** May 17: took final voyage for Liverpool-Brazil service. October: second Union sailing Southampton-Cape Town (arrived November 27). Continued to Algoa Bay (first time for Union Line) to pick up rebel chief Maqomo for imprisonment on Robben Island. **1862:** April: sold to Charles Lungley as part payment for new ships. **1864:** May: sold to Cornelis Balguerie & Zoon, Rotterdam and renamed GOTHENBURG. **1874:** Given new compound engine and boilers by D. Rowan, Glasgow - 90 h.p. **1875:** January 1: returned to British registry. Registered at Newcastle. New owner John Meek, Liverpool - reverted to CELT. **1881:** June 18: registered at Liverpool. **1889:** May: sold to Burgess & Co., Swansea. Registered at London. November: sold to Thames & Bristol Channel Trading Co., London. **1891:** April: sold to Shipping & General Property Co. Ltd., London. June: sold to McDowall & Barbour (from 1907 known as Hellenic Steam Nav. Co.), Piraeus - renamed POSSIDON. **1910:** Sold to J. Potamianos & Co., Constantinople - now known in Lloyds Register as POSEIDON. **1914:** No longer in list of Turkish vessels, so presumed scrapped - remained in Lloyds Register until 1932.

PHOEBE Iron screw steamer (Union 1858-1861)
O.N. 14943
Builders: Alexander Denny, Dumbarton (yard no: 17)
Tonnage: 613 gross 417 net
Dimensions: 172.8 x 25.5 x 15.6 feet
Engines: 2-cyl. simple by Tulloch & Denny (Engine No.1) 120 h.p. 8 knots
Passengers: Few saloon

1851: Named after Phoebe Watt one of the shareholders, PHOEBE was completed for Patrick Brenan & partners, Liverpool, trading as Preston & Co. Registered: September 11. Operated to the Mediterranean with Patrick Brenan, her master. **1857:** November: chartered by Union Line for Southampton-Cape Town service. **1858:** Arrived Cape Town: January 21. Registered Southampton: April 30. Bought later that year by Union as a stopgap. **1860:** Chartered to Lecisne & Co. for the London-Bordeaux trade. **1861:** April: after arrival of Union's first purpose-built mailship CAMBRIAN, sold to Charles Lungley who sold her to Z. C. Pearson, London. Based in Hull, she was supposed to be a blockade-runner during the American Civil War - this venture was a failure and ownership passed to the mortgagee. **1862:** September: bought by G. Fleming, London. December: purchased at Bermuda by the Intercolonial Royal Mail Steam Packet Co. Used on the trans-Tasman and New Zealand coastal route. **1863:** Refitted at Sydney to carry 54 first, 40 second. **1864:** With the award of a new subsidised mail contract, her owners were retitled Panama, New Zealand & Australia Royal Mail Co. Ltd., London. **1869:** January: after the failure of the company, she was sold to Thomas Henderson who operated the Circular Saw Line, Auckland. **1870:** Sold to John Martin of the Wreck Recovery Co. Ltd., Wellington. **1871:** John Martin's company was renamed the New Zealand Steam Shipping Co. Ltd. **1876:** June: New Zealand Steam taken over by Union S.S. Co. of New Zealand. **1879:** February: sold to James & A. Brown, Newcastle N.S.W. **1901:** Bought by Einerson & Jorgensen, Sydney and converted into hulk. **1904:** Broken up at Sydney.

ATHENS

ATHENS Iron screw steamer (Union 1858-1865)
O.N. 17836
Builders: Alexander Denny, Dumbarton (yard no.42)
Tonnage: 739 gross 502 net
Dimensions: 224.6 x 30.1 x 16.5 feet
Engines: 2-cyl. simple by Tulloch & Denny or builder 130 h.p. 8 knots
Passengers: not known

1856: Built for Liverpool–Constantinople service of J. P. Schilizzi., Liverpool. Registered: December 20. **1857:** March: after one round trip, returned to builders, possibly because owners defaulted on payment or were dissatisfied with the ship. **1858:** May: bought by Union Line for Southampton-Cape Town service. Arrived Cape Town: July 14. **1864:** November 18: inaugurated Cape-Mauritius mail service. **1865:** May 17: unable to sail out of Table Bay during the worst north-west gale for years, her fires were doused by the sea and she was blown onto the rocks between Mouille Point and Green Point where her remains can still be seen. All on board (29) lost their lives.

FIRST PURPOSE-BUILT UNION MAILSHIPS

Between 1860 and 1865 a series of six mailships over 1,000 gross toms were built on the Thames for the Union Line Cape mail service.

CAMBRIAN Iron screw steamer (Union 1860-1872)
O.N. 28108
Builders: Charles Lungley & Co., Deptford, London
Tonnage: 1,055 gross 868 net
Dimensions: 245.1 x 30.1 x 18.4 feet
Engines: 2-cyl. horizontal trunk direct-acting by Day, Summers & Co., Southampton 120 h.p. 8 knots
Passengers: 64 first, 40 fore-cabin

1860: Registered: September 26. Union's first purpose-built mailship and first over 1,000 tons. Arrived Cape Town: November 12. **1871:** Designed to carry sufficient coal for round trip but ran out of coal on voyage south and took 42 days to reach Cape Town. **1872:** March: sold to W. Banks & Cie., Havre. **1875:** Given 2-cyl.compound engine by Constructions Navals, Havre. New owners: A. Deglaire, Havre. **1877:** Owner: H. Deglaire, Havre. **1880:** Sold to Joannes Couvert, Havre. **1882:** October: 30: sank in the Bay of Biscay near Bordeaux - all crew rescued by the steamer IXIA.

PHOEBE

PHOEBE at Sydney in James & A. Brown colours later in the 19th century

CAMBRIAN

BRITON (2) Iron screw steamer (Union 1861-1873)
O.N. 29884
Builders: Charles Lungley & Co., Deptford, London
Tonnage: 1,164 gross 932 net
Dimensions: 248 x 30.7 x 23.9 feet
Engines: 2-cyl. horizontal trunk direct-acting by Day, Summers & Co., Southampton 120 h.p. 8.5 knots
Passengers: 60 first, 50 fore-cabin

1861: Registered October 31. First ocean going vessel built to Lungley's "unsinkable plan" i.e. 3 completely watertight decks plus usual transverse bulkheads. Arrived Cape Town: December 15. **1862**: May: fastest yet Plymouth-Cape Town voyage for Union Line: 31 days 14 hours. **1873**: November: sold to Admiralty as transport, renamed HMS DROMEDARY, and used on Ashantee War service. **1874**: After leaving Ascension, she broke down and had to return home under sail. Repair costs were too high and she was later relegated to a "sailing lighter" in Portsmouth. **1885**: Scrapped by Castle & Sons, London

SAXON (2) Iron screw steamer (Union 1863-1873)
O.N. 44905
Builders: Day, Summers & Co., Southampton
Tonnage: 1,141 gross 894 net
Dimensions: 245 x 31.8 x 23.7 feet
Engines: 2-cyl. horizontal trunk direct-acting by builder 220 h.p. 9 knots
Passengers: 60 first, 50 fore-cabin

1863: Registered March 27. On maiden voyage to the Cape, broke record: 31 days. Arrived Cape Town: May 9. **1865**: Reduced record to 28 days 12 hours. **1870**: May: fitted with a poop. Tonnage increased to 1,308gross 1,049 net. November 5: after hitting a rock near Cape Agulhas, she became the first mailship to use the new Alfred Dock in Cape Town, the first man-made harbour in South Africa. **1872**: Re-engined with 220 h.p. 2-cyl. compound engine by Maudslay, Sons & Field, London. **1873**: September: sold to Bailey & Leetham, Hull for Bailey & Co., Lisbon, and registered at Lisbon as BENGUELLA. The company had been awarded the mail contract between Lisbon and Southern Africa and traded as the Empreza Lusitana. October 5: first voyage to Angola with 72 passengers. **1876**: Re-engined again with 2-cyl. compound engine by Bailey & Leetham, Hull - speed raised to 12 knots. **1885**: September: sold to Empreza Insulana de Navegação,

Lisbon for a transatlantic service between Lisbon and New York via the Azores and Boston. The company's first ship in 1871 was DANE (2) of 1866. **1889**: Given new 145 h.p triple expansion engine and boilers by Earles' S.B. & E. Co., Ltd., Hull. **1890**: June 24: after springing a leak, her engine room flooded, and she was abandoned in the Atlantic (40N-49W) on a voyage from New York to Azores and Lisbon - all saved by the Italian barque MARIANNINA and were transferred to Spanish liner ALFONSO X111 on June 26 and landed at La Coruña. The flooding may have been a result of damaged hull plates caused when she went aground at New York whilst being towed out of her berth at low tide.

ROMAN (1) Iron screw steamer (Union 1863-1889)
O.N. 44906
Builders: Charles Lungley & Co., Deptford, London
Tonnage: 1,282 gross 1,027 net
Dimensions: 267 x 32.4 x 23.6 feet
Engines: 2-cyl. horizontal trunk direct-acting by Day, Summers & Co., Southampton 220 h.p. 9 knots
Passengers: 60 first, 60 fore-cabin

1863: Registered: April 30. On maiden voyage to the Cape (arrived Cape Town: June 6.), broke the southbound record set by SAXON (2) - Plymouth-Cape Town: 30 days 20 hours. **1869**: Used as an "extra" steamer. **1870**: Lengthened by 54 feet, fitted with a poop. Tonnage increased to 1,751gross 1,096 net. **1872**: Re-engined with 274 h.p., 2-cyl. compound engine by Maudslay, Sons & Field, London - speed raised to 11 knots. **1873**: May 25: homeward bound, she hit an uncharted rock off Dassen Island near Cape Town and continued her voyage. Two days later, taking in too much water, she turned back to Cape Town where she spent several weeks being repaired on the patent slipway. **1880**: Used on the Cape-Zanzibar route. **1888**: Placed on the fortnightly Southampton-Hamburg feeder service. **1889**: Bought by Essayan, Oondjian & Co., Constantinople, renamed ADANA (a Turkish town). **1895**: Sold again to Idare-i Mahsusa (Ottoman Steam Nav. Co.), Constantinople - the same company owned the former Castle coaster FLORENCE. **1910**: August: Idare-i Mahsusa was reorganised as Osmanli Seyrisefain Idaresi. **1911**: October: scuttled as blockship during the Italo-Ottoman War in the approaches to Yenikale (Gulf of Izmir).

ROMAN (AG)

BRITON

SAXON in Cape Town with tug GNU (SAL)

NORSEMAN (1) Iron screw steamer (Union 1865-1873)
O.N. 51290
Builders: Charles Lungley & Co., Deptford, London
Tonnage: 1,245 gross 960 net
Dimensions: 262.8 x 32.2 x 23.5 feet
Engines: 2-cyl. horizontal direct-acting by C. A. Day & Co., Southampton 220 h.p. 9 knots
Passengers: not known

1865: Designed for the mail service - also the last ship completed by Charles Lungley & Co. for Union Line. The yard was taken over by the Millwall Ironworks & Shipbuilding Co. in April 1866. Registered: December 20. **1866**: Arrived Cape Town: February 13. **1873**: June: sold initially to E. Bates, Liverpool and then to the newly formed Western & Brazilian Telegraph Co., London. Converted into a cable-laying vessel. Given new boilers and engines compounded by G. Watt & Co. - 200 h.p. **1880**: New 2-cyl. compound engine by George Clark, Sunderland -160 h.p. **1888**: Laid cable across the River Plate. **1892**: Suffered serious storm damage and was offered for sale. Her name was continued in three subsequent ships owned by the company (which later became the Western Telegraph Co.). **1896**: July: sold to A. C. S. Springer, London and then to M. S. Springer & Zoon, Amsterdam. **1898**: November: broken up at Harburg.

CELT (2) Iron screw steamer (Union 1866-1875)
O.N. 51296
Builders: Charles Lungley & Co., Deptford/Millwall Ironworks & Shipbuilding Co., London
Tonnage: 1,439 gross 864 net
Dimensions: 274.5 x 34.4 x 25.8 feet
Engines: 2-cyl. horizontal direct-acting by C. A. Day & Co., Southampton 300 h.p. 11 knots
Passengers: not known

1865: Designed for the mail service - last Union ship built on the Thames. Work underway in July but probably ceased following the bankruptcy of Charles Lungley's Rotherhithe works. **1866**: April: yard was taken over by the Millwall Ironworks & Shipbuilding Co. with Charles Lungley, as Managing Director. Registered: May 29. Arrived Cape Town: July 11. In September, the Millwall Ironworks & Shipbuilding Co. went bankrupt as a result of the collapse of the

Overend & Gurney Bank on *Black Friday*, May 11. **1874**: Cut in half and lengthened by 51 feet - new length 325.4 feet and tonnage: 2,095 gross 1,353 net. Also given new 300 h.p. compound engine by Maudslay, Sons & Field, London. **1875**: February 7: wrecked near Quoin Point, Cape Colony whilst on voyage to Algoa Bay - all were saved. Ironically, her main rival WINDSOR CASTLE met a similar fate the following year. Quoin Point (near the southern tip of Africa, Cape Agulhas) is also the place where TEUTON was lost in 1881 with great loss of life.

FLEET RECONSTRUCTION 1869-1876

Following the introduction of a twice-monthly Cape mail service in 1868, Union Line significantly increased the size of the fleet with new and second-hand ships.

NORTHAM Iron screw steamer (Union 1869-1876)
O.N. 21595
Builders: Day, Summers & Co. Southampton
Tonnage: 1,557 gross 958 net
Dimensions: 274 x 34.7 x 23.1 feet
Engines: 2-cyl. horizontal direct-acting by builder 300 h.p. 1,514 i.h.p. 13.5 knots
Passengers: 97 first, 30 second

1858: Launched: April 1 for Peninsular & Oriental S. N. Co., London. Registered: June 11. **1859**: April: placed on Suez-Mauritius-Sydney service. August 20: stranded near Jeddah and successfully refloated August 25. **1861**: Galle-Sydney-Melbourne service. **1866**: Suez-Bombay service. **1868**: December: sold to Day, Summers & Co. in part payment for HINDOSTAN. **1869**: January: bought by Union S. S. Co. and rebuilt for Cape mail service. Registered June 8. Arrived Cape Town: July 27. **1876**: February: sold to Sir James Malcolm, Liverpool and converted into a four-mast sailing ship, registered at London. **1878**: December 21: destroyed by fire in South Atlantic (09.40S-31.36W) whilst on voyage London-Sydney. Passengers and crew were rescued and landed at Montevideo.

NORSEMAN (AG)

CELT (AG)

CELT wrecked at Quion Point in 1875 (TH)

NORHAM (P&O)

SYRIA Iron screw steamer (Union 1870-1877)
O.N. 48568
Builders: Day, Summers & Co., Southampton
Tonnage: 1,932 gross 1,420 net
Dimensions: 312.5 x 36 x 25.8 feet
Engines: 2-cyl. oscillating by builder 450 h.p. 2,602 i.h.p. 13 knots
Passengers: 161 first, 34 second

1863: Launched: August 15 for Peninsular & Oriental S. N. Co., London as a two funnel paddle steamer for Southampton-Suez route (laid down as SCINDIA). November: completed. **1870:** Redundant with the opening of Suez Canal, sold to Caird & Co., Greenock in part payment for new steamers PEKIN and PESHAWUR. September: sold to Union S. S. Co. **1871:** Fitted with 2-cyl. compound engine by builders 300 h.p. (1,800 i.h.p.) and converted to screw. Her bunker and cargo capacity increased from 450 and 400 tons respectively to 1,000 and 1,200 tons. She was also Union Line's first ship with compound engines. Trials: May 18. Arrived Cape Town: June 21. On second voyage, broke the Southampton-Cape Town record: 26 days 18 hours. **1874:** On homeward voyage broke her shaft north of St. Helena. Reached Ascension under sail and was towed back to Southampton by AMERICAN which was hit by ARACAN (see AMERICAN for details). **1875:** Broke her shaft again near St. Helena and was towed back to England by tug ANGLIA. **1876:** November: inaugurated the Southampton-Port Elizabeth direct service - the first regular Intermediate service. **1877:** November: sold to James Laing, Sunderland in part payment for new steamer DURBAN. **1880:** April 4: on a charter voyage New Orleans-Liverpool with a cargo of cotton and oil-cake, she foundered in the North Atlantic (39.59N-56.1W).

DANUBE Iron screw steamer (Union 1871-1888)
O.N. 54753
Builders: Millwall Ironworks & Shipbuilding Co., London
Tonnage: 2,000 gross 1,260 net
Dimensions: 332 x 34 x 24.4 feet
Engines: 2-cyl. by Humphrys, Tennant & Dykes 400 h.p. 10 knots
Passengers: 140 first, 68 second, 30 third

1866: The last paddle steamer built for Royal Mail Steam Packet. Co., London, she originally had two funnels and was used on the Southampton-Rio de Janeiro-Buenos Aires route and later in the West Indies. Registered: September 18. **1871:** March: bought by Union S.S. Co. Converted by Day, Summers & Co. Southampton into a screw driven ship - one of her funnels was removed and she was fitted with new 300 h.p. (1800 i.h.p.) compound engines by Day, Summers. New tonnage: 2,039 gross, 1,462 net. **1872:** Arrived Cape Town: February 6. **1873:** March: made the fastest Southampton-Cape Town voyage for Union Line: 25 days 12 hours. **1879:** February: carried the French Prince Imperial, Louis Bonaparte to South Africa for the Zulu War campaign - he was later killed in a Zulu ambush. **1881:** Transferred to the South African coastal service. **1888:** February: sold to I. Cohen, London for breaking up.

EUROPEAN Iron screw steamer (Union 1872-1877)
O.N. 65556
Builders: Robert Napier & Sons, Glasgow (yard no: 145)
Tonnage: 2,242 gross 1,431 net
Dimensions: 307.2 x 37.7 x 27.7 feet
Engines: 2-cyl. compound by builder 350 h.p. 11 knots
Passengers: 55 first, 55 second

1869: September: completed as EUROPE. She and her sister AFRIQUE were built for a new service from Marseilles to Bombay operated by Cie. Marseillaise de Nav. à Vapeur (well known later as Cie. Fraissinet). November 18: took part in the inauguration ceremony for the opening of the Suez Canal. **1871:** The new route was not a success, especially after the Franco-Prussian War, and both ships were sold, the EUROPE going to John Ryde & Co., London who used her on a new London-Calcutta service. Registered: March 2. **1872:** Bought by Union S. S. Co. and renamed EUROPEAN. She was the company's first straight stemmed ship. Registered: April 25. Sailed from Southampton May 5 on her first Union voyage in the midst of a seamens' strike - she anchored down river the day before sailing and her crew were ferried aboard by local tugs. Arrived Cape Town: June 16. **1873:** Given new 350 h.p., 2-cyl. compound engines by Day, Summers, Southampton. **1877:** Fitted with iron bulwarks and a forecastle. December 5: homeward bound, was wrecked on Basse Meur Rock at the south-west tip of the island of Ushant with no loss of life.

ASIATIC Iron screw steamer (Union 1873-1888)
O.N. 68812
Builders: Whitehaven Shipbuilding Co. (yard no: 4)
Tonnage: 2,066 gross 1,520 net
Dimensions: 299.9 x 34.2 x 23.3 feet
Engines: 2-cyl. compound by Jack, Rollo & Co., Liverpool 274 h.p.
Trials: 12.2 knots
Passengers: 75 first, 55 second

1872: Launched: September 19 for unknown owners. Purchased on the stocks for mail service, her design was based on the model and specifications of a similar sized ship launched in May and completed as NIGRETIA for the African S.S. Co. (Elder Dempster). **1873:** Registered: January 24. Arrived Cape Town: February 23. **1879:** Chartered as a transport during Zulu War. **1880:** Became an "extra" steamer. **1884:** April 28: went aground near Mossel Bay but was refloated. **1888:** March: sold to H. Martini, Glasgow. Name unchanged and still registered at Southampton. **1890:** May: bought by George Tweedy & Co., London - renamed JAFFAR. Registered at London. **1891:** July: owners bought by The London Steamers Ltd. (Philip Wigham Richardson manager). **1895:** March: sold for scrap.

SYRIA (AG)

DANUBE (AG)

EUROPEAN Union Line's first straight stemmed ship (AG)

ASIATIC aground near Mossel Bay in 1884. In the background is the Castle Line coaster FLORENCE (BI)

AFRICAN (1) Iron screw steamer (Union 1873-1883)
O.N. 68814
Builders: John Key & Son, Kinghorn, Fife (yard no: 15)
Tonnage: 2,019 gross 1,258 net
Dimensions: 315.7 x 34.3 x 24.1 feet
Engines: 2-cyl. compound from builder's works at Kirkcaldy
280 h.p. 10 knots
Passengers: 60 first, 80 second

1872: Launched: December 31 for the mail service. After launching, she was towed to Leith to be fitted out. Key did not have a fitting out basin. **1873**: Registered: March 4. Arrived Cape Town: April 3. **1879**: January: after the Zulu victory at Isandlwana, carried relief troops from Cape Town to Durban. **1881**: Transferred to coastal service. **1883**: November: sold to J. Japp, Liverpool and J. M. Kirby, London. Name and registration unchanged. **1884**: Ownership now J. Japp, Liverpool, J. M. Kirby, London, and F. Stumore, London. **1887**: February 15: ran aground on the Abu Madaff reef (42 miles north of Jeddah) in the Red Sea whilst on voyage with a cargo of coal from Cardiff to Jeddah. February 26: broke in two.

TEUTON Iron screw steamer (Union 1873-1881)
O.N. 60927
Builders: William Denny & Bros., Dumbarton (yard no: 135)
Tonnage: 1,741 gross 1,088 net
Dimensions: 286.4 x 34.4 x 25.1 feet
Engines: 2-cyl. simple by Denny & Co. 300 h.p. 1,345 i.h.p.
Trials: 13.2 knots
Passengers: 20 first

1869: Launched: March 13 as for Robert Jardine (Matheson & Co.) GLENARTNEY for the Calcutta and Hong Kong trade - also fitted with two 12-pounder iron guns as protection against pirates. Registered: April 14. **1873**: February: bought by Union S.S. Co. for mail service - renamed TEUTON. Passenger accommodation increased to 250 in three classes. Registered: February 12. Arrived Cape Town: April 22. **1875**: Lengthened by 46 feet - new length 332.9 feet. Tonnage: 2,313 gross 1,466 net. Engines compounded by A. & J. Inglis, Glasgow. **1878**: Given new compound engines by Thomas Clark & Co., Newcastle. **1879**: Chartered as a transport during Zulu War. **1881**: Became an "extra". August 30: after leaving Cape Town bound for Algoa Bay, she struck a rock off Quoin Point (near Cape Agulhas) and sank with the loss of 236 passengers and crew - one of South Africa's worst maritime disasters.

ANGLIAN (2) Iron screw steamer (Union 1873-1894)
O.N. 68820
Builders: Aitken & Mansel, Whiteinch (yard no: 60)
Tonnage: 2,206 gross 1,453 net
Dimensions: 314 x 35.9 x 26.4 feet
Engines: 2-cyl. compound by J.& J. Thomson, Glasgow 270 h.p.
Trials: 11.5 knots
Passengers: 94 first, 50 second, 100 third

1873: Launched: March 3 as mail ship. Registered: July 2. Arrived Cape Town: August 2 - among her passengers was a then unknown, Barney Barnato. **1884**: February: chartered to carry troops to Egypt for the General Gordon Relief Expedition. **1886**: Engines converted to triple expansion and new boilers installed by T. Richardson, Hartlepool - the first such conversion by the company. She was also given a forecastle and iron bulwarks and her yards were removed. Transferred to coastal service. **1894**: September: sold to Huddart Parker Ltd., Melbourne for use on their Sydney-New Zealand service. December 17: arrived at Melbourne with a cargo of coal from Barry, South Wales. **1895**: January: entered service, name unchanged, after a refit which increased her passenger capacity to 200. **1897**: July: transferred to Sydney-Fremantle run but, following the loss of the TASMANIA later that month, she reverted to her original route. **1902**: With the arrival of the new VICTORIA, she was reduced to a cargo carrier. **1913**: Became a coal hulk in Adelaide. **1929**: After time as a coal hulk in Sydney, she was laid up in Berrys Bay, Sydney. **1933**: August 2: now sixty years old, she was towed outside Sydney Heads and scuttled.

TEUTON

AFRICAN

ANGLIAN

ANGLIAN in Huddart Parker ownership at Sydney

AMERICAN Iron screw steamer (Union 1873-1880)
O.N. 68822
Builders: Alexander Stephen & Sons, Dundee (yard no: 49)
Tonnage: 2,126 gross 1,357 net
Dimensions: 320 x 34.2 x 25.1 feet
Engines: 2-cyl. compound by Gourlay Bros. & Co., Dundee 320 h.p. 12 knots
Passengers: 100 first, 50 second, 100 third

1873: Launched: April 26 for the mail service. Registered: August: 16. Arrived Cape Town: September 21. **1874:** March 9: homeward bound, towing SYRIA with a broken shaft, she was hit amidships by Thos. & Jno. Brocklebank's sailing ship ARACAN near Portland, Dorset during poor visibility. The ARACAN sank and her crew was transferred to the Union ships. Although badly damaged, AMERICAN towed SYRIA back to Southampton where both were repaired. **1876:** April 17: broke the southbound record set by DUNROBIN CASTLE. Plymouth-Cape Town: 22 days 2 hours. In the same year, she was given a long poop (she was flush decked when built). New tonnage: 2,485 gross 1,599 net. **1879:** Chartered as a transport during Zulu War and carried the new commander-in-chief Lt-General Thesiger (later Lord Chelmsford) to South Africa. **1880:** March 17: arrived Southampton with 382 army personnel from Natal - the voyage from Cape Town to Plymouth took 21 days and 12 hours. April 23: sailing to the Cape, just north of the Equator (01.56N-9.50W), her shaft broke and severely damaged her hull. The 136 crew and passengers managed to get into lifeboats before she sank, and although the boats were separated, they were all eventually rescued by passing ships. May 12: one of the rescue vessels, the British & African Steam Navigation Co. steamer SENEGAL (1,625/1872), ran aground at Las Palmas and a survivor from AMERICAN, the Cape Parliament MP John Paterson was drowned - two years later, a new South African paddle tug JOHN PATERSON was named in his memory.

NYANZA Iron screw steamer (Union 1873-1880)
O.N. 50137
Builders: Thames Iron Works & Shipbuilding Co., Blackwall (yard no: 1f)
Tonnage: 2,082 gross 1,482 net
Dimensions: 327.3 x 36.2 x 27.6 feet
Engines: 2-cyl. oscillating by J. & G. Rennie, London 450 h.p.
2,304 i.h.p. 12 knots **Trials:** 13.6 knots
Passengers: 143 first, 34 second

1864: Launched: June 6. Completed for Peninsular & Oriental S. N. Co., London as a two funnel paddle steamer (their last) for Southampton-Alexandria route. Registered: November 3. **1870:** Laid up following the opening of the Suez Canal and the closure of the

Southampton-Alexandria service. **1873:** January: sold to Union S.S. Co. Fitted with a 2-cyl. compound engine by Gourlay Bros. & Co., Dundee (351 h.p.), she was converted to screw, and lengthened by 17 feet - she also now only had one funnel. New tonnages: 2,128 gross 1,421 net. **1874:** Arrived Cape Town: April 20. **1880:** Used briefly on the East African coastal run. October: sold to Sultan of Zanzibar for use as his private yacht. **1889:** Run down by unknown steamship in the Suez Canal - successfully repaired and sold her to Mahallah, Zanzibar. The same year, she was again acquired by the Sultan of Zanzibar. Operated Zanzibar-Bombay passenger service: 80 first, 40 second. **1904:** June: after a lengthy period of inactivity, she was broken up at Bombay.

NUBIAN Iron screw steamer (Union 1876-1892)
O.N. 72366
Builders: C. Mitchell & Co., Newcastle (yard no: 300)
Tonnage: 3,091 gross 1,998 net
Dimensions: 359 x 38.6 x 27.2 feet
Engines: 2-cyl. compound by Thomas Clark & Co., Newcastle 400 h.p.
1,800 i.h.p. 10 knots
Passengers: 150 first, 50 second

1876: Launched: February 28. Purchased on the stocks for mail service - a sister of their ST OSYTH, her original order came from Watts, Milburn & Co. She was Union's first two funnelled ship. Registered: August 11. Arrived Cape Town: September 11. **1883:** October: she joined ARAB on Union Line's short lived and unsuccessful Liverpool-Bermuda-Newport News (later Baltimore) service, and made four round trips before the line closed in April 1884. **1891:** Rebuilt with a single funnel. Her boilers were also replaced, and she was given a new 385 h.p. triple expansion engine by Day, Summers & Co., Southampton which increased her speed to 12 knots. **1892:** Became an intermediate ship. December 20: with a pilot on board, on a southbound voyage, she ran aground on the southern shore of the River Tagus, Lisbon and was a total loss - all were saved.

AMERICAN

NYANZA

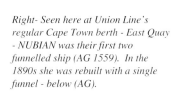

Right- Seen here at Union Line's regular Cape Town berth - East Quay - NUBIAN was their first two funnelled ship (AG 1559). In the 1890s she was rebuilt with a single funnel - below (AG).

FIRST CURRIE-OWNED MAILSHIPS

Although Donald Currie initially operated his Cape mail service with ships transferred from the family North Sea operation (see Chapter Seven Sail, Currie family and chartered ships), his first wholly-owned ships on the route were the second-hand WILLIAM MILLER and the trio designed for the London-Calcutta service.

WILLIAM MILLER Iron screw steamer (Castle 1872)
O.N. 62274
Builders: Randolph, Elder & Co., Glasgow (yard no: 100)
Tonnage: 889 gross 567 net
Dimensions: 215.8 x 27.7 x 20.5 feet
Engines: 2-cyl. compound by builder 100 h.p.
Passengers: not known

1869: Launched: April 10. Completed for Oriental Screw Collier Co. Ltd., Leith. Registered: May 5. **1872**: Oriental Screw Collier Co. went into liquidation and in February WILLIAM MILLER was bought by Donald Currie as a stopgap until arrival of new steamers. Registered: February 2. She was also the first Donald Currie-owned steamer seen at Cape. Sailing from London February 23, she arrived at Cape Town on March 28. December: sold to Bristol General Steam Navigation Co., Bristol. Renamed SAPPHO and used on the Bristol-Antwerp-Rotterdam-Amsterdam service. **1877**: Company restyled as Bristol Steam Navigation Co. Ltd. **1883**: May 17: ran ashore off Fort Bathe in the River Scheldt on voyage from Antwerp-Bristol with general cargo. Broke her back and declared constructive total loss.

DOVER CASTLE (1) Iron screw steamer (Castle 1872)
O.N. 65672
Builders: Barclay, Curle & Co., Stobcross (yard no: 215)
Tonnage: 2,341 gross 1,582 net
Dimensions: 327.7 x 36.4 x 27.9 feet
Engines: 2-cyl. compound by builder 217 h.p. 10 knots
Passengers: not known

1872: Launched: January 25 for London-Calcutta service. First steamer with CASTLE name and the lead ship in a group of four similar vessels. Registered: April 11. Chartered to the Pacific Steam Navigation Co. July 26: on her maiden voyage, homeward bound from Callao to Liverpool with a cargo of cotton, wool and hides, caught fire. The following day she was scuttled at Coquimbo, Chile. Earlier that month her new near sister, EDINBURGH CASTLE (1), had also been placed on charter with P.S.N.C.

EDINBURGH CASTLE (1) Iron screw steamer (Castle 1872-1880)
O.N. 65708
Builders: Robert Napier & Sons, Glasgow (yard no: 309)
Tonnage: 2,678 gross 1,734 net
Dimensions: 335.3 x 37.7 x 28.2 feet
Engines: 2-cyl. compound by builder 270 h.p. 10 knots
Passengers: not known

1872: Launched: March 27 for London-Calcutta service but never operated on the route. Registered: June 27. Joined DOVER CASTLE (1) on a Pacific Steam Navigation Co. charter. July 13: left Liverpool on her maiden voyage to South America. **1873**: July 4: after three South American voyages, arrived back at Liverpool. Placed on Cape mail run. Arrived Cape Town: August 16. **1880**: July: with arrival of KINFAUNS and GRANTULLY CASTLE, sold with WALMER CASTLE to Don José Campo, Marqués de Campo for his recently won Cádiz-Manila mail contract service - renamed ESPAÑA. **1882**: Inaugurated a new line between Spain and San Francisco via the Straits of Magellan. **1884**: March 14: Spain-Philippines mail contract transferred to Compañía General de Tabacos de Filipinas which was owned by Compañía Trasatlántica, Barcelona. **1885**: Sold to Compañía Trasatlántica - name unchanged. **1891**: One return voyage from Spain to Argentina. **1898**: Sold to Armement Bonnecroy, Marseilles for demolition. July: scrapped.

WINDSOR CASTLE (1) Iron screw steamer (Castle 1872-1876)
O.N. 65728
Builders: Robert Napier & Sons, Glasgow (yard no: 310)
Tonnage: 2,672 gross 1,732 net
Dimensions: 334.7 x 37.7 x 28.2 feet
Engines: 2-cyl. compound by builder 270 h.p. 10 knots
Passengers: not known

1872: Launched: April 25 for London-Calcutta service. Registered: August 19. The only ship of the quartet to operate on the India trade. On maiden voyage broke the England-Calcutta record. **1873**: After two voyages on Indian run, transferred to Cape mail service. Arrived Cape Town: May 16 having broken the Cape southbound record: 23 days 15 minutes. **1874**: October: bound for Cape Town, caught fire but managed to make La Coruña safely. **1876**: October 19: on voyage Dartmouth-Cape Town, wrecked near the Triangles, west of Dassen Island, 60 miles north of Cape Town - no lives were lost.

WALMER CASTLE (1) Iron screw steamer (Castle 1872-1880)
O.N. 65729
Builders: Barclay, Curle & Co., Stobcross (yard no: 216)
Tonnage: 2,439 gross 1,589 net
Dimensions: 327.8 x 36.4 x 27.9 feet
Engines: 2-cyl. compound by builder 217 h.p. 10 knots
Passengers: not known

1872: Launched: April 23 for London-Calcutta service but never operated on the route. Registered: August 19. First CASTLE named steamer seen at Cape. Arrived Cape Town: October 4 on voyage London-Bordeaux-Cape Town-Mauritius. Subsequently on regular Cape mail service. **1880**: May: with arrival of KINFAUNS and GRANTULLY CASTLE, sold with EDINBURGH CASTLE to Don José Campo, Marqués de Campo for his recently won Cádiz-Manila mail contract service. Renamed VALENCIA after the birthplace of the Marqués de Campo. **1884**: March 14: Spain-Philippines mail contract transferred to Compañía General de Tabacos de Filipinas which was owned by Compañía Trasatlántica, Barcelona. **1888**: Bought by T.Cuthbertson, West Hartlepool for China trade. Renamed GAW QUAN SIA. Engines tripled by Central Marine Engineering Co., West Hartlepool 190 h.p. **1889**: December 16: on voyage Singapore-Calcutta-Hamburg-London with general cargo, collided with the Nederlandsch Amerikaansche Stoomvaart Maatschappij (Holland America Line) steamer LEERDAM (2,796/1881) 23 miles north-east by north of Noord Hinder Lightship Belgian coast - both ships sank with loss of two lives on GAW QUAN SIA.

EDINBURGH CASTLE (LD)

WINDSOR CASTLE

WALMER CASTLE

FIRST CASTLE CAPE MAILSHIPS 1875-1877

DUNROBIN CASTLE Iron screw steamer (Castle 1875-1893)
O.N. 73612
Builders: Robert Napier & Sons, Glasgow (yard no: 346)
Tonnage: 2,811 gross 1,784 net
Dimensions: 342.3 x 38.3 x 28.3 feet
Engines: 2-cyl. compound by builder 300 h.p. 1,400 i.h.p. 11 knots
Passengers: 100 first, 50 second, 100 emigrants

1875: Launched: November as the first of Donald Currie's purpose-built Cape mailships. **1876**: Registered: January 29. Arrived Cape Town: April 15 having broken the Cape southbound record: 22 days 12 hours. **1877**: February 17: improved the Cape southbound record: 21 days 12 hours 49 minutes. **1879**: January 27: sailed Cape Town for St Vincent, Cape Verde Islands (the end of the telegraph cable to Europe) with first news of defeat at Isandlwana and request for troop reinforcements. **1883**: Transferred to intermediate mail service. **1892**: January 6: first ocean-going steamer to cross the bar at Durban. **1893**: May: sold to Barclay Curle & Co. Ltd. October: bought by the Association Notre Dame de France, a Roman Catholic organization which arranged pilgrimages to the Holy Land. Placed under the management of Armement Letocart & Cie., Marseille and converted into a 300 capacity pilgrim ship to Palestine (hence the blue cross on her funnel). Renamed NOTRE DAME DE SALUT. **1895**: February: chartered by French Government as a hospital ship during the war in Madagascar. **1896**: Resumed the Palestine pilgrim service. **1900**: Between August 10, 1900 and January 30, 1901, used as a 256-bed hospital ship during the Boxer Rebellion in China under the auspices of the French Red Cross. **1902**: Sold to L. Bertaux, Paris - remained on Marseille-Palestine run and renamed L'ÉTOILE. **1913**: Sold for scrap to G. Pittaluga fu J., Genoa. **1914**: 1st quarter broken up at Genoa.

BALMORAL CASTLE (1) Iron screw steamer (Castle 1877-1882)
O.N. 76935
Builders: Robert Napier & Sons, Glasgow (yard no: 356)
Tonnage: 2,948 gross 1,885 net
Dimensions: 344.8 x 39.4 x 29.1 feet
Engines: 2-cyl. compound by builder 300 h.p. 1,400 i.h.p. 11 knots
Passengers: 100 first, 50 second, 100 emigrants

1876: Launched: November 2 for Cape mail service. **1877**: Registered: February 15. Arrived Cape Town: March 31 with new Governor of the Cape Colony, Sir Bartle Frere. October 12: broke the Cape southbound record: 21 days, 11 hours 8 minutes - this was broken 5 days later by Union's GERMAN and Castle had to wait until 1890 for another record run. **1882**: June: sold with DUBLIN CASTLE to Don José Campo, Marqués de Campo for his recently won Cádiz-Manila mail contract service. Renamed SAN AUGUSTIN. They joined WALMER and EDINBURGH CASTLE, which were bought in 1880. **1883**: December 17: caught fire north of La Coruña (45.40N-7.23W)

on voyage from Manila to Liverpool. Abandoned by her crew, she was towed to La Coruña by the British steamer OPORTO (319/1870). **1884**: March 14: Spain-Philippines mail contract transferred to Compañía General de Tabacos de Filipinas which was owned by Compañía Trasatlántica, Barcelona. **1885**: June: after lengthy repairs at La Coruña, placed on Spanish West Indies service. **1887**: April: sold to J. MacMillan Jr., Dumbarton - reverted to BALMORAL CASTLE. June: sold to Balmoral Castle S.S. Co. Ltd. (J. Kilgour, manager), London. **1888**: March: arrived on the Clyde for engines to be tripled (383 h.p.) by D. Rowan & Sons, Glasgow. June 16: rammed the newly built Southampton-Isle of Wight paddle steamer PRINCESS OF WALES whilst both were undergoing trials on the Skelmorie measured mile on the Firth of Clyde - the paddler was cut in two and sank with the loss of 3 lives. **1891**: Visited Cape Town on Australian and New Zealand meat trade charter to the International Line. **1893**: March: sold to the Quebec Steam Ship Co., London - renamed MADIANA. **1903**: February 10: wrecked on coral reef about 10 miles north of Hamilton, Bermuda on voyage from New York to Bermuda and Kingston with passengers and general cargo - no lives lost. Her wreck lies one mile east of CARAQUET (ex GUELPH).

DUBLIN CASTLE Iron screw steamer (Castle 1877-1882)
O.N. 76971
Builders: Robert Napier & Sons, Glasgow (yard no: 361)
Tonnage: 2,911 gross 1,856 net
Dimensions: 344.9 x 39.4 x 28.7 feet
Engines: 2-cyl. compound by builder 300 h.p. 1,400 i.h.p. 11 knots
Passengers: not known

1877: May: launched for Cape mail service. Registered: June 12. On maiden voyage, carried Mr. and Mrs. Gladstone from London to Plymouth. Arrived Cape Town: August 4. **1882**: September: sold with BALMORAL CASTLE to Don José Campo, Marqués de Campo for his recently won Cádiz-Manila mail contract service - renamed SANTO DOMINGO. They joined WALMER and EDINBURGH CASTLE, which were purchased in 1880. **1884**: March 14: Spain-Philippines mail contract transferred to Compañía General de Tabacos de Filipinas which was owned by Compañía Trasatlántica, Barcelona. July 21: thirty miles north of Cape Finisterre, rescued survivors from the Compañía Trasatlántica GIJON (1,843/1872) which sank with much loss of life after three way collision in thick fog with R. Harrowing & Co.'s LAXHAM (1,295/1879) and W. H. Scott Bros' HUELVA (1,342/82) - both these ships also sank. **1896**: Transferred to the Cadiz-Havana-New York service. **1886**: Sold to Compañía Trasatlántica, Barcelona - name unchanged. **1898**: July 12: During the Spanish-American war, on a voyage from Vera Cruz to Havana with provisions and livestock, was intercepted by US gunboat EAGLE about 22N-83.45W and driven ashore on the Isle of Pines, Cuba and burnt.

BALMORAL CASTLE (AG)

DUNROBIN CASTLE (LD)

The pilgrim ship NOTRE DAME DE SALUT (ex DUNROBIN CASTLE) (TH)

DUBLIN CASTLE (AG)

WARWICK CASTLE (2) Iron screw steamer (Castle 1877-1897)
O.N. 77027
Builders: Robert Napier & Sons, Glasgow (yard no: 362)
Tonnage: 2,957 gross 1,892 net
Dimensions: 348.9 x 39.4 x 28.8 feet
Engines: 2-cyl. compound by builder 370 h.p. 12 knots
Passengers: not known

1877: Launched: August 24 for Cape mail service (name was announced as STIRLING CASTLE). Registered: October 24. Arrived Cape Town: December 8. **1889**: January 23: now on the intermediate run, inaugurated London-Flushing-South Africa route (Direct Flushing Service) for Dutch emigrants to the Transvaal Republic. **1891**: Engines tripled by Fairfield S.B. & E. Co. Ltd., Glasgow (400 h.p.). Funnel heightened and given bulwarks in place of rails and topgallant forecastle. **1892**: Chartered by Lord Ardilaun (Sir Arthur Guinness) for a cruise in the Mediterranean. **1897**: August - sold to Booth Line. Renamed JEROME, she joined AUGUSTINE (ex GRANTULLY CASTLE) which had been bought in 1896. In 1902 HAWARDEN CASTLE was purchased and renamed CYRIL. October: first voyage Liverpool-Amazon. **1910**: Sold to the Turkish government and commissioned by the navy as the mine transport GIRESUN (a Turkish town on the Black Sea). **1916**: Became a naval collier. **1917**: Laid up at Istanbul. **1919**: May: transferred to the Osmanli Seyrisefain Idaresi, Istanbul for commercial service she joined TIRIMÜJGAN (ex PEMBROKE CASTLE). **1924**: December: with Turkey now a republic, owners restyled Türkiye Seyrisefain Idaresi. **1927**: Sold to Ilhami Söker, Istanbul for demolition.

CONWAY CASTLE Iron screw steamer (Castle 1877-1893)
O.N. 77047
Builders: Robert Napier & Sons, Glasgow (yard no: 364)
Tonnage: 2,966 gross 1,899 net
Dimensions: 349 x 39.3 x 28.9 feet
Engines: 2-cyl. compound by builder 370 h.p. 12 knots
Passengers: not known

1877: Launched: September for Cape mail service. Registered: December 7. **1878**: Arrived Cape Town: February 14. **1885**: During the Sudanese War, she and PEMBROKE CASTLE were used as troopships. **1892**: Engines tripled by Fairfield S.B. & E. Co. Ltd., Glasgow (400 h.p. 3,188 i.h.p. trials: 14.4 knots max). Funnel was heightened and she was given bulwarks in place of rails. Placed on the Mauritius route. **1893**: May 10: on voyage London-Mauritius with general cargo, ran aground 50 miles south of Tamatave, Madagascar. No loss of life - all rescued 10 days later by Union Line's ARAB.

CONWAY CASTLE after her 1892 conversion (JC)

CONWAY CASTLE *as built (TT)*

WARWICK CASTLE *after her 1891 conversion (TT)*

NEW GENERATION OF UNION MAILSHIPS

Following the establishment of the joint mail contract, Union Line built ten fast superior mailships between 1877 and 1883 able to undertake the voyage to the Cape in 21 days.

GERMAN (1) Iron screw steamer (Union 1877-1896)
O.N. 76834
Builders: William Denny & Bros., Dumbarton (yard no: 195)
Tonnage: 3,028 gross 1,946 net
Dimensions: 350.6 x 39.4 x 29.6 feet
Engines: 2-cyl. compound by Denny & Co. 500 h.p. 2,760 i.h.p. 12 knots
Trials: 13.8 knots
Passengers: 72 first, up to 78 second (flexible)

1877: Launched: June 27 as the first of a new generation of fast, modern mail ships built for Union. Registered: August 3. October 17: when she arrived at Cape Town, not only had she shaved more than two days off BALMORAL CASTLE's record run, she was also the first mailship to complete the Southbound journey in less than twenty days: 19 days 8 hours 30 minutes. From now on, apart from a few occasions, the record in both directions remained with Union Line. **1880**: March: carried the ex-Empress Eugenie of France to Natal so that she could visit the site of her son's death. Prince Louis Bonaparte was killed during the Zulu War. **1889**: Became an intermediate steamer. **1895**: July: sold (via brokers H. E. Moss) to Soc. Metallurgica di Savona for scrapping, but as hull and machinery were in good condition, was bought by Navigazione Generale Italiana (N.G.I.), Genoa. **1896**: Renamed SEMPIONE, her accommodation was expanded to take 130 first, 1,150 steerage. December 16: first voyage Genoa-River Plate. **1899**: February 3: first voyage Genoa-Naples-New York. **1902**: October: became coal hulk in Genoa. **1903**: Scrapped in Genoa.

DURBAN Iron screw steamer (Union 1877-1893)
O.N. 76838
Builders: James Laing, Sunderland (yard no: 203)
Tonnage: 2,875 gross 1,685 net
Dimensions: 360 x 38.5 x 28.5 feet
Engines: 2-cyl. compound by R.& W. Hawthorn & Co., Newcastle 550 h.p. 12 knots
Passengers: 150 first, 55 second

1877: Launched: June 12. Purchased on the stocks for mail service - name announced as either GRECIAN or ARABIAN but DURBAN selected instead. Registered: November 12. November 23: shortly after leaving Plymouth, she sprang a leak during bad weather and had to abandon her maiden voyage. **1878**: Arrived Cape Town: January 11. **1880**: August 8: set new northbound record: 18 days 9 hours and subsequently became an intermediate steamer. **1883**: Because of the serious trade depression the 1880s, DURBAN was withdrawn from the route for five years. **1888**: Returned to South Africa as a cargo carrier. **1893**: June 11: northbound with cargo of wool, mohair, skins and hides, wrecked on south-east coast of Teneriffe, 15 miles south of Santa Cruz with no loss of life.

PRETORIA Iron screw steamer (Union 1878-1897)
O.N. 76844
Builders: William Denny & Bros., Dumbarton (yard no: 213)
Tonnage: 3,198 gross 2,040 net
Dimensions: 350 x 40.2 x 31.1 feet
Engines: 2-cyl. compound by Denny & Co. 500 h.p. 2,804 i.h.p. 12 knots
Trials: 13.6 knots
Passengers: 78 first, up to 112 second (flexible), 32 third

1878: Launched: August 14 as a repeat of GERMAN but with slightly different dimensions. Registered: October 22. Arrived Cape Town: December 12. **1879**: January: on the homeward run, she became the first mailship to complete the northbound run in less than twenty days. February: after the Zulu victory at Isandlwana, PRETORIA was refitted as a troopship in eight days and carried 942 men of the 91st Argyle Highlanders to Natal in record time: 24 days 6 hours (including 25 hours in Cape Town). September 7: again lowered the northbound record: 18 days 13 hours 14 minutes. October 29: reduced GERMAN's southbound record: 18 days 16 hours 48 minutes. **1881**: Carried troops for the first Boer War - went direct from Southampton to Durban in record time of just over 19 days. **1888**: Engines tripled by J. & J. Thomson, Glasgow (557 h.p.). She also had her yards removed, was fitted with a hurricane deck, and transferred to the intermediate service. **1897**: February: bought by the Quebec S.S. Co., presumably for their New York-West Indies run. Name unchanged. **1902**: March: on voyage New York-Bermuda, caught fire and returned to New York for repairs. **1907**: July: sold to the Khedivial Mail Steamship & Graving Dock Co. for use in the Eastern Mediterranean and Red Sea. Renamed SAIDIEH. **1915**: June 1: on a voyage from Alexandria to Hull, she was torpedoed by German submarine UB 6 and sunk in the mouth of the Thames, 6 miles north-east of Elbow Buoy - eight lives were lost.

ARAB Iron screw steamer (Union 1879-1900)
O.N. 79846
Builders: J. & G. Thomson, Clydebank (yard no: 168)
Tonnage: 3,170 gross 2,044 net
Dimensions: 350 x 40.2 x 31.1 feet
Engines: 2-cyl. compound by builder 500 h.p. 2,810 i.h.p. 12 knots
Trials: 14 knots
Passengers: 110 first, 90 second, 50 third

1879: Launched: January 23 for the mail service. Registered: May 3. Arrived Cape Town: June 14. **1882**: August 3: arrived at Southampton with the exiled Zulu King Cetshwayo. August 4 to December 5: chartered as a troop transport for the Egyptian Campaign. August 8: sailed from Southampton for Egypt as troopship No. 40 with 792 men and 55 horses. **1883**: September 15: started Union Line's short lived and unsuccessful Liverpool-Bermuda-Newport News (later Baltimore) service, and made four round trips (with NUBIAN) before the line closed in April 1884. **1885**: During the Sudanese War, she became the HQ ship for the Naval Transport Staff in Suakin, Sudan. Later, she carried Australian volunteer troops back to Sydney. **1889**: Engines tripled (557 h.p. 3,617 i.h.p.) and new boilers installed by her builder - her yards were removed. **1891**: She became an intermediate ship. December: inaugurated the Union Line Cape-Mauritius service. **1893**: May: returned to South Africa with passengers and crew from the wrecked CONWAY CASTLE. **1900**: March 8: transferred to Union-Castle - surplus to requirements. March 15: sold to German breakers. August: broken up at Harburg.

DURBAN

GERMAN (AG)

PRETORIA with ornate scrollwork adorning her bow (AM)

ARAB (AG)

TROJAN Iron screw steamer (Union 1880-1900)
O.N. 82404
Builders: J. & G. Thomson, Clydebank (yard no: 177)
Tonnage: 3,555 gross 2,285 net
Dimensions: 364.5 x 42.6 x 28.6 feet
Engines: 2-cyl. compound by builder 600 h.p. 3,531 i.h.p. 13 knots
Trials: 14.8 knots
Passengers: 116 first, 90 second, 50 third

1880: Launched: February 26. An improved ARAB, built for the mail service, and the first Cape liner to have electric light. Registered: April 22. Arrived Cape Town: June 10 and then proceeded to Natal to pick up the returning ex-Empress Eugenie of France who had come over on GERMAN in March to visit the site of her son's death during the Zulu War. **1887**: Her engines were tripled and boilers replaced by T. Richardson & Sons, Hartlepool. **1889**: November: became an intermediate ship. **1896**: Refrigerated space was added. **1899**: Converted into the Boer War Hospital Ship No.10 - employed between September 27, 1899 to October 18, 1900. **1900**: March 8: transferred to Union-Castle - surplus to requirements. Bought by Beaver Line (Elder Dempster & Co., managers) and renamed WASSAU. **1901**: January: with a changed passenger configuration (60 second, 650 third), she undertook her first voyage between Liverpool and Quebec. March 3: put into Queenstown with heavy weather damage. November: sold for scrap. **1902**: Sold to J. Goutte of Marseilles, and became ISLAM. **1904**: Scrapped at Marseilles.

SPARTAN Iron screw steamer (Union 1880-1900)
O.N. 82421
Builders: J. & G. Thomson, Clydebank (yard no: 182)
Tonnage: 3,491 gross 2,223 net
Dimensions: 363 x 43.2 x 28.9 feet
Engines: 2-cyl. compound by builder 600 h.p. 3,610 i.h.p. 13 knots
Trials: 14.6 knots
Passengers: 116 first, 90 second, 50 third

1881: Launched: June 12 as a sister to TROJAN. Registered: October 15. Arrived Cape Town: December 9. **1884**: August: broke her shaft near Madeira and had to be towed back to Madeira. **1886**: Engines tripled and new boilers installed by T. Richardson & Sons, Hartlepool. At the same time, her yards were removed. **1889**: She became an intermediate ship. **1899**: Converted into the Boer War Hospital Ship No.11 - employed between September 25, 1899 to October 29, 1900. **1900**: March 8: transferred to Union-Castle - surplus to requirements. December: Sold to A. Fragala of Catania, Sicily and renamed FIUME. **1902**: April: scrapped in Italy.

ATHENIAN Iron screw steamer (Union 1882-1897)
O.N. 82425
Builders: Aitken & Mansel, Whiteinch (yard no: 110)
Tonnage: 3,877 gross 2,493 net
Dimensions: 365 x 45.8 x 29 feet
Engines: 2-cyl. compound by J. & J. Thomson, Glasgow 600 h.p. 4,000 i.h.p. 13 knots
Passengers: 150 first, 90 second, 130 third

1881: Launched: December 7 for the mail service. **1882**: Registered: February 23. Arrived Cape Town: March 31. October 22: became the first ship to enter the new Robinson Graving Dock in Cape Town, which is still in regular use. **1887**: Engines tripled by T. Richardson & Sons, Hartlepool. Her funnel was also heightened and her yards removed. **1888**: She twice broke the northbound record: March 11: 17 days, 21 hours 5 minutes and June 3: 17 days, 9 hours 10 minutes. **1897**: December 29: sold with TARTAR to the Canadian Pacific Railway Company for use during the Klondike gold rush. Her name was unchanged. **1898**: February 12: left Southampton for Vancouver, via Cape Horn. With the gold rush almost over, both ships were laid up after only six voyages. October: ATHENIAN made a voyage to Vladivostok and was laid up in Hong Kong until spring 1899. **1899**: After further use across the Pacific, in July, ATHENIAN and TARTAR were chartered to the U.S. Government to carry supplies and troops from Seattle to the Philippines during the Spanish-American War. ATHENIAN was also used as such during the Boxer Revolution in China. **1901**: February: returned to her Pacific route and used to supplement the "White Empress" service. **1907**: August 22: last sailing from Vancouver. September: sold to K. Kishimoto, Osaka to be broken up. **1908**: Demolition complete.

SPARTAN

TROJAN as a Boer War hospital ship (AG)

ATHENIAN leaving Cape Town (CA AG 1814)

ATHENIAN in Canadian waters (CP)

MOOR Iron screw steamer (Union 1882-1900: UC 1900-1901)
O.N. 82428
Builders: J. & G. Thomson, Clydebank (yard no: 184) - subcontracted from Aitken & Mansel
Tonnage: 3,688 gross 2,229 net
Dimensions: 365.8 x 46.1 x 28.9 feet
Engines: 2-cyl. compound by J. & J. Thomson, Glasgow 600 h.p. 4,000 i.h.p. 13 knots **Trials**: 15.2 knots
Passengers: 150 first, 90 second, 130 third

1881: Launched: December 23 as a sister to ATHENIAN. **1882**: Registered: April 28. June 8: arrived Cape Town, having reduced PRETORIA's southbound record: 18 days 13 hours 17 minutes. **1884**: August 7: beat GERMAN's northbound record: 18 days, 2 hours 28 minutes. **1885**: April: with the possibility of war between Britain and Russia, she was converted in Simon's Town by the Admiralty into an armed auxiliary cruiser. October: after patrol duty on the East Africa Coast as squadron flagship, she returned to the mail service. **1888**: Engines tripled by T. Richardson & Sons, Hartlepool. **1894**: Lengthened by 65 feet to 420.6 feet - the inserted section was made from steel. She was also given two new funnels, the forward one a dummy. Gross tonnage increased to 4,664. December: her shaft broke and after repairs, she made for Dakar. **1900**: March 8: transferred to Union-Castle. Took the final sailing from Southampton for Union Line, and later became part of the intermediate fleet. **1901**: March: bought by Royal Mail Steam Packet. Co. for use on their Southampton-West-Indies service and renamed LA PLATA. **1908**: Sold to the Polytechnic Touring Association, London (R. Mitchell, manager) as the cruise ship THE VIKING. **1910**: June: went aground in Geiranger Fjord but was refloated three days later. **1912**: Sold to the Viking Cruising Co., Ltd. (S. J. Beckett, manager). Name unchanged. **1913**: February 14: arrived Zwijndrecht, Holland to be scrapped.

MEXICAN Iron screw steamer (Union 1883-1900)
O.N. 86330
Builders: James Laing, Sunderland (yard no: 273)
Tonnage: 4,668 gross 3,003 net
Dimensions: 378.2 x 47 x 29.3 feet
Engines: 2-cyl. compound by George Clark, Sunderland 600 h.p. 4,000 i.h.p. 13 knots
Passengers: 179 first, 156 second, 89 third

1882: Launched: August 1 for the mail service. Completion was delayed by strikes at the yard. **1883**: Registered: February 16. Arrived Cape Town: March 29 - then, the largest ship on the South African run. **1885**: Used as a troop transport to Hong Kong when war between

Britain and Russia seemed imminent. **1887**: Engines tripled by T. Richardson & Sons, Hartlepool. **1900**: April 5: Homeward bound and 80 miles north of Cape Town she collided with Lawther, Latta & Co.'s WINKFIELD in thick fog, and later sank. WINKFIELD (4,009 gross) was on her maiden voyage and carrying troops and horses of the Northumberland Yeomanry to Cape Town. This was the newly formed Union-Castle Line's first loss. Fortunately, all on board plus the mails were saved and transferred to WINKFIELD.

TARTAR Iron screw steamer (Union 1883-1897)
O.N. 86336
Builders: Aitken & Mansel, Whiteinch (yard no: 116)
Tonnage: 4,339 gross 2,754 net
Dimensions: 376.5 x 47.2 x 30.3 feet
Engines: 2-cyl. compound by J. & J. Thomson, Glasgow 650 h.p. 4,000 i.h.p. 14 knots
Passengers: 160 first, 160 second, 80 third

1883: Launched: January 25 as a replacement mailship for the lost TEUTON. First to have electric lighting, patent luffing davits, and first class amidships - the saloon was forward of the engines instead of aft. Registered: May 22. Arrived Cape Town: July 20. **1886**: August 2: beat MOOR's northbound record: 18 days 2 hours 21 minutes. **1888**: August 25: for the second time in 1888, reduced the northbound record: 17 days 6 hours 15 minutes. Engines converted to triple expansion by T. Richardson & Sons, Hartlepool (762 h.p.). Funnel heightened by 10 feet. **1897**: December 29: sold with ATHENIAN to the Canadian Pacific Railway Company for use during the Klondike Gold Rush. Her name was unchanged. **1898**: February 5: left Southampton for Vancouver, via Cape Horn. With the Gold Rush almost over, both ships were laid up after only six voyages. October the first C.P.R. ship to visit Hawaii. **1899**: After further use across the Pacific, in July, ATHENIAN and TARTAR were chartered to the U.S. Government to carry supplies and troops from Seattle to the Philippines during the Spanish-American War. **1900**: April: returned to her Pacific route. **1907**: October 17: in collision with C.P.R. coastal ship CHARMER (1,081/1887) and beached in English Bay British Columbia. **1908**: March broken up in Osaka.

TARTAR and the unique positioning of the saloon forward of the funnel

In 1894 MOOR was lengthened and given a second funnel. As built (above AG) - after conversion (right CA DRJ 562).

MEXICAN

CASTLE LINE CAPE "FLYERS"

Donald Curries response to the new Union mailships was a series of Castle Line "flyers" built between 1879 and 1883.

KINFAUNS CASTLE (1) Steel screw steamer (Castle 1879-1893)
O.N. 81599
Builders: John Elder & Co., Glasgow (yard no: 226)
Tonnage: 3,507 gross 2,244 net
Dimensions: 360.4 x 43 x 31 feet
Engines: 2-cyl. compound by builder 500 h.p. 3,000 i.h.p. 12 knots
Trials: 13.9 knots
Passengers: 120 first, 100 second, 160 third

1879: Launched: November 3 for Cape mail service. First steel ship built for the company and originally to be called CLUNY CASTLE. Also first ocean-going steel ship. Registered: December 17. **1880**: Arrived Cape Town: February 11. **1884**: March: bought by the Russian Volunteer Fleet, St. Petersburg as the transport MOSKVA. **1895**: July: became a Russian Navy training ship based in the Black Sea and renamed PRUTH. **1905**: June 30: mutiny aboard, off the Tendra Peninsula. Two officers killed and the mutiny ended at Sevastopol, July 2. **1908**: October: re-rated as transport. **1909**: December: converted into an operational minelaying training ship. **1914**: October 29: rather than be captured by the Turkish battle cruiser YAVUZ SULTAN SELIM (ex German GOEBEN), she was scuttled 10 miles south-west of Feolent (44.34N-33.01E) with the loss of her commander and 28 crew.

GRANTULLY CASTLE (1) Iron screw steamer (Castle 1879-1896)
O.N. 81601
Builders: Barclay, Curle & Co. Ltd., Whiteinch (yard no: 290)
Tonnage: 3,489 gross 2,234 net
Dimensions: 359.6 x 43.8 x 29.1 feet
Engines: 2-cyl. compound by builder 550 h.p. 12 knots
Passengers: 120 first, 100 second, 160 third

1879: Launched: November 13 for Cape mail service. Registered: December 27. **1880**: Arrived Cape Town: March 11. August: took Gladstone and party on cruise round Britain. **1887**: Engines tripled by T. Richardson & Sons, Hartlepool (550 h.p. 13.5 knots). **1889**:

February: left Cape Town with 320 boxes of fruit packed in special refrigerated chamber. This experiment was a failure with the fruit arriving in poor condition. **1896**: December: sold to Booth Line. Renamed AUGUSTINE, she was joined in 1897 by WARWICK CASTLE which became JEROME and in 1902 by HAWARDEN CASTLE as CYRIL. **1896**: January: first voyage Liverpool-Amazon. **1904**: October 2: 23 miles north-west of Ushant, rescued the crew of the Greek ship CLEMENTINE (ex SWAINBY) 2,608/1888. **1912**: August: sold for scrap at Falmouth.

GARTH CASTLE (1) Iron screw steamer (Castle 1881-1900 : UC 1900 - 1901)
O.N. 82849
Builders: John Elder & Co., Glasgow (yard no: 245)
Tonnage: 3,705 gross 2,381 net
Dimensions: 365 x 43.5 x 31.3 feet
Engines: 2-cyl. compound by builder 500 h.p. 3,180 i.h.p. 12.5 knots
Trials: 14.2 knots
Passengers: 166 first, 80 second, 126 third

1880: Launched: December 16 for Cape mail service. **1881**: Registered: February 14. Arrived Cape Town: April 23. July 25: attended the grand opening of the Leith docks. **1888**: Engines tripled by T. Richardson & Sons, Hartlepool (585 h.p. 13 knots). **1890**: Transferred to intermediate service. **1893**: Passenger capacity reduced to 52 first, 46 second to provide more cargo space. **1901**: June: surplus after the merger, sold to Elder Dempster & Co. for Bristol-Jamaica service but used across the Atlantic to Canada. Name unchanged. **1902**: Sold to Khedivial Mail Steamship & Graving Dock Co., London for their passenger routes in the Mediterranean - renamed ISMAILIA. **1914**: Between September 1 and November 4 used as an Indian Expeditionary Force transport. **1921**: Bought by Soc. Armatrice Radivo-Frausin, Trieste and renamed BRUNETTE. **1923**: Broken up.

KINFAUNS CASTLE - the first steel ocean-going ship

GRANTULLY CASTLE (TT)

GARTH CASTLE (ML)

DRUMMOND CASTLE Iron screw steamer (Castle 1881-1896)
O.N. 82861
Builders: John Elder & Co., Glasgow (yard no: 246)
Tonnage: 3,705 gross 2,381 net
Dimensions: 365 x 43.5 x 31.3 feet
Engines: 2-cyl. compound by builder 500 h.p. 3,000 i.h.p. 12.5 knots
Passengers: 166 first, 80 second, 126 third

1881: Launched: February 17 for Cape mail service. Sister of GARTH CASTLE. Registered: April 2. Arrived Cape Town: June 29. **1887:** Engines tripled by T. Richardson & Sons, Hartlepool (600 h.p. 3,500 i.h.p. 13.5 knots. Trials: 14.4 knots). **1894:** Transferred to intermediate service. **1896:** June 16: homeward bound, she struck the Pierres Vertes reef at the south entrance to the Fromveur Sound, Ushant. Sank within four minutes with the loss of 243 lives. There were only three survivors.

HAWARDEN CASTLE Iron screw steamer (Castle 1883-1900: UC 1900-1904)
O.N. 87076
Builders: John Elder & Co., Glasgow (yard no: 269)
Tonnage: 4,241 gross 2,722 net
Dimensions: 380.6 x 48.2 x 31.4 feet
Engines: 2-cyl. compound by builder 600 h.p. 3,900 i.h.p. 13 knots
 Trials: 14.6 knots
Passengers: 144 first, 84 second, 72 third

1883: Launched: January 11 for Cape mail service. Name advertised as ARDTORNISH CASTLE. First of a new class of three. Registered: April 4. Arrived Cape Town: May 17. **1891:** Engines tripled by Fairfield S.B. & E. Co. Ltd., Glasgow (850 h.p. 5,000 i.h.p. 15 knots). Funnel heightened and lifeboats lifted above the rails. **1893:** February: towed White Star's IONIC (4,753/1883) back to Cape Town after she broke her shaft. **1890:** Transferred to intermediate service. **1899:** Became Boer War transport. Employed between October 6, 1899 and October 12, 1901 and carried 6,146 men. **1904:** September: sold to Booth Line. Renamed CYRIL, she joined AUGUSTINE (ex GRANTULLY CASTLE and JEROME (ex WARWICK CASTLE). **1905:** January: first voyage Liverpool-Amazon. September 5: homeward bound with cargo of rubber sank after collision with Booth's ANSELM (3,563/1905) in the Amazon four miles below Curralinho.

NORHAM CASTLE Iron screw steamer (Castle 1883-1900: UC 1900-1903)
O.N. 87101
Builders: John Elder & Co., Glasgow (yard no: 270)
Tonnage: 4,241 gross 2,722 net
Dimensions: 380.6 x 48.2 x 31.4 feet
Engines: 2-cyl. compound by builder 600 h.p. 3,950 i.h.p. 13 knots
Trials: 14.6 knots
Passengers: 144 first, 84 second, 72 third

1883: Launched: February 26 for Cape mail service. Name advertised as ARMADALE CASTLE. Registered: May 16 (registered owner F. J. Mirrielees - Donald Currie's son-in-law). Arrived Cape Town:

July 12. **1888:** February 19: broke her shaft northbound and made St.Helena under sail. Towed back to England by the tug STORMCOCK, she arrived home in May. This was then, one of the longest tows ever. **1891:** Engines tripled by Fairfield S.B. & E. Co. Ltd., Glasgow (850 h.p. 5,700 i.h.p. 15 knots trials: 16.6 knots max). Funnel heightened and lifeboats lifted above the rails. **1895:** February 7: rescued the crew of the steel barque FASCADALE (2,083/1890) which was wrecked on the rocks south of Port Shepstone, Natal. **1902:** Replaced by KILDONAN CASTLE. **1903:** September: sold to Cie Générale Transatlantique (French Line) for their Central America service. Renamed MARTINIQUE. **1914:** Transferred to Bordeaux–Casablanca service. **1922:** August 1: rescued crew of the Lloyd Royal Belge steamer ITALIER (1,905/1908) wrecked on a reef near Cabo Villano. **1924:** Refitted as livestock carrier for trade between French Mediterranean ports and Algeria. **1932:** September: sold for scrap in Italy.

ROSLIN CASTLE (2) Iron screw steamer (Castle 1883-1900: UC 1900-1905)
O.N. 87126
Builders: Barclay, Curle & Co. Ltd., Whiteinch (yard no: 316)
Tonnage: 4,280 gross 2,746 net
Dimensions: 380 x 48.3 x 31.4 feet
Engines: 2-cyl. compound by builder 600 h.p. 3,900 i.h.p. 13 knots
Passengers: 158 first, 84 second, 72 third

1883: Launched: April 24 for Cape mail service. Name advertised as DUNNOTTAR CASTLE. (note spelling with two Ns). Registered: June 27 (registered owner John Napier). On maiden voyage initiated Castle's call at Lisbon. Arrived Cape Town: September 21. **1888:** Because of problems with rolling, she was fitted with a new stern and lengthened by 15 feet. Engines tripled by T. Richardson & Sons, Hartlepool (777 h.p. 14 knots) and electric light fitted. Her funnel was also heightened. **1889:** October 21: although her rolling problems continued, she reduced the northbound record: 16 days 22 hours 30 minutes. **1890:** November 22: reduced the northbound record further by 16 minutes. **1891:** June 5: took the final Castle sailing from Dartmouth. The mails were subsequently embarked at Southampton. **1899:** Became Boer War Transport No. 26. Employed between October 3, 1899 and October 3, 1902, and carried 12,775 men. **1905:** January: sold to M. Jebsen, Hamburg and chartered as a storeship for the Russian fleet. Renamed REGINA. March: stranded on the coast of Moçambique with cargo of coal. November: pulled free and towed to Durban by Rennies' ILLOVO (1890/1,930) where she arrived in January and was later repaired. **1907:** May 3: arrived in Genoa from Durban with heavy weather damage and was broken up locally.

DRUMMOND CASTLE (JC)

HAWARDEN CASTLE (AG)

NORHAM CASTLE (TT)

ROSLIN CASTLE (JC)

A FOUR-MASTER & A RECORD BREAKER

After the arrival of the only four-masted Cape mail ship PEMBROKE CASTLE, neither company built any new mailships because of the 1880s recession. DUNOTTAR CASTLE was the first to be built in the 1890s.

PEMBROKE CASTLE (2) Steel screw steamer (Castle 1883-1900: UC 1900-1906)
O.N. 87157
Builders: Barrow Shipbuilding Co., Barrow-in-Furness (yard no: 105)
Tonnage: 3,936 gross 2,560 net
Dimensions: 400.2 x 42.6 x 29.15 feet
Engines: 2-cyl. compound by builder 450 h.p. 3,200 i.h.p. 12.5 knots
Passengers: 40 first, 80 second, 100 third

1883: Launched: July 7. Bought on the stocks to replace KINFAUNS CASTLE (1) on Cape mail service. Her similarity to the DUKE OF WESTMINSTER of 1882 indicates that she may have been ordered for Ducal Line. She was the first Castle mailship with first class passengers amidships and the only one to have this layout until the CARISBROOK CASTLE of 1898. Soon after trials, took Donald Currie, Prime Minister Gladstone and party on the famous northern cruise which did not amuse Queen Victoria because Gladstone left these shores without her permission. Registered: September 6. Arrived Cape Town: October 29. **1885**: During the Sudanese War, she was used as a transport with CONWAY CASTLE. **1893**: Transferred to intermediate service. At some point in the 1890s, her funnel was heightened, an extra deckhouse was built on the bridge deck and her lifeboats were raised above deck level. **1904**: Laid up at Netley with HELIUS. **1906**: June: both ships sold to the Turkish Government. PEMBROKE CASTLE went to Idare-i Mahsusa (Ottoman Steam Nav. Co.), Constantinople and was renamed TIRIMÜJGAN (the mother of Sultan Abdülhamid II). **1908**: Transferred to the Ottoman Navy and converted into a destroyer depot and repair ship. **1910**: She became a transport. **1914**: Used as an engineering school. **1915**: May: became an ammunition storage vessel at Çanakkale. **1919**: February: used as a depot ship at Izmir. April: transferred to the Osmanli Seyrisefain Idaresi, Istanbul for commercial service where she was later joined by GIRESUN (ex WARWICK CASTLE). **1920**: March: 31: wrecked off Bafra Burnu, Black Sea on voyage Istanbul-Trabzon with military personnel.

DUNOTTAR CASTLE Steel screw steamer (Castle 1890-1900: UC 1900-1913)
O.N. 98152
Builders: Fairfield S.B. & E. Co. Ltd., Glasgow (yard no: 348)
Tonnage: 5,465 gross 3,069 net
Dimensions: 420 x 49.8 x 33 feet
Engines: Triple expansion by builder 1100 h.p. 6,700 i.h.p. 16 knots
Passengers: 170 first, 100 second, 100 third (expandable to 250)

1890: Launched: May 22 for Cape mail service. The first mailship over 5,000 gross tons. August: completed and undertook a cruise around the Western Isles for Donald Currie and guests. Arrived Cape Town: October 28 with a new Cape southbound record: 17 days 19 hours 50 minutes. December 6: reduced northbound record to 16 days 14 hours 15 minutes. **1891**: Until arrival of SCOT in August, both records reduced further. Southbound: 16 days 22 hours 30 minutes. Northbound: 15 days 17 hours. June 20: inaugurated Southampton as the port of departure for the mails instead of Dartmouth. **1894**: August: ran aground off the Eddystone Lighthouse but was later refloated. **1897**: Returned to builders where her yards were removed and her funnels heightened. **1899**: October: at the beginning of the Anglo-Boer War, carried General Buller, troops and Winston Churchill south and on the next outward trip with Lord Roberts aboard was diverted to Gibraltar to pick up Lord Kitchener. **1900**: Was the first vessel to fly the Union-Castle flag. **1901**: November: broke her shaft off Cape Verde and was towed to Dakar by White Star's RUNIC (12,482/1900). Towed to England by tug OCEANA. **1904**: Laid up at Netley. **1907**: June: chartered by the Panama Railroad Co., for passenger service between New York and Panama. **1909**: Chartered for three years by Sir Henry Lunn for cruises to Norway and the Mediterranean. **1911**: November: carried guests to the Delhi Durbar. **1913**: April: sold to Royal Mail Steam Packet. Co. as a cruise ship and renamed CARIBBEAN. **1914**: Requisitioned for war duty as a troop transport. September-October: brought over Canadian troops to Europe. December: became armed merchant cruiser. **1915**: June: purchased by the Admiralty and refitted as an accommodation ship for dockyard workers. September 27: sank during rough weather off Cape Wrath en route to Scapa Flow with the loss of 15 lives.

PEMBROKE CASTLE (TT)

DUNOTTAR CASTLE. As built - above (TT). After the 1897 refit - below (ML)

OLD FASHIONED CASTLE MAILSHIPS

The next group of Castle mailships were old fashioned single funnel and single screw vessels - a far cry from the attractive twin funnelled liners built during the 1890s for the progressive Union Line.

TANTALLON CASTLE (2) Steel screw steamer (Castle 1894-1900: UC 1900-1901)
O.N. 102855
Builders: Fairfield S.B. & E. Co. Ltd., Glasgow (yard no: 373)
Tonnage: 5,636 gross 3,048 net
Dimensions: 440.3 x 50.5 x 23.9 feet
Engines: Quadruple expansion by builder 1,129 h.p. 8,000 i.h.p. 16 knots
Trials: 17.3 knots
Passengers: 150 first, 100 second, 80 third

1894: Launched: January 23 for Cape mail service. April: completed as single funnel version of DUNOTTAR CASTLE and the first Castle liner with quadruple expansion engines. Arrived Cape Town: May 22. **1895**: June: cruised with Donald Currie and guests to attend the opening of the Kiel Canal. **1901**: May 7: at the end of her southbound voyage, ran aground in fog on Robben Island, Table Bay. All on board rescued safely but ship was a constructive total loss.

DUNVEGAN CASTLE (1) Steel screw steamer (Castle 1896-1900: UC 1900-1923)
O.N. 105854
Builders: Fairfield S.B. & E. Co. Ltd., Glasgow (yard no: 389)
Tonnage: 5,958 gross 3,428 net
Dimensions: 450.5 x 50.9 x 23.6 feet
Engines: Triple expansion by builder 1,152 h.p. 7,000 i.h.p. 16 knots **Trials**: 17.3 knots
Passengers: 287 first, 96 second, 130 third (later 200 first, 170 second)
Refrigerated space: 2,251 cubic feet

1896: Launched: April 14 for Cape mail service. July: completed as enlarged version of TANTALLON CASTLE (2). Arrived Cape Town: September 22. **1900**: Yards removed. **1901**: With SCOT, carried members of the House of Lords and Commons to the naval pageant held after Queen Victoria's death. **1902**: October: hit the Elbow at the entrance to the Victoria Basin, Cape Town and caused £10,000 worth of damage. **1904**: May: with arrival of KENILWORTH CASTLE,

placed in reserve fleet. **1913**: With CARISBROOK CASTLE, replaced GOTH and GUELPH on the Royal East Africa Service between London and Durban via Suez. September: offered for sale. **1914**: Replaced by LLANDOVERY CASTLE. August 6: requisitioned as a transport. **1915**: Converted into a 400-bed hospital ship. In service between October 6, 1915 and April 20, 1916. **1916**: Returned to Cape mail run. **1917**: Requisitioned under Liner Requisition scheme. **1918**: December 8: chartered to the French Government to carry prisoners of war. **1919**: January: used as cross channel troop transport. March 13: returned to owners for East Africa service. **1923**: Sold for scrap to Schweitzer & Oppler, Berlin. **1924**: January: reported awaiting demolition at Kiel.

CARISBROOK CASTLE Steel screw steamer (Castle 1898-1900: UC 1900-1922)
O.N. 108351
Builders: Fairfield S.B. & E. Co. Ltd., Glasgow (yard no: 400)
Tonnage: 7,626 gross 4,264 net
Dimensions: 485 x 56 x 23.6 feet
Engines: Quadruple expansion by builder 1,490 h.p. 9,000 i.h.p. 17.5 knots
Trials: 18.7 knots
Passengers: 250 first, 150 second, 220 third
Refrigerated space: 2,288 cubic feet

1897: Launched: October 28 for Cape mail service. Name advertised as CROOKSTON CASTLE, she was the last of Castle's single screw mailships and the first built without yards. **1898**: May: completed. Arrived Cape Town: June 28. **1899**: April 14: made the second fastest Cape northbound run: 14 days 17 hours 3 minutes. **1913**: With DUNVEGAN CASTLE, replaced GOTH and GUELPH on the Royal East Africa Service between London and Durban via Suez. **1914**: Replaced by LLANSTEPHAN CASTLE and requisitioned as a 439-bed naval hospital ship. In service as such from August 2 to September. Then became a military hospital ship from September 3, 1914 to April 15, 1917. **1917**: Used primarily as cross Channel ambulance transport. **1918**: May 27, 1918 to August 26, 1919: on duty as Mediterranean ambulance transport. **1919**: August: returned to her owners and used as a mailship. **1921**: Used briefly on East Africa service. **1922**: October: sold while laid up in River Blackwater. Scrapped in Germany.

TANTALLON CASTLE (TT)

DUNVEGAN CASTLE (TH)

CARISBROOK CASTLE (TH)

TWIN FUNNELLED MAILSHIPS 1890-1910

Although SCOT was a magnificent ship, she was a financial failure for Union Line. NORMAN, on the other hand, was a great success and became the lead ship for a series of twin funnelled mailships which culminated with EDINBURGH CASTLE in 1910.

SCOT Steel twin screw steamer (Union 1891-1900: UC 1900-1905)
O.N. 98845
Builders: William Denny & Bros., Dumbarton (yard no: 443)
Tonnage: 6,844 gross 3,168 net
Dimensions: 477 x 54.6 x 37.6 feet
Engines: Triple expansion by Denny & Co. 11,000 i.h.p. 17.5 knots
Trials: 18.8 knots
Passengers: 212 first, 105 second, 108 third

1890: Launched: December 30 as the first twin screw Cape liner and largest Union ship to date. **1891**: May: completed. Broke the southbound record set by DUNOTTAR CASTLE - Southampton-Cape Town: 15 days 9 hours 52 minutes. Arrived Cape Town: August 10. On return voyage, broke the Cape Town-Southampton record: 14 days 21 hours 25 minutes. **1893**: March 19: broke the southbound record again - Southampton-Cape Town: 14 days 18 hours 57 minutes. This record remained unbroken until the arrival of the STIRLING CASTLE in 1936. **1895**: December: her southbound voyage terminated at Vigo after breakdown and she was sent to Harland & Wolff, Belfast for repairs. **1896**: At Harland & Wolff, she was cut in two and lengthened by 54 feet to 531 feet. Gross tonnage increased to 7,815. Her funnels were also shortened and work was completed in July. **1901**: With DUNVEGAN CASTLE, carried members of the House of Lords and Commons to the naval pageant held after Queen Victoria's death. **1903**: September 12: final arrival at Southampton where she was laid up off Netley. Her replacement was ARMADALE CASTLE. **1905**: October: sold to Hamburg-Amerikanische-Packetfahrt-Actien-Gesellschaft (HAPAG), Hamburg and converted into a cruise ship OCEANA by Harland & Wolff. **1906**: April: first cruise from Lisbon. October: placed on HAPAG's Naples-Alexandria route. **1907**: Replaced PRINZESSIN VICTORIA LUISE (the world's first purpose-built cruise ship) which had been lost off Jamaica, December 16, 1906. **1911**: Replaced by the former Blue Riband record breaker DEUTSCHLAND which had been converted into the cruise ship VICTORIA LUISE. June: sold to the Bermuda-Atlantic S.S. Co. Ltd., of Toronto. Name unchanged, she ran between New York and Bermuda. June 24: first voyage from New York. **1912**: The service was a failure. May 8: final arrival from Bermuda - laid up at the Brooklyn yard of the Morse Dry Dock & Repair Co. Ltd., New York.

1914: Taken over by the Morse Dry Dock & Repair Co. Inc., presumably in lieu of berthing payments. September 10: registered under the US flag (US official number: 212529). December: chartered by a group of Bermudian merchants who formed the Bermuda American Steamship Co. Ltd., Bermuda to operate a new service between New York and Bermuda. December 26: left New York on first voyage for new company. **1915**: March: Bermuda American Steamship Co. Ltd. declared bankrupt and the ship was returned to her owners. September 22: sold to Compañía Trasatlántica, Barcelona as replacement for the lost ALFONSO XIII, she was given the same name. October: placed on the Cadiz-New York route. **1923**: November: with the arrival of a new ALFONSO XIII, she was renamed VASCO NUÑEZ DE BALBOA, and later transferred to Cadiz-Havana service. **1925**: Laid up in Cadiz. **1927**: July 6: arrived in La Spezia to be broken up.

NORMAN (2) Steel twin screw steamer (Union 1894-1900: UC 1900-1926)
O.N. 104042
Builders: Harland & Wolff Ltd., Belfast (yard no: 280)
Tonnage: 7,537 gross 4,005 net
Dimensions: 490.8 x 53.2 x 33.5 feet
Engines: Triple expansion by builder 1,293 h.p. 9,000 i.h.p. 17 knots
Passengers: 190 first, 114 second, 138 third
Refrigerated space: 9,885 cu. ft.

1894: Launched: July 18 for mail service. The first of a series of two funnelled liners built by Harland & Wolff for Union Line. October: completed. Arrived Cape Town: November 26. **1895**: July: grounded near Port Shepstone and, although damage was slight, Commodore Bainbridge was relieved of his command. **1904**: April: after a four month refit, returned to mail service. **1908**: July: carried the first large consignment of citrus fruit from South Africa. **1911**: With the arrival of EDINBURGH CASTLE, she was laid up at Netley as reserve ship. **1914**: August 10: after the outbreak of war, she was amongst the first ships to land men of the British Expeditionary Force in France. Shortly afterwards, she returned to the Cape mail run. **1917**: Taken over by the Shipping Controller under the Liner Requisition Scheme. **1918**: Troopship in Mediterranean. **1919**: After a voyage to Australia on charter to P. & O., returned to the mail service because of shortage of ships. **1923**: Transferred to the recently-started round Africa service. **1925**: Replaced by the new LLANDOVERY CASTLE and laid up. **1926**: March: arrived at Morecambe to be broken up by T. W. Ward Ltd.

The SCOT became the cruise ship OCEANA in 1905 and was used initially by HAPAG for Mediterranean cruising. (TH)

SCOT prior to lengthening

NORMAN

BRITON (3) Steel twin screw steamer (Union 1897-1900: UC 1900-1926)
O.N. 106919
Builders: Harland & Wolff Ltd., Belfast (yard no: 313)
Tonnage: 10,248 gross 5,154 net
Dimensions: 530.3 x 60.3 x 36.2 feet
Engines: Triple expansion by builder 1,712 h.p. 10,500 i.h.p. 17.5 knots
Passengers: 280 first, 182 second, 122 third
Refrigerated space: 9.982 cu. ft.

1897: Launched: June 5 for mail service. Based on NORMAN design, the first mailship over 10,000 gross tons and the largest liner running between Britain and her colonies. November: completed. Arrived Cape Town: December 21. With CARISBROOK CASTLE, was the fastest on the Cape mail run after SCOT. **1898**: June: ran aground briefly on the Shambles off Portland Bill, Dorset. **1899**: October: at the outbreak of the Boer War carried 1,500 troops to Cape Town in less than 15 days. **1914**: August 11 to September 25: requisitioned as troopship. Returned to the mail service. **1915**: December 16: again requisitioned as troopship, this time mainly in the Mediterranean. **1918**: February: transported Nigerian soldiers from Mombasa to Lagos. Later, carried American troops between Liverpool and US. **1919**: On service to New Zealand. **1920**: Returned to mail run. **1925**: January: laid up at Netley. October: made final voyage to the Cape during seamens' strike leaving Cape Town November 13. **1926**: May: arrived La Spezia for demolition.

SAXON (4) Steel twin screw steamer (UC 1900-1935)
O.N. 112713
Builders: Harland & Wolff Ltd., Belfast (yard no: 326)
Tonnage: 12,385 gross 6,336 net
Dimensions: 570.5 x 64.4 x 38.6 feet
Engines: Quadruple expansion by builder 2,040 h.p. 11,800 i.h.p. 17.5 knots
Passengers: 310 first, 203 second, 286 third
Refrigerated space: 10,874 cu. ft. (1910: 49,001 cu. ft.)

1899: Launched: December 21 as mailship, the last with a Union name. **1900**: June: completed. Arrived Cape Town: July 3. **1914**: August: the last mailship to leave Cape Town before the outbreak of war. **1916**: Requisitioned as troopship. **1917**: Trooping duties in the Mediterranean and later in East Africa. **1918**: On North Atlantic,

she and WALMER CASTLE carried US troops. **1919**: Returned to mail service. **1920**: September: collided with a barge in Cape Town and lost her rudder. **1921**: August: on southbound voyage carrying General Smuts, fire broke out in coal bunkers after leaving Madeira. Her voyage terminated in Freetown, Sierra Leone where KENILWORTH CASTLE was diverted to pick up stranded passengers. SAXON was later escorted to the Cape by ARMADALE CASTLE. **1931**: April: on completion of WARWICK CASTLE, was withdrawn from mail fleet. Used on one intermediate voyage and then laid up at Netley in reserve. **1935**: April 9: arrived in Blyth, Northumberland for scrap by Hughes Bolckow Shipbreaking Co. Ltd.

WALMER CASTLE (2) Steel twin screw steamer (UC 1901-1932)
O.N. 114839
Builders: Harland & Wolff Ltd., Belfast (yard no: 342)
Tonnage: 12,546 gross 6,463 net
Dimensions: 570.5 x 64.4 x 38.6 feet
Engines: Quadruple expansion by builder 2,040 h.p. 12,000 i.h.p. 16.5 knots
Passengers: 336 first, 174 second, 244 third
Refrigerated space: 9,461 cubic feet (1913: 34,884 cubic feet; 1920s: 60,542 cubic feet)

1900: An improved SAXON, laid down as CELT (3) for Union Line but renamed WALMER CASTLE after merger. **1901**: Launched: July 6. **1902**: January: completed as mailship. Arrived Cape Town: April 1. **1917**: April: requisitioned as troopship. **1918**: On North Atlantic, she and SAXON carried American troops. **1919**: Returned to mail service. **1931**: January: after arrival of WINCHESTER CASTLE, was withdrawn from mail fleet and laid up at Netley in reserve. **1932**: Sold to Hughes Bolckow Shipbreaking Co. Ltd., Blyth, Northumberland for scrap. February 8: arrived Blyth.

WALMER CASTLE (TH)

BRITON

SAXON (LD)

KINFAUNS CASTLE (2) Steel twin screw steamer (Castle 1899-1900: UC 1900-1927)
O.N. 110173
Builders: Fairfield S.B. & E. Co. Ltd., Glasgow (yard no: 407)
Tonnage: 9,664 gross 5,063 net
Dimensions: 515.3 x 59.2 x 34.7 feet
Engines: Quadruple expansion by builder 1,663 h.p. 9,800 i.h.p. 17.5 knots
Trials: 18.2 knots
Passengers: 266 first, 171 second, 198 third
Refrigerated space: 7,536 cubic feet (1913: 22,001 cubic feet)

1899: Launched: May 12 as the first twin screw Castle mailship. August: completed. Arrived Cape Town: October 18. **1902**: April: stranded on the Isle of Wight for several days. **1914**: August: requisitioned as an armed merchant cruiser. In service as HMS KINFAUNS CASTLE from August 5, 1914 to September 16, 1915. **1915**: October 2: transferred to trooping duties, mainly in the Mediterranean and to Mesopotamia. In service as such until January 26, 1918. **1918**: July 13: requisitioned as a minelayer and was being converted at Millwall when the war ended. **1919**: February: returned to her owners. **1920**: Carried to Cape Town the new Governor-General of the Union, Prince Arthur of Connaught. **1922**: September 8: off the coast of Portugal, among the ships which rescued the passengers and crew of the foundering HAPAG liner HAMMONIA (7,291/1909). With the completion of WINDSOR CASTLE (2), was laid up at Netley after one voyage to the East with troops. **1925**: October: because of the disruption caused to the mail schedule by the shipping strike, recommissioned with BRITON for one mail trip to the Cape. November 17: left Cape Town for the last time. **1927**: January to April: chartered for trooping voyage Southampton-Shanghai and back. September: sold to Dutch breakers N.V. Frank Rijsdijk's Industrieele Ondernemingen. Broken up at Hendrik-Ido-Ambacht (near Rotterdam).

KILDONAN CASTLE Steel twin screw steamer (Castle 1899-1900: UC 1900-1931)
O.N. 112615
Builders: Fairfield S.B. & E. Co. Ltd., Glasgow (yard no: 408)
Tonnage: 9,652 gross 5,105 net
Dimensions: 515.3 x 59.2 x 34.7 feet
Engines: Quadruple expansion by builder 1,663 h.p. 9,800 i.h.p. 17.5 knots
Trials: 18.5 knots
Passengers: 266 first, 171 second, 198 third
Refrigerated space: 7,536 cubic feet (1913: 21,970 cubic feet)

1899: Launched: August 22 as the last Castle Line Cape mail steamer. Sister of KINFAUNS CASTLE. October: with the outbreak of the Boer War, completed as Troop Transport No. 44. Employed between October 5, 1899 and May 23, 1901, and carried 20,429 men. Arrived Cape Town: November 22. **1901**: Returned to builders for completion as mailship. December: first voyage on Cape mail run. **1915**: Converted into hospital ship. In service as HMHS KILDONAN CASTLE from October 6, 1915 to March 10, 1916. **1916**: Commissioned as an armed merchant cruiser in the 10th Cruiser Squadron. In service as HMS KILDONAN CASTLE from March 25, 1916 to January 16, 1919. **1917**: Carried a secret mission to Russia. **1919**: January: decommissioned as an armed merchant cruiser but continued to be used as a troopship. **1921**: December 31: returned to her owners. **1926**: Put into reserve with the arrival of CARNARVON CASTLE (2). **1927**: January to April: carried the Devon Regiment to Shanghai. **1929**: Used for one voyage as a cargo carrier. **1930**: May: with the delay in the delivery of DUNBAR CASTLE (2), was used on the intermediate run for one voyage. **1931**: Sold for scrap to Norwegian breakers, Stavanger Skibs-Ophugnings Co. A/S. May 18: arrived at Stavanger.

ARMADALE CASTLE (2) Steel twin screw steamer (UC 1903-1936)
O.N. 118350
Builders: Fairfield S.B. & E. Co. Ltd, Glasgow (yard no: 424)
Tonnage: 12,973 gross 7,264 net
Dimensions: 570.1 x 64.5 x 39.0 feet
Engines: Quadruple expansion by builder 2,212 h.p. 12,500 i.h.p. 16.5 knots
Passengers: 350 first, 200 second, 270 third
Refrigerated space: 18,667 cubic feet (1921: 49,496 cubic feet; 1928:145,456 cubic feet)

1903: Launched: August 11 as mailship similar to WALMER CASTLE. November: completed. Replaced SCOT. Arrived Cape Town: December 22. **1904**: June 26: first mailship to cross the bar at Durban. **1914**: August 2: commissioned as an armed merchant cruiser HMS ARMADALE CASTLE and placed on the Cape station. September: took part in the South-West Africa campaign. **1915**: On patrol off German East Africa. **1916**: September: carried gold and specie worth £7 million from Simon's Town to Halifax, Nova Scotia. **1917**: After refit, joined the 10th Cruiser Squadron for blockade duties between the Shetland Islands and Norway. **1918**: Escort duty on North and South American routes and West Africa. **1919**: September 11: end of war service. After reconditioning on the Clyde, which included a fully enclosed bridge (the only one of her class), returned to mail service with passenger capacity: 261 first, 271 second, 274 third. **1930**: Fitted with Oertz streamlined rudder. **1936**: Replaced WINCHESTER CASTLE for one voyage after her stranding at Portland, Dorset. April 10: final departure from Cape Town. June: sold to Hughes Bolckow Shipbreaking Co. Ltd. Blyth, Northumberland for scrap. June 12: arrived Blyth.

KINFAUNS CASTLE (TH)

KILDONAN CASTLE (TH)

ARMADALE CASTLE (BI)

KENILWORTH CASTLE (2) Steel twin screw steamer (UC 1904-1936)
O.N. 118433
Builders: Harland & Wolff Ltd., Belfast (yard no: 356)
Tonnage: 12,974 gross 6,463 net
Dimensions: 570.2 x 64.7 x 38.6 feet
Engines: Quadruple expansion by builder 2,175 h.p. 12,000 i.h.p. 16.5 knots
Passengers: 255 first, 269 second, 270 third
Refrigerated space: 17,206 cubic feet (1921: 45,642 cubic feet; 1928:140,982 cubic feet)

1903: Launched: December 5 as mailship similar to WALMER CASTLE. **1904**: May: completed. Arrived Cape Town: June 14. **1914**: August 11: requisitioned as troopship. In service until January 7, 1915. **1915**: January: returned to mail service. **1918**: Undertook one voyage to Australia with repatriated troops. June 4: 35 miles off Plymouth, collided with destroyer HMS RIVAL while zigzagging. Destroyer was cut in two and depth charges exploded under KENILWORTH CASTLE's bow. 15 lives were lost and she sailed to Plymouth for repairs. **1919**: Returned to mail service. **1930**: Fitted with Oertz streamlined rudder. **1936**: Withdrawn after the arrival of STIRLING CASTLE (2). April 24: final departure from Cape Town. December: sold to Hughes Bolckow Shipbreaking Co. Ltd. Blyth, Northumberland for scrap. **1937**: January 8: arrived Blyth.

BALMORAL CASTLE (2) Steel twin screw steamer (UC 1910-1939)
O.N. 129074
Builders: Fairfield S.B. & E. Co Ltd, Glasgow (yard no: 468)
Tonnage: 13,361 gross 7,512 net
Dimensions: 570 x 64.5 x 38.9 feet
Engines: Quadruple expansion by builder 2,050 h.p. 12,500 i.h.p. 16.5 knots
Passengers: 317 first, 220 second, 268 third
Refrigerated space: 28,000 cubic feet (1921: 49,076 cubic feet; 1928:142,302 cubic feet)

1909: Launched: November 13 as a larger version of WALMER CASTLE mailship class. **1910**: February: completed, the first mailship with wireless telegraphy. Arrived Cape Town: April 19. October: commissioned as a royal yacht to carry the Duke and Duchess of Connaught to South Africa for the inauguration of the Union of South Africa - her funnels were painted yellow and a cross tree was fitted to her foremast. **1914**: August 21 to September 19: requisitioned as a troopship, then resumed her mailship duties. **1917**: Taken over as a transport under the Liner Requisition Scheme, she was used extensively including the carrying of US troops across the Atlantic under Cunard management. **1919**: February: undertook a voyage to Australia via the Cape under Federal and Shire management. Later that year, she returned to the mail service with passenger capacity: 235 first, 296 second, 268 third. **1937**: March: sent to Durban to take the homeward round Africa sailing of LLANDOVERY CASTLE which had been damaged by a mine. **1939**: With the completion of the mailship-rebuilding programme, withdrawn from service. January 6: final departure from Cape Town. June 19: arrived Newport, Monmouthshire for scrapping by John Cashmore Ltd.

EDINBURGH CASTLE (2) Steel twin screw steamer (UC 1910-1941)
O.N. 129088
Builders: Harland & Wolff Ltd., Belfast (yard no: 410)
Tonnage: 13,330 gross 7,364 net
Dimensions: 570.2 x 64.7 x 38.7 feet
Engines: Quadruple expansion by builder 2,174 h.p. 12,500 i.h.p. 16.5 knots
Passengers: 320 first, 220 second, 250 third
Refrigerated space: 28,000 cubic feet (1921: 49,996 cubic feet; 1928:155,736 cubic feet)

1910: Launched: January 27. Sister of BALMORAL CASTLE. April: completed. Arrived Cape Town: June 7. **1914**: September 4: commissioned as an armed merchant cruiser and saw service mainly off the east coast of South America. **1916**: September: refitted at Simon's Town. **1918**: April: transferred to the North Atlantic for convoy duty. **1919**: July 12: decommissioned. After refit at Belfast, returned to the mail run with passenger capacity: 235 first, 295 second, 250 third. **1939**: With the completion of the mailship-rebuilding programme, withdrawn from service. January 19: final departure from Cape Town, the last of the pre World War I mailships. Requisitioned by the Admiralty for use as an accommodation vessel at Freetown, Sierra Leone. **1941**: June: sold to the Admiralty. **1944**: May: paid off and reduced to care and maintenance. **1945**: November 24: towed out of Freetown by HMS LAUNCESTON CASTLE and tug EMPIRE LAWN. November 25: in deep water, 60 miles from Freetown, sunk by gunfire from HMS FAL and other Royal Navy vessels.

BALMORAL CASTLE as royal yacht in 1910 (TH))

EDINBURGH CASTLE (JC)

KENILWORTH CASTLE laid up at Netley

BALMORAL CASTLE (TH))

ARUNDEL CASTLE (3) Steel twin screw steamer (UC 1921-1958)
O.N. 145175
Builders: Harland & Wolff Ltd., Belfast (yard no: 455)
Tonnage: 19,023 gross 11,222 net
Dimensions: 630.5 x 72.5 x 41.5 feet
Engines: Single reduction geared steam turbines by builder 3,055 hp.
14,500 s.h.p. 16 knots
Passengers: 234 first, 362 second, 274 third
Refrigerated space: 74,729 cubic feet (1928: 146,994 cubic feet)

1919: Ordered in February 1913. Laid down in 1915 as mailship
AMROTH CASTLE but construction ceased during the war.
Launched: September 11 as ARUNDEL CASTLE. She and her sister
WINDSOR CASTLE (2) were the last four funnelled liners ever built
and the only ones with cruiser sterns. **1921**: April: completed. Arrived
Cape Town: May 9. **1937**: January: returned to builders for rebuild.
Funnels reduced to two, fitted with raked bow (new length 661.3 feet)
and new single-reduction, oil-fired 24,000 s.h.p. steam turbines which
increased her speed to 19 knots. Tonnage was now 19,118 gross and
11,438 net. Passenger capacity: 219 first, 167 second, 194 tourist.
Gantry davits were also removed. October: back in service. **1940**:
January 1: requisitioned by the Ministry of Shipping (Ministry of War
Transport from May 1941) for use as a troopship. **1943**: Took part in
the North Africa campaign. **1944**: September: under diplomatic
protection, undertook a round trip voyage between Liverpool and
Göteborg, Sweden with exchange prisoners of war. **1948**: April 1:
decommissioned. Used on the immigrant service to South Africa as
an 846-berth "austerity" emigrant ship. **1949**: After one trooping
voyage to the Mediterranean, sent back to builders in September for
post-war refit. **1950**: September: returned to mail service. Passenger
capacity: 168 first, and 371 tourist. **1958**: December 5: final departure
from Cape Town - the longest serving mailship (37 years 8 months).
December: sold to Hong Kong Towage & Salvage Co. Ltd. Replaced
by PENDENNIS CASTLE. **1959**: February 6: arrived at Hong Kong
for demolition by the Hong Kong Chiap Hua Manufactory Co. Ltd.

WINDSOR CASTLE (2) Steel twin screw steamer (UC 1922-1941)
O.N. 146535
Builders: John Brown & Co. Ltd., Glasgow (H. & W. yard no: 456c)
Tonnage: 18,967 gross 11,295 net
Dimensions: 632.4 x 72.5 x 41.6 feet
Engines: Single reduction geared steam turbines by builder 3,055 h.p.
14,500 s.h.p. 16 knots
Passengers: 243 first, 360 second, 275 third
Refrigerated space: 73,855 cubic feet (1928: 146,640 cubic feet)

1921: Ordered in February 1913 and laid down in 1919 as mailship.
Construction was subcontracted to John Brown & Co. Ltd.. Launched:
March 9. **1922**: March: completed. Arrived Cape Town: May 9. **1937**:
March: sent to Belfast for rebuild. Funnels reduced to two, fitted with
raked bow (new length 661.3 feet) and new single-reduction, oil-fired
24,000 s.h.p. steam turbines, which increased her speed to 19 knots.
Tonnage was now 19,141 gross and 11,462 net. Passenger capacity:
219 first, 167 second, 194 tourist. Gantry davits were also removed.
1938: April: back in service. **1939**: September: requisitioned by the
Ministry of Shipping (Ministry of War Transport from May 1941) as
a troopship. **1940**: November 3: survived air attack west of Ireland
(54.12N-13.18W). **1943**: March 23: whilst in convoy 110 miles north-
west of Algiers, sunk by torpedo from enemy aircraft (37.27N-01.10E).
2,699 troops and 290 crew rescued - one life was lost.

ARUNDEL CASTLE (LD)

WINDSOR CASTLE. As built leaving Cape Town - right (LD) and after her late 1930s coversion - above (LD). Below - ARUNDEL CASTLE at Hong Kong awaiting demolition. (LD).

THE MOTORSHIP ERA

CARNARVON CASTLE (2) Steel twin screw motorship (UC 1926-1962) **O.N.** 148766
Builders: Harland & Wolff Ltd., Belfast (yard no: 595)
Tonnage: 20,063 gross 12,089 net
Dimensions: 630.7 x 73.5 x 41.5 feet
Engines: Burmeister & Wain design oil 4S DA 8-cyl. by builder 3,364 h.p.
13,000 b.h.p. 16 knots **Trials**: 18.4 knots
Passengers: 311 first, 276 second, 263 third
Refrigerated space: 122,000 cubic feet (1928: 209,921 cubic feet)

1926: Launched: January 14 as mailship. Ordered as a steamer, she
was not only the company's first motorship but also their first ship
over 20,000 gross tons. June: completed. Arrived Cape Town: August
2. **1937**: October: returned to builders for rebuild. Funnels reduced to
one, fitted with raked bow (new length 686 feet) and new 24,000 b.h.p.
2S DA 10-cyl. oil engines which increased her speed to 20 knots.
Tonnage was now 20,122 gross and 12,989 net. Passenger capacity:
226 first, 245 second, 188 tourist. **1938**: July: returned to service.
September: reduced STIRLING CASTLE's southbound record to 12
days 13 hours 38 minutes. **1939**: September 8: requisitioned by the
Admiralty and converted at Simon's Town into an armed merchant
cruiser HMS CARNARVON CASTLE. **1940**: December 5: in action
with German raider THOR (ex SANTA CRUZ 3,862/1938) but
managed to escape although six were killed. Repairs were carried at
Cape Town and Simon's Town. **1942**: Admiralty considered buying
her with DUNNOTTAR CASTLE and PRETORIA CASTLE for
conversion into an aircraft carrier but only the latter was converted.
1943: November 29: decommissioned as an armed merchant cruiser
and handed over to the Ministry of War Transport for conversion at
New York into a troopship. **1947**: January 1: decommissioned.
Returned to owners. June: inaugurated the post-war immigrant service
to South Africa as a 1,283-berth "austerity" emigrant ship. **1949**:
January 5: sent to builders for post-war refit. **1950**: June: returned to
mail service. Passenger capacity: 216 first, 401 tourist. **1960**: Mainmast
reduced in height. **1962**: Surplus with arrival of TRANSVAAL
CASTLE. June 18: final departure from Cape Town. July: sold to
Japanese breakers for scrap. September 8: arrived at Mihara for
demolition by Seibu Ogyo K.K.

CARNARVON CASTLE

CARNARVON CASTLE in three different guises. Top - as built with a pair of handsome motorship funnels (LD). Left - as an armed merchant cruiser. Below - single funnel mailship (LD).

WINCHESTER CASTLE (1) Steel twin screw motorship (UC 1930-1960)
O.N. 162489
Builders: Harland & Wolff Ltd., Belfast (yard no: 825)
Tonnage: 20,109 gross 12,228 net
Dimensions: 631.6 x 75.5 x 37.5 feet
Engines: Burmeister & Wain design oil 4S DA 8-cyl. by builder 3,336 h.p.
13,000 b.h.p. 16 knots
Passengers: 259 first, 243 second, 254 third (tourist from 1934)
Refrigerated space: 216,267 cubic feet

1929: Ordered with WARWICK CASTLE (3) after the agreement of
the new 1928 freight contract. An improved version of CARNARVON
CASTLE (2), she was launched: November 19. **1930**: October:
completed. Arrived Cape Town: November 10. **1936**: February 16:
went aground briefly off the Portland Bill Lighthouse, Dorset. One
round trip to South Africa cancelled for repair work - ARMADALE
CASTLE (2) brought out of reserve as replacement. **1938**: April:
returned to builders for rebuild. Funnels reduced to one and given
new 24,000 b.h.p. 2S DA 10-cyl. oil engines which increased her speed
to 20 knots. Tonnage was now 20,012 gross and 12,189 net. Passenger
capacity: 254 first, 228 second, 211 tourist. **1939**: January: back in
service. **1940**: December 8: requisitioned by the Ministry of Shipping
(Ministry of War Transport from May 1941) as a troopship. **1941**:
Used in Loch Fyne and the Clyde area as a training ship for marines
and commandos, preparing for *Operation Ironclad*, the invasion of
Vichy-held Madagascar. **1942**: May: took part in the successful
invasion of Madagascar and after a refit in New York, returned to
Scotland in September. November: carried troops for the North Africa
campaign. **1943**: During the next two years was involved in the
invasions of Italy and Southern France. **1947**: April 22: end of war
service. Used on the immigrant service to South Africa as an 877-
berth "austerity" emigrant ship - arrived Cape Town: May 16. **1948**:
November: sent to builders for post-war refit. **1949**: September:
returned to mail service. Passenger capacity: 189 first, 389 tourist.
1960: Surplus with the arrival of WINDSOR CASTLE (3). September
9: final departure from Cape Town. Sold to Japanese breakers for
scrap. November 5: arrived at Mihara for demolition by Nichimen
K.K.

WARWICK CASTLE (3) Steel twin screw motorship (UC 1931-1942)
O.N. 162527
Builders: Harland & Wolff Ltd., Belfast (yard no: 840)
Tonnage: 20,445 gross 12,443 net
Dimensions: 651.5 x 75.5 x 37.4 feet
Engines: Burmeister & Wain design oil 4S DA 8-cyl. by builder 3,364 h.p.
13,000 b.h.p. 16 knots
Passengers: 260 first, 240 second, 246 third (tourist from 1934)
Refrigerated space: 207,450 cubic feet

1930: Ordered with WINCHESTER CASTLE (1) after the agreement
of the new 1928 freight contract. An improved version of
CARNARVON CASTLE, she was launched: April 29. **1931**: January:
completed. Although a sister to WINCHESTER CASTLE, she was
20 feet longer. Arrived Cape Town: February 16. **1938**: January:
returned to builders for rebuild. Funnels reduced to one and given
new 24,000 b.h.p. 2S DA 10-cyl. oil engines which increased her speed
to 20 knots. Tonnage was now 20,109 gross and 12,240 net. Passenger
capacity: 256 first, 231 second, 211 tourist. October: back in service.
1940: January 8: requisitioned by the Ministry of Shipping (Ministry
of War Transport from May 1941) for use as a troopship. **1941**: August
6: collided with WINDSOR CASTLE in thick fog whilst in convoy -
repairs at Halifax took four weeks. **1942**: November 14: after taking
part in the invasion of North Africa and in a convoy returning home,
she was torpedoed and sunk by German submarine U 413, 200 miles
off the coast of Portugal (39.16N-13.25W). 63 lives were lost including
her commander. She was the largest Union-Castle vessel lost during
the war.

WINCHESTER CASTLE as built (LD)

WARWICK CASTLE leaving Cape Town before the war - top (LD) and during the war - right (BI). Below - WINCHESTER CASTLE after her conversion

STIRLING CASTLE (2) Steel twin screw motorship (UC 1936-1966)
O.N. 164570
Builders: Harland & Wolff Ltd., Belfast (yard no: 941)
Tonnage: 25,550 gross 15,687 net
Dimensions: 696 x 82.5 x 41.45 feet
Engines: Burmeister & Wain design oil 2S DA 10-cyl. by builder 4,650 h.p.
24,000 b.h.p. 19.5 knots
Passengers: 246 first, 538 cabin (tourist from 1947)
Refrigerated space: 336,666 cubic feet

1935: Launched: August 15 as mailship, the first to carry only first
and cabin class passengers. **1936**: January: completed. Arrived Cape
Town: February 23. September 4: arrived in Cape Town after reducing
SCOT's 43-year old southbound record from 14 days 21 hours 25
minutes to 13 days 6 hours 30 minutes. October 9: arrived Southampton
with new northbound record: 13 days 8 hours 38 minutes - this was
further reduced December 31, 1937 to 12 days 22 hours 18 minutes.
1939: March 10: arrived Southampton with new northbound record:
12 days 17 hours 30 minutes (net) - this remained in place until 1968
when reduced to less than 12 days by WINDSOR CASTLE and
successive mailships. **1940**: October 19: requisitioned by the Ministry
of Shipping (Ministry of War Transport from May 1941) for use as a
5,000-berth troopship. **1942**: Was the commodore ship for the first
convoy to leave Brazil after it declared war against the Axis powers.
1943: Used across the Atlantic to ferry US troops - on one such voyage
from New York, she carried 6,160 men. **1946**: Undertook three round
trip trooping voyages to Australia. **1947**: January 17: decommissioned
and sent to builders for post-war refit. October: returned to mail service.
1965: Too slow for accelerated eleven and a half-day mail service.
Along with ATHLONE CASTLE and CAPETOWN CASTLE,
replaced by SOUTHAMPTON CASTLE and GOOD HOPE CASTLE
(2). November 14: final departure from Cape Town. Sold to Taiwanese
breakers but deal fell through. **1966**: February: after two North African
cruises from Southampton, sold to Japanese breakers for scrap. March
3: arrived at Mihara for demolition by Nichimen K.K.

ATHLONE CASTLE Steel twin screw motorship (UC 1936-1965) **O.N.**
164625
Builders: Harland & Wolff Ltd., Belfast (yard no: 942)
Tonnage: 25,564 gross 15,688 net
Dimensions: 696 x 82.5 x 41.45 feet
Engines: Burmeister & Wain design oil 2S DA 10-cyl. by builder 4,650 h.p.
24,000 b.h.p. 19.5 knots
Passengers: 246 first, 538 cabin (tourist from 1957)
Refrigerated space: 337,178 cubic feet

1935: Launched: November 28 as mailship. **1936**: May: completed.
Arrived Cape Town: June 7. **1937**: April 14: arrived Cape Town:
with new southbound record: 13 days 0 hours 51 minutes. November
5: inaugurated the regular berthing for mailships in the Buffalo River,
East London - this marked the end of the basket and tender era (see
Chapter Five Tugs & Tenders). **1940**: December 27: requisitioned by
the Ministry of Shipping (Ministry of War Transport from May 1941)
for use as a troopship. During the next six years she carried 148,113
troops and passengers. **1942**: November: ferried troops for the North
Africa campaign. **1943**: Used across the Atlantic with US troops.
1945: August: arrived in Cape Town with the first contingent of
repatriated South African prisoners of war. **1946**: Undertook two round
trip trooping voyages to Australia and one to Singapore. September
17: decommissioned and sent to builders for post-war refit. **1947**:
May: returned to mail service. **1965**: Too slow for accelerated eleven
and a half-day mail service. Along with STIRLING CASTLE and
CAPETOWN CASTLE, replaced by SOUTHAMPTON CASTLE and
GOOD HOPE CASTLE (2). July 23: final departure from Cape Town.
August: sold to Taiwanese breakers for scrap. September 13: arrived
at Kaohsiung for demolition by China Steel Corporation.

ATHLONE CASTLE

STIRLING CASTLE (LD)

ATHLONE CASTLE (LD)

CAPETOWN CASTLE Steel twin screw motorship (UC 1938-1967)
O.N. 166402
Builders: Harland & Wolff Ltd., Belfast (yard no: 986)
Tonnage: 27,000 gross 16,454 net
Dimensions: 702.9 x 82.5 x 41 feet
Engines: Burmeister & Wain design oil 2S DA 10-cyl. by builder 4,650 h.p.
24,000 b.h.p. 19.5 knots
Passengers: 292 first, 499 cabin
Refrigerated space: 344,619 cubic feet

1937: Launched: September 23 as mailship. Enlarged version of
STIRLING CASTLE and ATHLONE CASTLE. She was one of three
new ships named after South African cities - the others were DURBAN
CASTLE and PRETORIA CASTLE. **1938**: April: completed. Arrived
Cape Town: May 13. **1940**: November 26: requisitioned by the
Ministry of Shipping (Ministry of War Transport from May 1941) for
use as a troopship. During the next six years she carried 164,000
troops and passengers. **1942**: November: carried troops for the North
Africa campaign. **1943**: Used across the Atlantic to ferry US troops.
1946: July 29: decommissioned and sent to builders for post-war refit.
1947: January: returned to mail service. Accommodation: 244 first,
553 cabin (tourist from 1957). **1960**: October 17: off Las Palmas, an
explosion in her engine room killed six engineering staff. **1965**:
January: two gold bars stolen from strong room but later recovered.
Too slow for an accelerated eleven and a half-day mail service. Along
with ATHLONE CASTLE and STIRLING CASTLE replaced by
SOUTHAMPTON CASTLE and GOOD HOPE CASTLE (2). Placed
on intermediate fifteen-day service as a one-class 776-passenger ship.
1966: May 10: went aground in the entrance to Flushing harbour and
was refloated at high tide by five Dutch tugs. September: made two
cruises from Southampton to Palma. With the late delivery of GOOD
HOPE CASTLE (2), she returned briefly to the mail service. **1967**:
August 23: final departure from Cape Town. Sold to Terrestre
Marittima S.p.A for scrap. September 26: arrived at La Spezia for
demolition.

Unlike the previous pair of mailships CAPETOWN CASTLE had no first class promenade on D deck. Below - post-war guise with white masts (all photos LD)

WORLD WAR TWO LOSS REPLACEMENTS

PRETORIA CASTLE (2) Steel twin screw steamer (UC 1948-1965)
O.N. 181944
Builders: Harland & Wolff Ltd., Belfast (yard no: 1332)
Tonnage: 28,705 gross 16,713 net
Dimensions: 717.4 x 84 x 43.8 feet
Engines: Double reduction geared steam turbines by builder 7,873 h.p.
35,000 s.h.p. 22 knots
Passengers: 227 first, 478 cabin (tourist from 1957)
Refrigerated space: 326,050 cubic feet

1947: Launched: August 19 as mailship. Built with EDINBURGH
CASTLE as replacements for the WINDSOR CASTLE and
WARWICK CASTLE, which had been lost in the war. Design based
on CAPETOWN CASTLE but with larger funnel and steam powered.
1948: July: completed. Arrived Cape Town: August 5. **1962**: January:
two month refit to improve crew and passenger accommodation.
Passenger capacity changed to: 154 first, 491 tourist class. **1965**: May:
as part of the accelerated eleven and a half day mail service, she
underwent a refit which included: shot-blasting of hull, engine and
propeller modifications - this increased her speed by one knot. She
was also given a mast layout similar to the PENDENNIS CASTLE
i.e. reduced foremast; no mainmast, and a signal mast abaft of the
bridge. **1966**: January 1: sold to the South African Marine Corp. Ltd.
UK subsidiary Safmariner and renamed S.A. ORANJE. Her crew and
management remained Union-Castle. **1969**: March 17: ownership
transferred from UK subsidiary to parent company South African
Marine Corp. Ltd - registered at Cape Town. **1975**: September: sold
to Taiwanese breakers for scrap. October 11: final departure from
Durban with a skeleton crew. November 2: arrived at Kaohsiung for
demolition by Chin Tai Steel Enterprises Co. Ltd. **1976**: January 24:
demolition commenced.

EDINBURGH CASTLE (3) Steel twin screw steamer (UC 1948-1976)
O.N. 182892
Builders: Harland & Wolff Ltd., Belfast (yard no: 1333)
Tonnage: 28,705 gross 16,713 net
Dimensions: 717.4 x 84 x 43.8 feet
Engines: Double reduction geared steam turbines by builder 7,873 h.p. 35,000
s.h.p. 22 knots
Passengers: 227 first, 478 cabin (tourist from 1957)
Refrigerated space: 326,050 cubic feet

1947: Launched: October 16 as mailship. Sister of PRETORIA
CASTLE. **1948**: November: completed. Arrived Cape Town:
December 23. **1954**: January: reduced southbound record: 11 days 21
hours 30 minutes. **1962**: April: two month refit to improve crew and
passenger accommodation. Passenger capacity changed to: 152 first,
491 tourist class. **1965**: June: as part of the accelerated eleven and a
half day mail service, she underwent a refit which included: shot-
blasting of hull, engine and propeller modifications - this increased
her speed by one knot. She was also given a mast layout similar to the
PENDENNIS CASTLE i.e. reduced foremast; no mainmast, and a
signal mast abaft of the bridge. **1976**: Sold to Taiwanese breakers for
scrap. En route to Taiwan, she carried cargo only to South Africa.
May 7: final departure from Cape Town. June 4: arrived at Kaohsiung
for demolition by Chou's Iron & Steel Co. Ltd.

PRETORIA CASTLE (LD)

EDINBURGH CASTLE (LD)

*Above - PRETORIA CASTLE with her new mast layout
in 1965 (LD). Right - S.A. ORANJE leaving Durban for
the breakers (IS).*

FINAL MAILSHIPS

PENDENNIS CASTLE Steel twin screw steamer (UC 1958-1976)
O.N. 300793
Builders: Harland & Wolff Ltd., Belfast (yard no: 1558)
Tonnage: 28,582 gross 15,600 net
Dimensions: 716 x 83.9 x 32.2 feet
Engines: Double reduction steam turbines by builder 46,000 s.h.p. 24 knots
Passengers: 182 first, 493 tourist (plus variable accommodation)
Refrigerated space: 339,840 cubic feet

1956: Designed as updated PRETORIA CASTLE class. After construction had started, the new owners of the company (British & Commonwealth Shipping Co. Ltd.) modified the plans, and she was lengthened on the stocks by 16 feet to incorporate Denny-Brown stabilisers. **1957**: Launched without ceremony December 24 as mailship. Her planned launch (December 10) was postponed because of a strike at the yard and a naming ceremony took place instead. The result of this embarrassment was the end of shipbuilding for Union-Castle by Harland & Wolff. **1958**: November: completed. **1959**: Arrived Cape Town: January 15. Replaced ARUNDEL CASTLE (4). **1968**: Reduced the northbound record: 10 days 15 hours 21 minutes. **1969**: August 12: arrived Cape Town, after setting the final southbound record for the company: 10 days and 11 hours 46 minutes, a far cry from the 31 days achieved by the line's first record breaker SAXON (2) in 1863. **1976**: June 2: final departure from Cape Town. June: sold to Ocean Queen Navigation Corp., Panama for possible use as a cruise ship out of Hong Kong. Renamed OCEAN QUEEN, arrived in Hong Kong August 9 and was laid up. **1977**: Sold to Kinvarra Bay Shipping Co., Liberia. (principal: Gulf Shipping Lines Ltd, London (Abbas K., Murtaza K., & Mustafa Gokal). Renamed first SINBAD and later that year, SINBAD I. Given the links the Gokal brothers had with government agencies in Islamic countries such as Indonesia, it is quite possible that she was bought for conversion into a pilgrim ship. Gulf Shipping Lines were the major debtors in the 1991 collapse of the Bank of Credit and Commerce International (B.C.C.I.). **1980**: April: after almost four years of inactivity, sold to Taiwanese breakers for scrap at Kaohsiung.

WINDSOR CASTLE (3) Steel twin screw steamer (UC 1960-1977)
O.N. 301167
Builders: Cammell Laird & Co. (Shipbuilders & Engineers) Ltd, Birkenhead (yard no: 1287)
Tonnage: 37,640 gross 20,948 net
Dimensions: 730 x 92.6 x 31.8 feet
Engines: Pametrada designed double reduction geared steam turbines by builder 45,000 s.h.p. 23 knots **Trials**: 24.7 knots
Passengers: 238 first, 585 tourist (interchangeable)
Refrigerated space: 348,485 cubic feet

1959: Launched: June 23 as the largest ever mailship. **1960**: June: completed. Inaugural voyage delayed because of seamen's strike. Arrived Cape Town: August 22. Replaced WINCHESTER CASTLE. **1965**: July 16: inaugurated the accelerated eleven and a half day mail service. Reduced both the southbound and northbound records to 11 days 14 hours. **1966**: April 27: arrived at Southampton two and a half days late due to engine trouble. **1977**: September 6: final departure from Cape Town. The last Union-Castle passenger mailship departure. Arrived in Southampton: September 19. October: sold to Margarita Shipping & Trading Corp. (principal - John Latsis Group), Piraeus. Renamed MARGARITA L. and registered at Panama. Converted at Piraeus into an 852-berth floating accommodation ship at Jeddah. **1978**: Ownership transferred to Santa Marianna Shipping & Trading Corp. S.A. (Bilinder Marine Corp S.A., Panama, managers), Panama. **1979**: January: moored at Jeddah for use by the construction company Petrola International S.A. She replaced MARIANNA VI (ex AUREOL 14,083/1951). **1991**: June: after returning to Greece, she was laid up at Eleusis Bay. **1999**: Still laid up.

Above and right - WINDSOR CASTLE (LD)

PENDENNIS CASTLE (LD)

TRANSVAAL CASTLE Steel twin screw steamer (UC 1962-1966)
O.N. 302850
Builders: John Brown & Co. (Clydebank) Ltd., (yard no: 720)
Tonnage: 32,697 gross 17,932 net
Dimensions: 700 x 90.2 x 32 feet
Engines: Pametrada designed double reduction geared steam turbines by builder 40,000 s.h.p. 23 knots **Trials**: 24.7 knots
Passengers: 729 one-class
Refrigerated space: 360,730 cubic feet

1961: Launched: January 17 as a one-class mailship. December: completed. **1962**: Arrived Cape Town: February 1. Replaced CARNARVON CASTLE (2). **1966**: January 1: sold to the South African Marine Corp. Ltd. UK subsidiary Safmariner and renamed S.A. VAAL. Her crew and management remained Union-Castle. **1969**: February 12: ownership transferred from UK subsidiary to parent company South African Marine Corp. Ltd., and registered at Cape Town. **1977**: September 27: final departure from Cape Town. September: sold to Festivale Maritime Inc., Panama. Operated by Carnival Cruise Lines, Miami. Rebuilt at Kawasaki Heavy Industries Ltd., Sadaike, Japan as 1,300-passenger cruise ship, FESTIVALE (Panamanian registered). **1978**: September: sailed for Miami. **1987**: Overhauled and passenger capacity increased to 1,750. **1996**: May: chartered to Dolphin Cruise Lines as ISLANDBREEZE. **1997**: Dolphin Cruise Lines taken over by Premier Cruises. July: after SOLAS refit at Genoa, chartered to Thomson Cruises for Mediterranean cruising. **1999**: Still in service.

Above - TRANSVAAL CASTLE leaving Southampton on her maiden voyage (LD). Left - S.A. VAAL.

Chapter Two
INTERMEDIATES & EXTRAS

DUNLUCE CASTLE at East Pier, Cape Town (CA E8659)

There has long been confusion about the terms "intermediate" and "extra" when used to describe passenger ships on the Union Line, Castle Packets and Union-Castle services. Originally, the "extra" vessels were those which operated on an ad hoc basis between the contract mail sailings. These ships also called at a wider range of ports and tended to be slower than the mailships. As the routes served by the "extra" ships became more popular, a regular line was introduced, which became known as the intermediate service. In many instances, the vessels were outdated or redundant mailships which were demoted to the intermediate service. In 1901, an extra service, which operated "as the trade requires" was started, and continued up to the outbreak of World War I. Thereafter the term applied to cargo sailings until the mid 1960s.

First intermediates and extras

After the introduction of the first joint mail contract in 1876, and the reduction in their annual mail contract sailings from 36 to 26, Union Line had a number of surplus ships, which were used on extra sailings. The first regular intermediate service was the Southampton-Port Elizabeth direct line, which was inaugurated by SYRIA in November 1876.

Donald Currie, introduced his first newly built extras in 1877 and 1879 respectively, with the arrival of TAYMOUTH CASTLE and DUART CASTLE. These were followed in 1883 by another pair of Barclay Curle-built ships, DUNBAR CASTLE and METHVEN CASTLE.

In January 1881, soon after the expiry of the eight-year Zanzibar contract (see Chapter Four Coasters & Feederships), Union Line introduced a fortnightly intermediate service to South Africa from Southampton, which alternated with the mailship sailings. The following month, the service commenced from Hamburg, and later included Antwerp in the schedule setting the pattern for west coast intermediate sailings right up to 1939.

After gold was discovered on the Witwatersrand in 1886, President Kruger of the Transvaal Republic encouraged Dutch immigrants to his country, and the Union Line intermediates started to call at Rotterdam, en route to Southampton. With London as a base port, Castle Line, however, had an advantage over Union as their ships were able to pick up Dutch passengers after leaving England and sail direct to South Africa. WARWICK CASTLE inaugurated the direct service from Vlissingen (Flushing) to South Africa on January 23, 1889. A short time later, they were also awarded the Dutch mail contract to carry mails to Southern Africa.

Union Line "G" class

To cope with new traffic brought about by the gold rush, Union bought two second-hand ships, DANE and ROMAN in 1889 and 1890. In 1891, William Pirrie, then a partner in Harland and Wolff, visited South Africa on a fact finding tour, gathering information for a new type of cargo-passenger ship for the Union Line intermediate service. With a large cargo capacity, the vessels also required a shallow draft for crossing the sand bars at the harbour entrances to East London and Durban. The result was a highly successful and profitable group of twin-screw ships, the famous "G" class, ten of which were built between 1893 and 1900.

Meanwhile, Donald Currie decided to build on the experience he had gained from his coastal service between South Africa and Mauritius which had operated since 1879, and ordered his first purpose-built intermediate ships. These were the DOUNE CASTLE and LISMORE CASTLE of 1890 and 1891 which were designed for the monthly Europe-Mauritius and Madagascar service - the latter was discontinued after the French annexation of Madagascar in 1896.

After the arrival of the innovative "G" class intermediates, Currie responded in the same backward looking way as he had done after NORMAN in 1894, with a series of three old fashioned style four-masted vessels, with yards on the foremast and driven by a single screw. Yards on Castle intermediates were in fact, only dispensed with on the last one built for the company in 1898, the BRAEMAR

CASTLE. Of the seven intermediate ships built by Castle Line between 1894 and 1898, only three remained in company service after 1905.

Until about 1890, calls at St. Helena and Ascension were made by the contract mail ships. These islands were subsequently served during the summer months by the intermediates of both companies which also called at the Canary Islands (the mailships stopped en route at Madeira). The intermediate service operated every four weeks and terminated at Delagoa Bay (Lourenço Marques, now called Maputo) where the new railway linking the port and Pretoria offered the shortest route to the Transvaal. Passengers wishing to travel up the east coast could connect with one of the Deutsche Ost-Afrika-Linie or British India Line ships.

Castle Line also now called at Southampton whilst the continental Europe calls ceased mainly because of the success of the Deutsche Ost-Afrika-Linie (D.O.A.L.) formed by Adolph Woermann in 1887 to serve the recently acquired German territories in East Africa. Although the D.OA.L four-weekly service via Suez initially terminated at Lourenço Marques, the close links between Woermann-Linie on the West Africa run and D.OA.L. ensured a gradual pincer movement southwards until in 1894, the first round Africa service took place.

The development of D.OA.L. was also inextricably linked with the German "scramble for Africa." From 1900 to the outbreak of the First World War, the pace of growth was phenomenal, so that by 1913 the German company operated 45 round Africa sailings from Hamburg, alternating via Suez or around the west of Africa. Up to 25 ports of call were included in each voyage and when one of these was Dover in 1904 (later changed to Southampton), they came into direct competition with Union-Castle Line.

Royal East African Service

Unlike the German company which was heavily subsidised, Union-Castle was unable to obtain any government support for services to East Africa but despite this, the intermediate terminating port was extended from Lourenço Marques to Mombasa in January 1910 - the first sailing was taken by DUNLUCE CASTLE. Support for the service grew and by August 1910 the British Government threw its weight behind an East African service via the Suez Canal. Although no subsidy was forthcoming, government passengers and freight would be carried in the ships, a move which provided a base income for the ships. Thus, on September 13, 1910, GUELPH inaugurated the monthly Royal East African Service, which terminated at Durban. Four of the "Gs" built in the 1890s were used initially on the run. Following complaints from the Colonial Office, however, about the unsuitability of their passenger accommodation for the route, two of these (GOTH and GUELPH) were replaced by the former mail ships, DUNVEGAN CASTLE and CARISBROOK CASTLE in 1913.

Post Boer War west coast intermediates and extras

Soon after the 1900 merger, Currie announced to the Union-Castle Council, as the board of directors was known, that he had ordered six new ships "at his own risk and on his own responsibility." As usual, he had not involved the Council in any of the planning or preparation for this order and the new cargo-passenger vessels of the ALNWICK CASTLE-class, designed for the post Boer War emigrant boom which never happened, ended up being used mainly as extras on the west coast and Mauritius run.

In 1903 and 1904, a new group of three faster and more comfortable ships was built for the weekly west coast intermediate service - the "D" class, which had the bridge set back, giving a very distinctive look to the series. These were followed in 1909 by a new "G" class which was designed to replace the original "G" class of the 1890s - five of these were built between 1909 and 1911, with the last in the series, GALWAY CASTLE, being the final passenger ship built under Donald Currie & Company management.

Royal Mail ownership

The first ships ordered in 1912 by Union-Castle's new owners, Royal Mail Steam Packet Company were two liners of just over 11,000 tons gross, specially designed for the Royal East African service. Their names reflecting the Welsh origins of the chairman Sir Owen Philipps, LLANDOVERY CASTLE and LLANSTEPHAN CASTLE were both completed at the beginning of 1914.

Although all the mailships survived World War I, the extra and intermediate fleet was badly hit, with six including LLANDOVERY CASTLE torpedoed by German submarines. After the war, the political map of Africa had also changed with German South-West Africa becoming a protectorate of South Africa, whilst the former German colony of Tanganyika formed part of British East Africa.

Despite these changes, regular west coast intermediate sailings only resumed in 1922. Instead of weekly departures for Southern Africa from London via Southampton, the ships sailed fortnightly from London, with no call at Southampton. At the same time, the East African service which had operated a restricted schedule since 1919, was extended to continue round Africa, with sailings in both directions. By 1931, the company offered a four-weekly passenger service round Africa in each direction and a four-weekly west coast service which terminated at Beira. The round Africa service via Suez was still called the Royal East African Service, whilst round Africa sailings in the opposite direction were referred to as the Intermediate Service via the west coast.

New motorships

Poor economic conditions in the early 1920s meant that it was only in 1925 that the first new post-war East Africa intermediate was completed - a smaller replacement LLANDOVERY CASTLE. She was followed by a sister, LLANDAFF CASTLE in 1926, and three years later by what was planned to be the first of two ships, the two-funnelled LLANGIBBY CASTLE, the first intermediate motorship. The first oil engine intermediate for the west coast was DUNBAR CASTLE, a smaller version of LLANGIBBY CASTLE.

The Great Depression and the failure of the Kylsant group of companies put paid to plans for a sister for LLANGIBBY CASTLE, and no new intermediates were built for six years. In 1936 two new look single funnelled intermediates were completed, the 15,000 gross ton DUNNOTTAR CASTLE and DUNVEGAN CASTLE which were designed for the round Africa service. These were followed in 1938 by a larger and faster pair for the west coast run - DURBAN CASTLE and PRETORIA CASTLE, the first intermediate ships named after South African cities. The size, speed and names of the last two ships must have been influenced by the arrival of D.OA.L.'s crack liners PRETORIA and WINDHUK in 1936 and 1937 on the Hamburg-Southampton-Las Palmas-Walvis Bay-Cape Town-Durban-Lourenço Marques route (see Chapter One Passenger Mailships).

Not long after the completion of Union-Castle's rebuilding programme, war broke out and the British Government soon had many of these new and reconditioned ships under requisition. DUNNOTTAR CASTLE, DUNVEGAN CASTLE and PRETORIA CASTLE were converted into armed merchant cruisers, whilst most of the remaining intermediates were used as troop transports. PRETORIA CASTLE was converted into an aircraft carrier in 1942, whilst four ships were lost, including DUNVEGAN CASTLE, LLANDAFF CASTLE, DUNBAR CASTLE and GLOUCESTER CASTLE.

Post-war optimism

After the war, there was considerable optimism about the opportunities in South and East Africa. The government of General Smuts actively promoted an assisted passage scheme for migrants to South Africa, and in 1947, Union-Castle placed the three oldest mailships on an "austerity" emigrant service to South Africa. Encouraged by the South African Government, the company also decided that one of the four replacement intermediate vessels would be a purpose-built emigrant carrier. The original plan for BLOEMFONTEIN CASTLE featured a well deck forward similar to the pre-war intermediates, but with the election of the Afrikaner-led

Nationalist Party in 1948, and the subsequent abolition of the emigrant scheme, her plans were modified and she was completed as a one class west coast intermediate ship.

In Tanganyika, an elaborate plan to develop three million acres of land for the production of groundnuts was introduced after the war. Heavily financed by the British Government, the *Groundnuts Scheme* also included the building of a railway in southern Tanganyika. Encouraged by this and other economic indicators, Union-Castle ordered three cabin class round Africa steamships, which were smaller versions of the DURBAN CASTLE and WARWICK CASTLE. These were completed in 1951 and 1952 as RHODESIA CASTLE, KENYA CASTLE and BRAEMAR CASTLE. Unfortunately, as had been the case with BLOEMFONTEIN CASTLE, the timing of the order for these ships was very bad as the *Groundnuts Scheme* was a major failure because of poor initial planning, and was subsequently carried out on a much-reduced scale. The 1950s also saw the first glimpses of the *winds of change*, which would sweep through Africa, with the stability of Kenya seriously disrupted after the outbreak of the Mau Mau Rebellion.

The Winds of Change

In 1950, only BLOEMFONTEIN CASTLE operated on the west coast intermediate run which terminated at Beira - this ended with her sale in 1959. The rest of the intermediate fleet were placed on the round Africa run. With the completion of BRAEMAR CASTLE in 1952, the last of the LLANs, LLANDOVERY CASTLE and LLANGIBBY CASTLE were sold for scrap, and the round Africa service was operated by six ships, with the twice-monthly sailings from London alternating via Suez and via the west coast. By the early 1960s, however, with many former colonies gaining independence, there was no longer any need for colonial administrators, the mainstay of the East African run. Also, air travel was now a serious alternative to the long sea journey, and by 1962 the service only operated from London to Durban, via Suez. This was the beginning of the end, and in 1965 BRAEMAR CASTLE was withdrawn leaving only RHODESIA CASTLE and KENYA CASTLE in service. A brief arrangement was made with the British India Steam Navigation Company for these two ships to operate a schedule with UGANDA and KENYA, but two years later when the RHODESIA CASTLE arrived in London in May 1967, the intermediate service finally came to an end. BRAEMAR CASTLE and RHODESIA CASTLE were sold for scrap after only fourteen and sixteen years of service respectively. On the other hand, their former running mates KENYA CASTLE (AMERIKANIS) and DUNNOTTAR CASTLE (PRINCESA VICTORIA) have celebrated their 47th and 63rd birthdays this year as cruise ships.

Union-Castle passenger ships were rarely used for cruising, and the only cruise ship managed and eventually owned by the company was the REINA DEL MAR, a popular vessel which became uneconomic with the rise in fuel prices in the 1970s. It is interesting to speculate that had the company been prepared to diversify into the cruise market, it might have been like P. & O., one of the leading cruise lines of today. The irony is that TRANSVAAL CASTLE, the last passenger ship built for the company was a major factor in the early success of Ted Arison's Carnival Cruise Lines which is now the biggest cruise company in the world.

CASTLE EXTRAS-INTERMEDIATES 1877-1894

TAYMOUTH CASTLE Iron screw steamer (Castle 1877-1890)
O.N. 769471
Builders: Barclay, Curle & Co. Ltd., Whiteinch (yard no: 270)
Tonnage: 1,827 gross 1,172 net
Dimensions: 300.1 x 33.8 x 25 feet
Engines: 2-cyl. compound by builder 190 h.p. 950 i.h.p. 10.5 knots
Passengers: 50 first

1877: Launched: March 17 as an "extra" steamer but because of the loss of the WINDSOR CASTLE was used initially on the Cape mail service. Registered: April 18. Arrived Cape Town: May 28 with cases of smallpox and was sent to quarantine at Saldanha Bay for 6 weeks. Shortly afterwards, towed brand-new Castle Line coaster MELROSE from Mossel Bay to Cape Town after she broke down. **1878**: Became an "extra" steamer. **1890**: December: sold to Sir Christopher Furness who also bought DUART CASTLE the following year. **1892**: February: both ships sold to Robert Pickford & William Black, Halifax Nova Scotia. Registered at London - name unchanged. **1900**: Renamed OCAMO and placed on the newly-won subsidised mail and cargo route between Canada and the British West Indies. Owners restyled Pickford & Black S.S. Co. Ltd. **1913**: Royal Mail Steam Packet. Co. awarded the Canada and the British West Indies contract (see GOTH) and Pickford & Black ships were withdrawn from route. **1915**: December: sold to Newport S.S. Co., Halifax, Nova Scotia (Continental Trading Co., New York, managers) - name unchanged. **1921**: October: sold for scrap in Germany.

DUART CASTLE Iron screw steamer (Castle 1879-1891)
O.N. 79148
Builders: Barclay, Curle & Co. Ltd., Whiteinch (yard no: 284)
Tonnage: 1,825 gross 1,186 net
Dimensions: 301.5 x 33.2 x 25.1 feet
Engines: 2-cyl. compound by builder 230 h.p. 11 knots
Passengers: 50 first

1878: Launched: June 29 for Seater, White & Co., Leith as ADJUTANT for their Indian service. Her sister GANNET had been chartered by Castle earlier that year as an "extra" steamer. Registered: September 9. **1879**: January: after one voyage to India, bought by Donald Currie as an "extra" steamer - renamed DUART CASTLE. Arrived Cape Town: February 14. **1891**: March: sold to Sir Christopher Furness who bought TAYMOUTH CASTLE the previous year. **1892**:

February: both ships sold to Robert Pickford & William Black, Halifax Nova Scotia. Registered at London - name unchanged. **1900**: Renamed ORURO and placed on the newly-won subsidised mail and cargo route between Canada and the British West Indies. Owners restyled Pickford & Black S.S. Co. Ltd. **1913**: Royal Mail Steam Packet. Co. awarded the Canada and the British West Indies contract (see GOTH) and Pickford & Black ships were withdrawn from route. **1915**: December: sold to Bedford S.S. Co., Halifax, Nova Scotia, (Continental Trading Co., New York, managers) - name unchanged. **1920**: Bought by Anglo-India & Colonial Nav. Co., Bombay (registered London) - same name. **1922**: December: sold to Dada Mia Khandwani & Co., Bombay. **1924**: 4th quarter: broken up at Bombay.

DUNBAR CASTLE (1) Iron screw steamer (Castle 1883-1896)
O.N. 87166
Builders: Barclay, Curle & Co. Ltd., Whiteinch (yard no: 317)
Tonnage: 2,682 gross 1,741 net
Dimensions: 335 x 38.2 x 27.2 feet
Engines: 2-cyl. compound by builder 270 h.p. 1,750 i.h.p. 11 knots
Trials: 12.2 knots
Passengers: not known

1883: Launched: August 2 as an extra steamer. Name advertised as DOUNE CASTLE. Registered: September 22 (registered owner F. J. Mirrielees - Donald Currie's son-in-law). Arrived Cape Town: November 28. **1894**: Broke her shaft, and reached Las Palmas under sail. She was later towed home. **1896**: May: taken over by Fairfield S.B. & E. Co. Ltd., Glasgow in part payment for new ships. December: transferred to the Scottish American S.S. Co., Glasgow which operated as the Northern Pacific S.S. Co. formed by Sir William Pearce (2) in 1892 to provide a Tacoma-Far East service using ships which had been given in part payment to Fairfield (including two ex-Cunarders, PARTHIA and BATAVIA, and ex-Guion Line, ARIZONA. Renamed OLYMPIA - her registered owner was R. Barnwell, William Pearce's executor. **1898**: With the outbreak of the Spanish-American war, she was transferred to US flag as part of the North American Mail S.S. Co., Tacoma. Remained on same service. **1901**: Sold to a new Northern Pacific S.S. Co. which was owned by the Northern Pacific Railroad. **1904**: Sold to the Northwestern S.S. Co., Seattle for Seattle-Nome, Alaska service. **1908**: Company merged with Alaska Steam to form the Alaska S.S. Co. **1910**: December 11: hit a submerged reef in heavy snowstorm near Bligh Island, Prince William Sound. No lives were lost but ship was a constructive total loss. **1922**: February: after remaining on rocks on an even keel for 12 years, she finally slipped off and sank.

TAYMOUTH CASTLE (AG)

DUART CASTLE (AG)

DUNBAR CASTLE (TT)

METHVEN CASTLE Iron screw steamer (Castle 1883-1897)
O.N. 87198
Builders: Barclay, Curle & Co. Ltd., Whiteinch (yard no: 318)
Tonnage: 2,681 gross 1,740 net
Dimensions: 335 x 38.2 x 27.2 feet
Engines: 2-cyl. compound by builder 270 h.p. 1,700 i.h.p. 11 knots
Trials: 12.6 knots
Passengers: not known

1883: Launched: September 19 as an extra steamer. Sister of DUNBAR CASTLE. Name advertised as ARUNDEL, CLUNY and NORHAM CASTLE. Registered: November 9. **1884**: Arrived Cape Town: January 10. **1896**: March: taken over by Fairfield S.B. & E. Co. Ltd., Glasgow in part payment for new ships. **1897**: Transferred like DUNBAR CASTLE (1) to the Scottish American S.S. Co., Glasgow which operated as the Northern Pacific S.S. Co. formed by Sir William Pearce (2) in 1892 to provide a Tacoma-Far East service using ships which had been given in part payment to Fairfield (including two ex-Cunarders, PARTHIA and BATAVIA, and ex-Guion Line, ARIZONA. Renamed COLUMBIA. **1898**: With the outbreak of the Spanish-American war, transferred to US flag as part of the North American Mail S.S. Co., Tacoma. She remained on same service. Later sold to the U.S. Army as the troop transport ROSECRANS (Civil War General William Starke Rosecrans 1819-1898). **1903**: Converted into a tanker. June: bought by Matson Navigation Co. Transported oil from California to Hawaii, returning with molasses. **1905**: June: sold to National Oil & Transportation Co. which later became Associated Oil Co. **1912**: March 12: went aground during storm at Alcatraz, California, 22 miles north of Santa Barbara with a loss of 2 lives. She was successfully salvaged and returned to service 6 months later. **1913**: January 7: wrecked on Peacock Spit, Columbia River bar, Oregon whilst on a voyage from Monterey, California to Portland, Oregon. This time, all but 4 of her 33 crew lost their lives.

FINLAND Steel screw steamer (Castle 1886-1887)
O.N. 91954
Builders: A. McMillan & Son, Dumbarton (yard no: 272)
Tonnage: 1,363 gross 969 net
Dimensions: 230.6 x 33 x 23.2 feet
Engines: Triple expansion by Hutson & Corbett, Glasgow 117 h.p. 10 knots
Passengers: 30 first

1886: Laid down as NATAL MERCHANT for the Cape & Natal Merchants' Line but with demise of the company, was bought before completion and renamed FINLAND. Launched: July 16. (Her sister CAPE MERCHANT was bought by the Indo-China Steam Navigation Co. Ltd., London as PAUMBEN – she lasted in various guises until wrecked in 1930) Registered: September 9. Chartered to the South African Line. Arrived Cape Town: December. **1887**: April 26: on coastal voyage from Cape to Mauritius with general cargo and passengers, was wrecked 16 miles east of Kowie River on Great Fish Point, Eastern Cape. Cargo recovered and no lives lost.

DOUNE CASTLE Steel screw steamer (Castle 1890-1900: UC 1900-1904) **O.N.** 98174
Builders: Barclay, Curle & Co. Ltd., Whiteinch (yard no: 362)
Tonnage: 4,046 gross 2,613 net
Dimensions: 396 x 43.2 x 28.5 feet
Engines: Triple expansion by builder 463 h.p. 3,200 i.h.p. 12 knots
Passengers: 30 first, 42 second, 80 third

1890: Launched: August 4 for Mauritius intermediate service. Completed: November. Arrived Cape Town: December 20. **1904**: May: sold to Barclay, Curle & Co., with LISMORE and RAGLAN CASTLE in part payment for new ships - given temporary name BELLMOUNT but never sailed as such. October: sold to A/S Det Vestindiske Kompagni Copenhagen for their West Indies service - renamed ST. DOMINGO. **1905**: Det Vestindiske Kompagni was taken over by the A/S Det Østasiatiske Kompagni (East Asiatic Co.), Copenhagen. Transferred first to the A/S Det Østasiatiske Kompagni, but not registered in Denmark and then in February to their Russian subsidiary Russisk-Østasiatiske Dampskibsselskab, St. Petersburg and renamed CURONIA. Used on services between Black Sea and Baltic ports and the Far East, she was joined by ARUNDEL CASTLE as A/S Det Østasiatiske Kompagni's BIRMA, whilst RAGLAN CASTLE took her place on the West Indies service and was given her former name ST. DOMINGO. **1913**: April: sold to Goshi Kaisha Kishimoto Shokai, Dairen as KAIJO MARU. **1918**: Bought by Madrigal & Co., Manila as SUSANA II. **1928**: Sold to An Kee S.S. Co., Amoy - renamed SUSANA. **1932**: Sold again to Chit Soon On Co., (Limin S.S. Co. managers), Amoy - renamed ASIA. **1935**: Sold to Japanese breakers - delivered as TOA MARU and broken up during 2nd quarter.

Wreck of FINLAND (CA DR J489)

METHVEN CASTLE (TT)

DOUNE CASTLE (TT)

LISMORE CASTLE Steel screw steamer (Castle 1891-1900: UC 1900-1904)
O.N. 98199
Builders: Barclay, Curle & Co. Ltd., Whiteinch (yard no: 363)
Tonnage: 4,046 gross 2,606 net
Dimensions: 396 x 43.2 x 28.5 feet
Engines: Triple expansion by builder 479 h.p. 3,200 i.h.p. 12 knots
Passengers: 30 first, 42 second, 80 third

1890: Launched: October 30 for Mauritius intermediate service. Sister of DOUNE CASTLE. **1891**: January: completed. Arrived Cape Town: March 20. **1899**: Converted into hospital ship for Boer War. Employed between October 3, 1899 and September 4, 1900. **1904**: May: taken over by her builder with DOUNE and RAGLAN CASTLE in part payment for new ships. Given temporary name WESTMOUNT but never sailed as such. September: sold to Compañía Trasatlántica, Barcelona and named after its founder's brother C. LÓPEZ Y LÓPEZ. Ran between Spain and the Philippines (32 first, 40 second, 400 third). **1916**: Placed on the Spain-New York run. Later transferred to Mexican service. **1930**: October 7: arrived in Genoa for scrapping at Savona.

HARLECH CASTLE Steel screw steamer (Castle 1894-1900: UC 1900-1904)
O.N. 102867
Builders: Barclay, Curle & Co. Ltd., Whiteinch (yard no: 389)
Tonnage: 3,264 gross 2,083 net
Dimensions: 350 x 42.5 x 25.8 feet
Engines: Triple expansion by builder 367 h.p. 2,600 i.h.p. 11 knots
Passengers: 44 first, 250 third

1894: Launched: February 22 as an extra streamer. Completed: May. Arrived Cape Town: July 1. **1899**: Became Boer War Transport No. 27. Employed between October 3, 1899 and October 4, 1902, and carried 2,934 men. **1904**: Bought by Earl Fitzwilliam for use in a hunt for buried treasure on the Cocos Islands. Renamed VERONIQUE. **1905**: November: sold to the Peruvian government as the naval auxiliary IQUITOS. **1922**: Bought by Cia. Peruana de Vapores y Dique del Callao, Callao and renamed AMAZONAS. **1934**: Broken up.

LISMORE CASTLE (TT)

HARLECH CASTLE

LISMORE CASTLE (JC)

UNION SECOND-HAND INTERMEDIATES

DANE (3) Iron screw steamer (Union 1889-1894)
O.N. 63614
Builders: Caird & Co., Greenock (yard no: 153)
Tonnage: 3,648 gross 2,288 net
Dimensions: 381.9 x 44.7 x 33 feet
Engines: 2-cyl. compound by builder 600 h.p. 2,626 i.h.p. 11 knots
Passengers: 180 first, 75 second

ROMAN (2) Iron screw steamer (Union 1890-1891)
O.N. 63553
Builders: Day, Summers & Co., Southampton
Tonnage: 2,994 gross 1,642 net
Dimensions: 348 x 40.3 x 33.2 feet
Engines: 2-cyl. simple by builder 600 h.p. 2,500 i.h.p. 10 knots
Passengers: 172 first, 58 second and 43 third

1870: Launched: April 21 for Peninsular & Oriental S. N. Co., London as AUSTRALIA (1) for P. & O. China and Australia services, although laid down as MIRZAPORE. Registered: June 23. **1876**: Engines compounded by builder. **1879**: October 16: shaft broke in English Channel outward bound from Southampton - towed into Plymouth by naval tugs TRUSTY and GRINDER. **1889**: July: because of shortage of ships, bought at auction by Union S.S. Co. for intermediate service and renamed DANE (3). Arrived Cape Town: September 22. **1893**: December: with arrival of first of the new "G" class of intermediate steamers was sold to Messrs. George Cohen & Sons of Woolwich for scrap.

1870: Built for Royal Mail Steam Packet. Co., London as NILE. Used on the West Indies service, she was the last in the fleet with single expansion engine. **1878**: Engines compounded by builder. **1890**: May: bought by Union S.S. Co. for intermediate service and renamed ROMAN (2). Arrived Cape Town: September 8. **1891**: Planned to be kept with DANE (3) until arrival of the new "G" class of intermediate steamers but was found to be unsuitable and was sold to Messrs. George Cohen & Sons of Woolwich for scrap.

Below - DANE and above as AUSTRALIA

Below - ROMAN (WSS) and above as NILE

UNION LINE "G" CLASS INTERMEDIATES

GAUL Steel twin screw steamer (Union 1893-1900: UC 1900-1906)
O.N. 98863
Builders: Harland & Wolff Ltd., Belfast (yard no: 261)
Tonnage: 4,745 gross 3,047 net
Dimensions: 400.5 x 47.2 x 26.7 feet
Engines: Triple expansion by builder 324 h.p. 2,200 i.h.p. 11.5 knots
Passengers: 38 first, 60 second, 65 third

1893: Launched: February 16 for intermediate service as the first of the new "G" class. May: completed. Arrived Cape Town: June 10. **1906**: Sold with GREEK to Royal Mail Steam Packet Co. for a new Southampton-Cuba-Mexico service. Renamed SABOR. **1909**: June: transferred with SEGURA (ex GREEK) to Shire Line of Steamers Ltd. for use on the Far East routes (Royal Mail were joint owners of the service with Thos. & Jno. Brocklebank Ltd.). Renamed CARMARTHENSHIRE. **1911**: July: Royal Mail become sole owners of Shire Line of Steamers Ltd. **1913**: October: transferred to new R.M.S.P.'s Canadian Government-subsidized fortnightly passenger, mail and cargo service between Canada and West Indies via Bermuda. Name changed to CHALEUR. Her running mates were ex "G"s - COBEQUID (ex GOTH), CHIGNECTO (ex GREEK) and CARAQUET (ex GUELPH). **1927**: July: after the loss of the contract to the newly formed Canadian National Steamships, she and CHIGNECTO were sold to Dutch breakers N.V. Frank Rijsdijk's Industrieele Ondernemingen. August: arrived in Rotterdam. Broken up at Hendrik-Ido-Ambacht (near Rotterdam).

GOTH Steel twin screw steamer (Union 1893-1900: UC 1900-1913)
O.N. 98866
Builders: Harland & Wolff Ltd., Belfast (yard no: 263)
Tonnage: 4,738 gross 3,035 net
Dimensions: 400.5 x 47.2 x 26.7 feet
Engines: Triple expansion by builder 324 h.p. 2,200 i.h.p. 11.5 knots
Passengers: 38 first, 60 second, 65 third

1893: Launched: March 16 for intermediate service. June: completed. Arrived Cape Town: July 23. **1910**: Joined GUELPH, GASCON and GOORKA on the new monthly Royal East Africa Service between London and Durban via Suez. **1913**: October: because of complaints from the Colonial Office about the suitability of their passenger accommodation for the route, both GOTH and GUELPH were replaced by former mail ships, DUNVEGAN CASTLE and CARISBROOK CASTLE, and transferred by the new owners of Union-Castle, Royal Mail Steam Packet. Co. to R.M.S.P.'s Canada and West Indies route. Renamed COBEQUID. November 23: sailed from Halifax at the start of the new service. **1914**: January 13: on return from first voyage to West Indies, with cargo of sugar and molasses, was wrecked on Trinity Ledges, at the entrance to the Bay of Fundy, with no loss of life.

GREEK Steel twin screw steamer (Union 1893-1900: UC 1900-1906)
O.N. 98870
Builders: Harland & Wolff Ltd., Belfast (yard no: 268)
Tonnage: 4,757 gross 3,036 net
Dimensions: 400.5 x 47.2 x 26.7 feet
Engines: Triple expansion by builder 324 h.p. 2,200 i.h.p. 11.5 knots
Passengers: 38 first, 60 second, 65 third

1893: Launched: May 18 for intermediate service. August: completed. Arrived Cape Town: October 17. **1906**: March: sold with GAUL to Royal Mail Steam Packet. Co. for new Southampton-Cuba-Mexico service. Renamed SEGURA. **1909**: June: transferred with SABOR (ex GAUL) to Shire Line of Steamers Ltd. for use on the Far East routes (Royal Mail were joint owners of the service with Thos. & Jno. Brocklebank Ltd.). Renamed PEMBROKESHIRE. **1911**: July: Royal Mail become sole owners of Shire Line of Steamers Ltd. **1913**: Transferred to R.M.S.P.'s new Canadian West Indies service. Renamed CHIGNECTO. **1918**: September 22: on a voyage to Britain, loaded with explosives, was badly damaged in collision with dock wall at St. John, New Brunswick. **1927**: July: after the loss of the contract to the newly formed Canadian National Steamships, she and CHALEUR were sold to Dutch breakers N.V. Frank Rijsdijk's Industrieele Ondernemingen. July: left London in tow for Rotterdam. Broken up at Hendrik-Ido-Ambacht (near Rotterdam).

GUELPH Steel twin screw steamer (Union 1894-1900: UC 1900-1913)
O.N. 104040
Builders: Harland & Wolff Ltd., Belfast (yard no: 284)
Tonnage: 4,917 gross 3,112 net
Dimensions: 400.5 x 47.3 x 26.7 feet
Engines: Triple expansion by builder 324 h.p. 2,200 i.h.p. 11.5 knots
Passengers: 40 first, 67 second, 87 third

1894: Launched: June 26 for intermediate service. Differed from the three earlier "G"s by having three masts instead of two. September: completed. Arrived Cape Town: October 29. **1910**: September 13: started the new monthly Royal East Africa Service between London and Durban via Suez. Her running mates were GOTH, GASCON and GOORKA. **1913**: October: because of complaints from the Colonial Office about the suitability of their passenger accommodation for the route, both GOTH and GUELPH were replaced by former mail ships, DUNVEGAN CASTLE and CARISBROOK CASTLE, and transferred by the new owners of Union-Castle, Royal Mail Steam Packet. Co. to R.M.S.P.'s Canada and West Indies route. Renamed CARAQUET. **1923**: June 25: wrecked on reef north of Hamilton, Bermuda, while on voyage from Halifax, Nova Scotia to West Indies with flour and general cargo - no loss of life.

GUELPH (LD)

GAUL (AG)

GREEK

GOTH

GASCON (2) Steel twin screw steamer (Union 1897-1900: UC 1900-1928)
O.N. 106907
Builders: Harland & Wolff Ltd., Belfast (yard no: 304)
Tonnage: 6,278 gross 3,975 net
Dimensions: 430 x 52.2 x 29 feet
Engines: Triple expansion by builder 508 h.p. 2,750 i.h.p. 11.5 knots
Passengers: 60 first, 87 second, 95 third
Refrigerated space: 7,665 cubic feet

1896: Launched: August 25 for intermediate service. The first in a new series of larger, three masted "G" class ships. **1897**: February: completed. Arrived Cape Town: April 11. Took part in the Diamond Jubilee Spithead Review. **1905**: Made first Union-Castle call at Lobito, Angola with contractors for the Benguela Railway. **1910**: Joined GUELPH, GOTH and GOORKA on the new monthly Royal East Africa Service between London and Durban via Suez. **1914**: August: as a temporary mail ship, was the first to sail for South Africa after the outbreak of war. September 20: off Zanzibar narrowly escaped attack by the German cruiser KÖNIGSBERG which sank HMS PEGASUS. Under Red Cross flag, GASCON picked up wounded from the British ship and transported them to Simon's Town. She later became a full time hospital ship. **1920**: July 29: returned to owners at the end of war duty. August: returned to intermediate service. **1926**: January: laid up in Southampton water. September: recommissioned. **1928**: May: laid up with GAIKA in East India Dock. September: arrived Inverkeithing for scrap by T. W. Ward.

GAIKA Steel twin screw steamer (Union 1897-1900: UC 1900-1929)
O.N. 106908
Builders: Harland & Wolff Ltd., Belfast (yard no: 305)
Tonnage: 6,278 gross 3,975 net
Dimensions: 430 x 52.2 x 29 feet
Engines: Triple expansion by builder 508 h.p. 2,750 i.h.p. 11.5 knots
Passengers: 60 first, 89 second, 91 third
Refrigerated space: 8,966 cubic feet

1896: Launched: September 22 for intermediate service. **1897**: April: completed. Arrived Cape Town: May 23. **1902**: November: ran aground on her southbound voyage at Las Palmas - returned home for

repairs. **1913**: Transferred to Royal East Africa Service between London and Durban via Suez. **1914**: Carried troops between Cape Town and German South-West Africa. **1915**: April: returned to owners and was used as a mail steamer. **1916**: January to February: transport on east Coast of Africa. **1917**: Requisitioned by the Shipping Controller under the Liner Requisition Scheme and used on Australia-UK run. **1919**: Returned to intermediate service. **1922**: April 22: in thick fog ran aground briefly opposite the Green Point lighthouse, Cape Town. **1926**: Laid up in Southampton water. **1928**: May: laid up in East India Dock. **1929**: March: arrived in Savona, Italy for demolition.

GOORKHA Steel twin screw steamer (Union 1897-1900: UC 1900-1926)
O.N. 106917
Builders: Harland & Wolff Ltd., Belfast (yard no: 311)
Tonnage: 6,278 gross 3,975 net
Dimensions: 430 x 52.2 x 29 feet
Engines: Triple expansion by builder 508 h.p. 2,750 i.h.p. 11.5 knots
Passengers: 60 first, 89 second, 91 third
Refrigerated space: 8,014 cubic feet

1897: Launched: January 23 for intermediate service - first Union ship with stockless anchors. August: completed. Arrived Cape Town: September 26. **1913**: Transferred to Royal East Africa Service between London and Durban via Suez. **1914**: August: requisitioned as transport. October: commissioned as 408-bed hospital ship. **1917**: October 17: with 400 wounded from Salonika, she hit a mine but managed to reach Malta for repairs. **1919**: December 9: returned to owners. **1920**: Returned to intermediate service. **1926**: May: sold for scrap. June 2: arrived in Genoa.

GASCON (AG)

GAIKA (AG)

GOORKHA (ML)

GERMAN (2)/**GLENGORM CASTLE** Steel twin screw steamer (Union 1898-1900: UC 1900-1930)
O.N. 109290
Builders: Harland & Wolff Ltd., Belfast (yard no: 334)
Tonnage: 6,763 gross 4,221 net
Dimensions: 440.3 x 53.2 x 29.6 feet
Engines: Triple expansion by builder 497 h.p. 2,900 i.h.p. 12 knots
Passengers: 76 first, 105 second, 98 third
Refrigerated space: 7,779 cubic feet

1898: Launched: August 4 for intermediate service. With two masts, the first of the final "G" class series. November: completed. November 16: collided with and sank Wilson Line's CORSO (895/1894) in the River Elbe. Shortly afterwards she collided with the barque SAVERNAKE with minor damage. **1899**: Arrived Cape Town: January 29. **1914**: September: converted into 423-bed hospital ship - because of anti-German sentiment, name was changed to GLENGORM CASTLE. **1921**: Among the last hospital ships to be decommissioned. Apart from one mail voyage to South Africa, continued in government service as a troopship. **1925**: Returned to intermediate service. **1930**: March: sold to Dutch breakers N.V. Frank Rijsdijk's Industrieele Ondernemingen - the last survivor of the "G" class. April 11: sailed London for Rotterdam. Broken up at Hendrik-Ido-Ambacht (near Rotterdam).

GALEKA Steel twin screw steamer (Union 1899-1900: UC 1900-1916)
O.N. 110265
Builders: Harland & Wolff Ltd., Belfast (yard no: 347)
Tonnage: 6,767 gross 4,299 net
Dimensions: 440.3 x 53.2 x 29 feet
Engines: Triple expansion by builder 508 h.p. 2,900 i.h.p. 12 knots
Passengers: 78 first, 106 second, 65 third
Refrigerated space: 7,753 cubic feet

1899: Launched: October 21 for intermediate service. December: completed. **1900**: Arrived Cape Town: January 28 under Union Line flag - thereafter, she flew Union-Castle colours. **1914**: August 7: requisitioned as a troopship. **1915**: June: commissioned as 366-bed hospital ship. **1916:** October 27: arriving 19.00 hours at Le Havre, was unable to contact port examination vessel and had to steam off the coast all night. The following day, struck a mine (laid 2 days earlier by German submarine UC 26) 5 miles north-west of Cap de la Hève (near Le Havre). Nineteen lives were lost. Beached, she became a total loss.

GALICIAN/GLENART CASTLE Steel twin screw steamer (UC 1900-1918)
O.N. 113334
Builders: Harland & Wolff Ltd., Belfast (yard no: 348)
Tonnage: 6,757 gross 4,297 net
Dimensions: 440.3 x 52.2 x 29 feet
Engines: Triple expansion by builder 508 h.p. 2,900 i.h.p. 12 knots
Passengers: 70 first, 105 second, 91 third
Refrigerated space: 7,164 cubic feet

1900: Launched: September 20 for intermediate service. Ordered by Union Line, but completed in December as Union-Castle vessel - the last of the "G" class. **1901**: Arrived Cape Town: January 14. **1914**: August: 15: shortly after outbreak of war, was stopped near Teneriffe by the famous Norddeutscher Lloyd Blue Riband liner, KAISER WILHELM DER GROSSE, now a German armed merchant cruiser. After boarding was released because of the women and children on board. September: like GERMAN, was renamed for political reasons. As GLENART CASTLE, she was commissioned as a 453-bed hospital ship. **1917:** March 1: carrying wounded from Le Havre to Southampton, she hit a mine but managed to stay afloat and was towed into Portsmouth for repairs. **1918**: February 26: en route from Newport, South Wales to Brest was torpedoed by the German submarine UC 56 in Bristol Channel, 20 miles west of Lundy. Sank within five minutes, with loss of 168 lives.

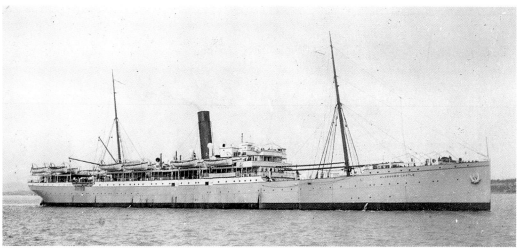

GLENGORM CASTLE (ex GERMAN)

GALICIAN (TT)

GALEKA (AG)

CASTLE RESPONSE TO UNION "G" CLASS

Castle's response to the "G"s was a series of old-fashioned looking intermediate vessels.

ARUNDEL CASTLE (2) Steel screw steamer (Castle 1894-1900: UC 1900-1901)
O.N. 104827
Builders: Fairfield S.B. & E. Co. Ltd., Glasgow (yard no: 377)
Tonnage: 4,588 gross 2,879 net
Dimensions: 415 x 45.8 x 27.9 feet
Engines: Triple expansion by builder 568 h.p. 3,300 i.h.p. 13 knots
Trials: 14.2 knots
Passengers: 96 first, 124 second, 150 third

1894: Launched: October 2 for intermediate service. December: completed. **1895**: Arrived Cape Town: May 9. **1905**: May: sold to the A/S Det Østasiatiske Kompagni (East Asiatic Co.), Copenhagen and renamed BIRMA. October: fitted out in Copenhagen as a troop transport for the Russian Army, she undertook two round voyages (each with almost 2,000 men) between Vladivostock and Odessa. **1906**: April 26: end of trooping service, laid up at Copenhagen. June: chartered by DFDS (The United Steamship Company), Copenhagen for three 12 day cruises to Norway and the midnight sun in connection with the celebration of the coronation of the Danish Prince Carl as the Norwegian King Håkon VII. October: left Copenhagen on a special promotion trip to the Far East with the Danish princes Valdemar and Georg and the founder of Det Østasiatiske Kompagni, H. N. Andersen and other distinguished Danish guests. **1907**: March: returned to Copenhagen after a trip of 127 days during which she had sailed 21,794 nautical miles. July 21: left Copenhagen on charter to the Danish Ministry of Naval Affairs as a cruise ship for the Danish King Frederik VIII and Queen Louise's official visit to the Faroe Islands and Iceland. During the visit, BIRMA was escorted by the Danish warships HEKLA and GEYSIR. September: undertook a Mediterranean cruise with the Danish Prime Minister, H. N. Andersen and the King of Siam. **1908**: Still under the Danish flag, completed one round trip with emigrants between Libau, Latvia and New York for the Russian East Asiatic Steamship Co.'s new Russian American Line. **1909**: Transferred to company's Russian flagged subsidiary, Russisk-Østasiatiske Dampskibsselskab, St. Petersburg. Placed on the Libau-New York service - her passenger capacity was 59 first; 94 second and 869 steerage. **1914**: Renamed MITAU (or MITAWA), with the outbreak of war, she was laid up at Kronstad (St. Petersburg), and later seized by the Russian Government. Unable to leave port because of the activities of the German Navy in the Baltic, she remained laid up. **1918**: April: when in Helsinki to be fitted out as a hospital ship for trooping service of wounded prisoners of war between Russia and Germany, she was ordered to hoist the Russian flag aft and the Danish and Red Cross flag at the mainmast to indicate that she was under Red Cross protection. November: after much negotiation between the Finnish and Danish authorities, A/S Det Østasiatiske Kompagni was acknowledged as her owner, and she was allowed to proceed to Copenhagen for repairs and transfer to the Danish flag. She later was chartered by the British Government to repatriate British prisoners of war from Danzig to Leith via Copenhagen. **1919**: Returned to Far East service and was used across the Atlantic to the U.S. Gulf. **1920**: June 15: laid up at Copenhagen. **1921**: February: sold to the Polish Navigation Inc. of New York for a new service between Poland and New York – renamed JÓZEF PILSUDSKI (70 second and 740 third). After only one voyage, was arrested at Kiel and the company went bankrupt in November. **1923**: Sold to H. Hellmers, Kiel and renamed FRANCK HELLMERS. Resold to Algemeine Reed G.m.b.H., Hamburg. **1924**: Sold to Wilh. Boelstler & Co., G.m.b.H., Hamburg as WILBO. December 10: arrived in Genoa to be scrapped. **1925**: Broken up.

TINTAGEL CASTLE (1) Steel screw steamer (Castle 1896-1900: UC 1900-1912)
O.N. 105900
Builders: Fairfield S.B. & E. Co. Ltd., Glasgow (yard no: 393)
Tonnage: 5,513 gross 3,542 n.
Dimensions: 425.2 x 50 x 22.2 feet
Engines: Triple expansion by builder 620 h.p. 3,500 i.h.p. 13.5 knots
Trials: 14.7 knots
Passengers: 78 first, 98 second, 150 third
Refrigerated space: 2,870 cubic feet

1896: Launched: September 12 for intermediate service. Completed: November. Arrived Cape Town: December 27. **1912**: August: sold with AVONDALE CASTLE to the newly formed Cie. de Nav. Sud Atlantique, Bordeaux and renamed LIGER. October: first sailing from Bordeaux to South America. **1923**: With the arrival of new ships, sold for scrap in Genoa and arrived March 1.

AVONDALE CASTLE Steel screw steamer (Castle 1897-1900: UC 1900-1912)
O.N. 108160
Builders: Fairfield S.B. & E. Co. Ltd., Glasgow (yard no: 394)
Tonnage: 5,513 gross 3,542 net
Dimensions: 425.2 x 50 x 22.2 feet
Engines: Triple expansion by builder 620 h.p. 3,500 i.h.p. 13.5 knots
Trials: 14.2 knots
Passengers: 78 first, 98 second, 150 third
Refrigerated space: 2,787 cubic feet

1896: Launched: November 5 for intermediate service. December: completed. **1897**: Arrived Cape Town: February 22. **1899**: October 9: arrived at Lourenço Marques with £250,000 in specie intended for the Transvaal Government. Intercepted by HMS PHILOMEL and escorted to Durban where the cargo was landed. **1912**: August: sold with TINTAGEL CASTLE to the newly formed Cie. de Nav. Sud Atlantique, Bordeaux and renamed GARONNA. October: first sailing from Bordeaux to South America. **1923**: Broken up at Bordeaux.

The four-masted Castle intermediates were: AVONDALE CASTLE - below opposite; ARUNDEL CASTLE - top and TINTAGEL CASTLE - below (TH)

DUNOLLY CASTLE Steel screw steamer (Castle 1897-1900: UC 1900-1905)
O.N. 108163
Builders: Barclay, Curle & Co. Ltd., Whiteinch (yard no: 407)
Tonnage: 4,167 gross 2,636 net
Dimensions: 368 x 46.3 x 20 feet
Engines: Triple expansion by builder 419 h.p. 2,600 i.h.p. 12.5 knots
Passengers: 36 first, 110 second, 130 steerage

1896: Launched: November 4 for intermediate service. **1897:** January: completed. Arrived Cape Town: March 21. **1905:** February: sold to Max Jebsen, Hamburg and renamed JULIETTE. August: resold to the A/S Det Østasiatiske Kompagni (East Asiatic Co.) Copenhagen and transferred to the company's Russian flagged subsidiary Russisk-Østasiatiske Dampskibsselskab, St. Petersburg. Used initially on Far East route before being placed on the new Russian American Line emigrant service between Libau, Latvia and New York. Later renamed ARCONIA, only three round voyages to New York were carried out. **1908:** With a decline in emigrant traffic, she became surplus to requirements. **1911:** February: sold to Swan, Hunter & Wigham Richardson, Newcastle as down payment for new tonnage. July: sold to Continentale Rederei A.G., Hamburg and renamed HITTFIELD. **1913:** Sold to National Greek Line (National Steam Nav. Co. Ltd. of Greece) as IOANNINA for Piraeus-New York service. **1917:** December 15: captured and scuttled by German submarine U 156, about 150 miles north-west of Madeira (35N-19W) whilst on voyage from Piraeus to New York.

RAGLAN CASTLE Steel screw steamer (Castle 1897-1900: UC 1900-1905)
O.N. 108187
Builders: Barclay, Curle & Co. Ltd., Whiteinch (yard no: 408)
Tonnage: 4,324 gross 2,743 net
Dimensions: 383.5 x 46.3 x 20 feet
Engines: Triple expansion by builder 419 h.p. 2,600 i.h.p. 12.5 knots
Passengers: 36 first, 110 second, 130 steerage

1897: Launched: January 20 for intermediate service. March: completed. Arrived Cape Town: May 8. **1904:** August: taken over by her builder with LISMORE and DOUNE CASTLE in part payment for new ships. **1905:** Sold to the Russian Navy for use as a store-carrier, but February: sold to A/S Det Vestindiske Kompagni, Copenhagen for their West Indies service just before the company was taken over by the A/S Det Østasiatiske Kompagni (East Asiatic Co.), Copenhagen. Renamed ST. DOMINGO (replaced DOUNE

CASTLE which had been briefly given the same name) she undertook one round trip to the West Indies. **1906:** February-August: chartered as a troop ship between Vladivostock and Odessa. **1907:** September 23: arrived at Greenock after sale to Barclay, Curle & Co. **1909:** Reverted to her original name. **1910:** January: bought by Pythia S.S. Co., Glasgow (Donaldson Bros. managers). Most of the shares were owned by Barclay, Curle & Co. Renamed PYTHIA. **1911:** November: sold to A/S Dominion Whaling Co. Ltd., (T. Dannevig & Co.), Sandefjord and converted into a whale oil refinery. Name unchanged. **1919:** Same owner - Chr. Christensen jr., managers. **1920:** Sold to A/S Odd (Chr. Christensen jr., managers) Sandefjord. **1923:** Same owner - I. Bryde & L. Thorsen managers. **1925:** Same owner - Thor Dahl, managers. **1929:** April 18: capsized whilst being repaired at Sandefjord by Framnaes M.V. who took her over and repaired her. **1930:** Sold to Hvalfanger A/S Africa (B. Gundersen, manager), Sandefjord and renamed READY. **1933:** Same owners, new manager F. Bettum. **1934:** July: sold to Metal Industries Ltd., Rosyth for scrap. September 12: arrived Rosyth under tow and demolition commenced in October.

BRAEMAR CASTLE (1) Steel screw steamer (Castle 1898-1900: UC 1900-1924)
O.N. 108381
Builders: Barclay, Curle & Co. Ltd., Whiteinch (yard no: 409)
Tonnage: 6,266 gross 3,964 net
Dimensions: 450 x 52.2 x 22.5 feet
Engines: Quadruple expansion by builder 756 h.p. 4,400 i.h.p. 13.5 knots. Trials: 15.3 knots
Passengers: 70 first, 130 second, 160 third
Refrigerated space: 2,297 cubic feet

1898: Launched: February 23 as the first Castle intermediate ship without yards and last single screw passenger ship. July: completed. Arrived Cape Town: September 4. **1902:** January: stranded on the Isle of Wight for two days. **1909:** Chartered by British Government as peacetime troop transport - painted white with blue hull band and yellow funnel. **1914:** August: requisitioned as transport. **1915:** Converted into a 421-bed hospital ship. In service between October 7, 1915 and August 1, 1919. **1916:** November 23: hit a mine in the Mykonos Channel and beached on Tinos Island. Four lives were lost. **1917:** Refloated, she was towed to Malta where she arrived in February. Because the dockyard was busy, she was later repaired at La Spezia. **1918:** Became the base hospital at Murmansk. **1920:** Made one voyage as an intermediate before being requisitioned again as a troop transport. **1922:** Took part in peace keeping force during Turko-Greek war. **1924:** Sold for scrap in Italy. October 12: arrived Genoa.

DUNOLLY CASTLE (JC)

RAGLAN CASTLE - above (JC) ended her career as the whale oil refinery READY - right (LD).

BRAEMAR CASTLE (LD)

POST BOER WAR EXTRAS

HELIUS Steel screw steamer (UC 1904-1906)
O.N. 118066
Builders: Fairfield S.B. & E. Co. Ltd., Glasgow (yard no: 336)
Tonnage: 4,527 gross 2,950 net
Dimensions: 387.4 x 46.7 x 31.1 feet
Engines: Triple expansion by builder 2,800 i.h.p. 13 knots
Passengers: 38 first, 20 second, 1,759 steerage ('tweendecks)

1888: Launched: December 1 as DRESDEN, the first in a new series of cargo and passenger ships built by Fairfield for Norddeutscher Lloyd, Bremen - all were named after German cities. **1889:** January: delivered. **1903:** November: sold to British and South American Steam Nav. Co. Ltd. (R. P. Houston & Co., managers), Liverpool for their cargo and passenger service to South Africa. Renamed HELIUS. **1904:** After one voyage, Houstons agreed to drop this service after they were admitted to the conference lines. March: sold to Union Castle. Laid up at Netley with PEMBROKE CASTLE and never used. **1906:** June: both ships sold to the Turkish Government. HELIUS became the navy transport BEZMI-I ALEM (Council of the Universe). **1914:** November 6: en route from Istanbul to Trabzon with troops and stores, sunk by Russian destroyers near Kandilli in the Black Sea (41.23N-31.32E). In the same attack, the transports BAHRIYE AMER (ex ROLAND 3,603/1893) and MITHAT PASA (ex PORT ROYAL 4,455/1900) were also sunk.

ALNWICK CASTLE Steel twin screw steamer (UC 1901-1917)
O.N. 114784
Builders: William Beardmore & Co. Ltd., Glasgow (yard no: 475)
Tonnage: 5,893 gross 3,796 net 8,000 deadweight
Dimensions: 400.4 x 50.2 x 26.8 feet
Engines: Triple expansion by builder 475 h.p. 3,400 i.h.p. 11.5 knots
Passengers: 12 first, 29 second, 42 third

1901: Launched: September 27. November: completed as the first in a new series of cargo-passenger "extras" for anticipated post Boer War emigrant boom, but was used primarily on the west coast and Mauritius runs. Arrived Cape Town: December 21. **1914:** September 26: requisitioned as a troop transport. **1915:** March: arrived at the Dardenelles with men of the Royal Naval Division for the Gallipoli campaign. **1916:** June 16: returned to owners and placed on the South Africa run. **1917:** March 19: torpedoed and sunk by German submarine U 81 in Atlantic 310 miles south-west of Bishop Rock (47.38N-13.24W) on voyage from London to Cape Town. 40 lives were lost.

BERWICK CASTLE Steel twin screw steamer (UC 1902-1920)
O.N. 114822
Builders: William Beardmore & Co. Ltd., Glasgow (yard no: 476)
Tonnage: 5,893 gross 3,788 net 8,000 deadweight
Dimensions: 398.2 x 50 x 26.8 feet
Engines: Triple expansion by builder 476 h.p. 3,400 i.h.p. 11.5 knots
Passengers: 12 first, 29 second, 42 third

1901: Launched: December 7. **1902:** January: completed as a cargo-passenger "extra" for anticipated post Boer War emigrant boom but was used primarily on the west coast and Mauritius runs. Sister of ALNWICK CASTLE. Arrived Cape Town: March 26. **1904:** March 8: on voyage from Southampton to Hamburg, rammed and sank the British submarine A1 off the Nab Lightship in the Solent with the loss of all her crew. **1915:** Carried part of the Nigerian Brigade from Lagos to Mombasa for the East Africa campaign. **1919:** October 16: beached after fire at Port Reitz, Kilindini on voyage to Beira and UK with general cargo. October 19: fire extinguished. November 1: refloated and laid up at Mombasa. **1920:** April: under her own steam, reached Durban where she was auctioned in October. Unsold, she was purchased in December by the Andora Soc. Anon. di Construzione ed Imprese Navale, Genoa who hoped to use her as an emigrant ship to South America. **1921:** June: renamed ANDORA CASTLE, she arrived at Porto Maurizio (Imperia), North Italy and was laid up. **1925:** June: moved from Porto Maurizio to La Spezia for scrapping.

CAWDOR CASTLE Steel twin screw steamer (UC 1902-1926)
O.N. 114823
Builders: Barclay, Curle & Co. Ltd., Whiteinch (yard no: 429)
Tonnage: 6,235 gross 4,052 net 8,000 deadweight
Dimensions: 414.7 x 51.2 x 28 feet
Engines: Triple expansion by builder 430 h.p. 3,400 i.h.p. 11.5 knots
Trials: 13.6 knots
Passengers: 12 first, 29 second, 42 third

1901: Launched: December 7. **1902:** January: completed as a cargo-passenger "extra" for anticipated post Boer War emigrant boom but was used primarily on the west coast and Mauritius runs. Arrived Cape Town: March 10. **1914:** August 8: requisitioned as a transport. **1915:** December 13: attacked by enemy submarine in Mediterranean but managed to escape. German submarine U 38 reported attacking a British steamer on this date in the Ionian Sea, but this was called off as steamer was better armed than the submarine. **1917:** May 5 to June 19: carried horses and wheat from Canada to Europe. **1918:** First ship to reach Cape Town with repatriated South African troops. **1923:** Laid up. **1924:** Returned to service as a cargo carrier. **1926:** July 30: on voyage Hamburg-London-Mauritius with general cargo, ran aground at Conception Bay, South-West Africa. All crew were saved but ship was a constructive total loss.

HELIUS laid up at Netley (AG)

ALNWICK CASTLE (AM)

BERWICK CASTLE (AG)

CAWDOR CASTLE

NEWARK CASTLE Steel twin screw steamer (UC 1902-1908)
O.N. 115806
Builders: Barclay, Curle & Co. Ltd., Whiteinch (yard no: 430)
Tonnage: 6,224 gross 4,036 net 8,000 deadweight
Dimensions: 414.1 x 51.2 x 28 feet
Engines: Triple expansion by builder 430 h.p. 3,400 i.h.p. 11.5 knots
Passengers: 12 first, 29 second, 42 third

1902: Launched: March 22. April: completed as a cargo-passenger "extra" for anticipated post Boer War emigrant boom but was used primarily on the west coast and Mauritius runs. Sister of CAWDOR CASTLE. Arrived Cape Town: July 4. **1908**: March 12: six hours after leaving Durban for Mauritius via Delagoa Bay with soldiers for the Mauritius garrison, general cargo and a large amount of paper money, she went ashore 4 miles from the coast near Port Durnford, Natal. Abandoned, the wreck later drifted seven miles and ran aground on a sandbank outside the Umhlatuzi Lagoon (Richards Bay) and was a constructive total loss. Three lives were lost when one of the boats was swamped.

CLUNY CASTLE (2) Steel twin screw steamer (UC 1903-1924)
O.N. 118323
Builders: Barclay, Curle & Co. Ltd., Whiteinch (yard no: 441)
Tonnage: 5,147 gross 3,303 net 7,270 deadweight
Dimensions: 419.1 x 50.2 x 28.2 feet
Engines: Triple expansion by builder 548 h.p. 2.900 i.h.p. 11.5 knots
Passengers: 8 first, 20 second, 140 third

1903: Launched: August 10. September: completed as a cargo-passenger "extra" for anticipated post Boer War emigrant boom but was used primarily on the west coast and Mauritius runs. Arrived Cape Town: November 2. **1915**: Placed on the East African coastal

run. **1917**: July: requisitioned as a transport under the Liner Requisition Scheme, she was used extensively including a trip to New Zealand. **1924**: December: sold with COMRIE CASTLE to the Union-Castle subsidiary Bullard King & Co. Ltd. (Natal Line), London. Converted into a one-class vessel and given a taller funnel. **1925**: February: renamed UMKUZI. **1938**: July: sold to Hughes Bolckow Shipbreaking Co. Ltd. for scrap. August 3: arrived Blyth.

COMRIE CASTLE Steel twin screw steamer (UC 1903-1924)
O.N. 118342
Builders: Barclay, Curle & Co. Ltd., Whiteinch (yard no: 442)
Tonnage: 5,167 gross 3,311 net 7,270 deadweight
Dimensions: 419.3 x 50.2 x 28.3 feet
Engines: Triple expansion by builder 548 h.p. 2,900 i.h.p. 11.5 knots
Passengers: 8 first, 20 second, 140 third

1903: Launched: October 5. November: completed as a cargo-passenger "extra" for anticipated post Boer War emigrant boom but was used primarily on the west coast and Mauritius runs. Sister of CLUNY CASTLE. Arrived Cape Town: December 29. **1914**: August 6: requisitioned as a troopship. **1916**: August: used during the East African campaign. **1918**: March 16: torpedoed in the English Channel on voyage from London to New York. Nine lives were lost and she was towed to Portsmouth for repairs. **1924**: December: sold with CLUNY CASTLE to the Union-Castle subsidiary Bullard King & Co. Ltd. (Natal Line), London. Converted into a one-class vessel. **1925**: February: renamed UMVOTI. August: took the homeward mail sailing during the seaman's strike. **1940**: Requisitioned by Admiralty. July 29: sunk as blockship at Folkestone. **1943**: Wreck was broken up on the beach at Folkestone.

NEWARK CASTLE (JC)

CLUNY CASTLE

*COMRIE CASTLE - left (AG) was
sold to Natal Line and became
UMVOTI - below (CA E8871)*

"D" CLASS INTERMEDIATES

DURHAM CASTLE Steel twin screw steamer (UC 1904-1917)
O.N. 118387
Builders: Fairfield S.B. & E. Co. Ltd., Glasgow (yard no: 433)
Tonnage: 8,217 gross 5,177 net
Dimensions: 475.4 x 56.7 x 31.6 feet
Engines: Quadruple expansion by builder 969 h.p. 5,200 i.h.p. 13 knots
Passengers: 230 first, 270 third, 300 steerage (1920s: reduced 177 first, 186 tourist)
Refrigerated space: 9,379 cubic feet (1920s: 21,602 cubic feet)

1903: Launched: December 17 as the first of the new "D" class series of west coast intermediate ships. **1904**: February: completed. Arrived Cape Town: April 10. **1910**: West coast intermediate service extended to Mombasa. **1914**: Remained in company service throughout the war. **1931**: November: placed on round Africa service. **1939**: June: sold to Metal Industries Ltd., Rosyth for scrap. Towed from London and arrived Rosyth: July 10. October: a week after the start of demolition, requisitioned by the Admiralty as a blockship at Scapa Flow. **1940**: January 26: on tow to Scapa Flow by HMS WATERMEYER (South African Railways & Harbours' tug T. H. WATERMEYER on hire to Admiralty as rescue tug), hit a mine and sunk off Cromarty.

DOVER CASTLE (2) Steel twin screw steamer (UC 1904-1917)
O.N. 118409
Builders: Barclay, Curle & Co. Ltd., Whiteinch (yard no: 443)
Tonnage: 8,271 gross 5,219 net
Dimensions: 476.4 x 56.7 x 31.9 feet
Engines: Quadruple expansion by builder 969 h.p. 5,200 i.h.p. 13 knots
Passengers: 230 first, 270 third, 300 steerage
Refrigerated space: 8,397 cubic feet

1904: Launched: February 4 for west coast intermediate service. April: completed. Arrived Cape Town: May 22. **1910**: West coast intermediate service extended to Mombasa. **1914**: September 2: requisitioned as a transport. **1915**: August 11: commissioned as a 607-bed hospital ship HMHS DOVER CASTLE. **1917**: May 26: on voyage from Malta to Gibraltar, torpedoed and sunk by German submarine UC 67, fifty miles north of Bona, Algeria (37.54N-07.36E). Seven lives were lost.

DUNLUCE CASTLE Steel twin screw steamer (UC 1904-1939)
O.N. 118490
Builders: Harland & Wolff Ltd., Belfast (yard no: 361)
Tonnage: 8,114 gross 5,105 net
Dimensions: 475.5 x 56.9 x 31.7 feet
Engines: Quadruple expansion by builder 965 h.p. 5,200 i.h.p. 13 knots
Passengers: 230 first, 270 third, 300 steerage (By 1939: reduced to 149 first & 186 tourist)
Refrigerated space: 8,600 cubic feet (1920s: 20,433 cubic feet)

1904: Launched: April 31 for west coast intermediate service. September: completed. Arrived Cape Town: November 6. **1910**: West coast intermediate service extended to Mombasa. **1915**: July: converted into a 755-bed hospital ship. In service from July 6, 1915 to April 2, 1919 during which time she operated in the Mediterranean, East Africa, across the English Channel and to Australia and India. **1920**: Returned to company service. **1931**: October: placed on round Africa service. **1939**: June: sold for scrap to Smith & Houston Ltd., Port Glasgow, but requisitioned by the Admiralty. Initially used as an accommodation vessel at Immingham, and later as a depot ship at Scapa Flow. **1940**: April: purchased by Admiralty. **1945**: July: arrived at Inverkeithing for demolition by T. W. Ward Ltd.

DURHAM CASTLE (FH)

DUNLUCE CASTLE at Cape Town - above (ML) and as a depot ship at Scapa Flow during World War Two - below. DOVER CASTLE - right (TH)

SECOND "G" CLASS INTERMEDIATES

GRANTULLY CASTLE (2) Steel twin screw steamer (UC 1910-1939)
O.N. 129058
Builders: Barclay, Curle & Co. Ltd., Whiteinch (yard no: 477)
Tonnage: 7,606 gross 4,794 net
Dimensions: 450.7 x 54.3 x 30.7 feet
Engines: Quadruple expansion by builder 625 h.p. 3,250 i.h.p. 12 knots
Passengers: 75 first, 110 second, 194 third
Refrigerated space: 7,400 cubic feet (1921: 22,181 cubic feet)

1909: Launched: October 11 as the first of a new class of "G" west coast intermediate ships designed to replace the Union built "G"s of the 1890s. She also reintroduced three classes on the intermediate service. **1910**: January: completed. Arrived Cape Town: February 14. **1910**: West coast intermediate service extended to Mombasa. **1915**: June: converted into a 552-bed hospital ship. In service from June 22, 1915 to March 11, 1919 during which time she operated in the Mediterranean, across the English Channel and to the West Indies. **1919**: September: returned to company service. **1923**: All intermediates became two class: first and third. **1930**: February: placed on round Africa service - used mainly as such between periods of lay-up. **1932**: February laid up in reserve fleet. **1933**: August: returned to west coast intermediate service. **1934**: Third became tourist. **1939**: July: sold for scrap to P. & W. MacLellan Ltd. July 20: arrived Bo'ness.

GARTH CASTLE (2) Steel twin screw steamer (UC 1910-1939)
O.N. 129078
Builders: Barclay, Curle & Co. Ltd., Whiteinch (yard no: 478)
Tonnage: 7,610 gross 4,791 net
Dimensions: 452.6 x 54.3 x 30.7 feet
Engines: Quadruple expansion by builder 647 hp. 3,250 i.h.p. 12 knots
Passengers: 75 first, 110 second, 194 third
Refrigerated space: 13,510 cubic feet (1921: 22,359 cubic feet)

1910: Launched: January 13 for west coast intermediate service. March: completed. Arrived Cape Town: April 25. **1910**: West coast intermediate service extended to Mombasa. **1914**: November 4:

commissioned as a naval hospital ship based mainly at Scapa Flow. **1919**: October 24: returned to her owners. **1923**: All intermediates became two class: first and third. **1926**: March 25: ran ashore at English Bay, Ascension and flooded one of her holds. Passengers were transferred to KENILWORTH CASTLE on March 30, and she was later repaired at Cape Town. **1931**: September: laid up until February 1932. **1939**: June: sold to Hughes Bolckow Shipbreaking Co. Ltd. for scrap. June 14: arrived Blyth.

GLOUCESTER CASTLE Steel twin screw steamer (UC 1911-1942)
O.N. 132592
Builders: Fairfield S.B. & E. Co. Ltd., Glasgow (yard no: 478)
Tonnage: 7,999 gross 4,974 net
Dimensions: 452.7 x 56.2 x 30.7
Engines: Quadruple expansion by builder 722 h.p. 3,750 i.h.p. 12 knots
Passengers: 87 first, 130 second, 195 third
Refrigerated space: 14,500 cubic feet (1920: 20,851 cubic feet)

1911: Launched: May 13. August: completed for west coast intermediate service. Arrived Cape Town: September 15. **1914**: September: converted into a 410-bed hospital ship. In service from September 24, 1914 to September 9, 1919 during which time she operated mainly in the Mediterranean and across the English Channel. **1917**: March 31: torpedoed in the English Channel by German submarine UB 32 whilst carrying patients between Le Havre and Southampton. Down at the stern, she was later towed to Portsmouth for repairs. **1920**: Returned to intermediate service and later placed on round Africa service until arrival of LLANDAFF CASTLE in 1926. **1923**: All intermediates became two class: first and third. **1939**: June: laid up. August: recommissioned for service. **1942**: July 15: on voyage from Birkenhead to Cape Town, was attacked and sunk by German raider MICHEL (4,740/1939) 750 miles from Ascension (approximately 08S-01E). 93 lives were lost and the survivors were sent to Japan for internment.

GRANTULLY CASTLE (FH)

GARTH CASTLE (FH)

GLOUCESTER CASTLE (TH)

GUILDFORD CASTLE Steel twin screw steamer (UC 1911-1933)
O.N. 132611
Builders: Barclay, Curle & Co. Ltd., Whiteinch (yard no: 488)
Tonnage: 8,036 gross 5,055 net
Dimensions: 452.1 x 56.2 x 30.8 feet
Engines: Quadruple expansion by builder 720 h.p. 3,750 i.h.p. 12 knots
Passengers: 87 first, 130 second, 195 third
Refrigerated space: 8,400 cubic feet (1921: 21,833 cubic feet)

1911: Launched: August 11 for west coast intermediate service. October: completed. Arrived Cape Town: November 11. **1914**: September: converted into a 427-bed hospital ship. In service from September 22, 1914 to November 19, 1918 during which time she operated mainly in the Mediterranean and in East Africa. **1918**: March 10: at the end of a voyage from Cape Town to Avonmouth, torpedoed twice at the entrance to the Bristol Channel. The first torpedo missed, whilst the second failed to explode - submarine is believed to be German submarine U 110. **1920**: Returned to intermediate service. **1922**: Placed on round Africa service until arrival of LLANGIBBY CASTLE in 1929. **1923**: All intermediates became two class: first and third. **1933**: May 30: on a voyage from Hamburg to London, whilst under a German pilot, collided with Blue Funnel's STENTOR (6,626/1926) near Oste Riff in the River Elbe, and sank the following day. Three lives were lost.

GALWAY CASTLE Steel twin screw steamer (UC 1911-1918)
O.N. 132616
Builders: Harland & Wolff Ltd., Belfast (yard no: 419)
Tonnage: 7,988 gross 4,967 net
Dimensions: 452.3 x 56.3 x 30.8 feet
Engines: Quadruple expansion by builder 722 h.p. 3,750 i.h.p. 12 knots
Passengers: 87 first, 130 second, 195 third
Refrigerated space: 8,400 cubic feet

1911: Launched: April 12 for west coast intermediate service. October: completed. The last passenger ship built under Donald Currie & Co. management and the final ship in the second "G" series. Arrived Cape Town: November 19. **1914**: September: carried troops from Cape Town at the start of the German South-West Africa campaign. **1915**: Because of the shortage of ships, became a mailship. **1916**: August 3: was attacked by German aircraft off the Gull Lightship but escaped serious damage. **1917**: October 12: ran aground on the Orient Beach, East London, South Africa. Refloated a few days later. **1918**: September 12: on voyage from Plymouth to South Africa with mail and passengers, torpedoed by German submarine U 82, 160 miles south of the Fastnet Rock (48.50N-10.40W). 150 lives were lost, many unnecessarily during the evacuation of the ship, which although suffering a broken back, remained afloat for another 3 days.

GALWAY CASTLE (ML)

GUILDFORD CASTLE - above (FH) sank in 1933 after a collision in the River Elbe.

ROYAL EAST AFRICA SERVICE

LLANDOVERY CASTLE (1) Steel twin screw steamer (UC 1914-1918)
O.N. 135302
Builders: Barclay, Curle & Co. Ltd., Whiteinch (yard no: 504)
Tonnage: 11,423 gross 7,128 net
Dimensions: 500.1 x 63.3 x 37.2 feet
Engines: Quadruple expansion by builder 1,135 h.p. 5,800 i.h.p. 14 knots
Passengers: 234 first, 116 second, 100 third
Refrigerated space: 3,295 cubic feet

1913: Launched: September 3 as the first Union-Castle liner specially designed for the Royal East African service which operated between London and East Africa (via Suez). Also, the first ship ordered for the company's new owners, Royal Mail Steam Packet Company, under the chairmanship of the Welshman Sir Owen Philipps, hence the LLAN nomenclature. **1914**: January: completed. Arrived Durban (via Suez): March 6. Because of the shortage of ships after the outbreak of war, placed on the mail service. **1915**: December: requisitioned as a troop transport. **1916**: July: converted into a 622-bed hospital ship. In service from July 27. December 7: set alight by German prisoners of war on voyage from Tilbury to France - fires extinguished at Dover. **1918**: June 27: on voyage from Halifax to Liverpool, torpedoed and sunk by German submarine U 86, 116 miles south-west of the Fastnet Rock. All were evacuated safely, but U 86 surfaced and opened fire on life boats. Only 24 were rescued out of 258.

LLANSTEPHAN CASTLE Steel twin screw steamer (UC 1914-1952)
O.N. 135315
Builders: Fairfield S.B. & E. Co. Ltd., Glasgow (yard no: 494)
Tonnage: 11,293 gross 7,021 net
Dimensions: 500.5 x 63.3 x 37.2 feet
Engines: Quadruple expansion by builder 1,157 h.p. 5,800 i.h.p. 14 knots
Passengers: 195 first, 165 second, 100 third (1923: 357 first, 74 third; 1934: 301 first, 140 tourist)
Refrigerated space: 3,210 cubic feet (1920s: 25,466 cubic feet)

1913: Launched: August 29 for the Royal East African service which operated between London and East Africa (via Suez). Sister of LLANDOVERY CASTLE. **1914**: February: completed. Arrived Durban (via Suez): April 2. Because of the shortage of ships, after the outbreak of war placed on the west coast mail service. **1917**: Requisitioned by the Shipping Controller as a troop transport. **1918**: At the end of the war, was once again put into service as mailship. **1920**: Returned to East African service. **1922**: Round Africa service commenced. **1923**: All intermediates two class: first and third. **1939**: Converted to oil fuel. **1940**: September 17 to December 11: chartered by Ministry of Shipping as transport. **1941**: Requisitioned by Ministry of War Transport as a transport and supply ship. August: acted as the commodore ship of the first convoy to Russia. **1943**: Operated in the Indian Ocean. **1944**: Transferred to the Royal Indian Navy as an auxiliary. **1946**: July: sent to builders for refit. **1947**: August: refit complete. September: returned to round Africa service. Passenger capacity: 231 first, 198 tourist. **1952**: Sold to the British Iron & Steel Corporation (BISCO) for scrap. March 1: arrived Newport, Monmouthshire to be broken up by John Cashmore Ltd. Longest serving ship in company history 38 years 1 month.

Whilst LLANDOVERY CASTLE - above - did not survive the First World War. Her sister LLANSTEPHAN CASTLE - right and below opposite (LD) - became the longest serving Union-Castle ship. She also served as a transport during World War Two - below

LLANDOVERY CASTLE (2) Steel twin screw steamer (UC 1925-1952)
O.N. 148678
Builders: Barclay, Curle & Co. Ltd., Whiteinch (yard no: 606)
Tonnage: 10,609 gross 6,501 net
Dimensions: 471.1 x 61.7 x 39 feet
Engines: Quadruple expansion by builder 1,085 h.p. 5,500 i.h.p. 14 knots
Trials: 15.5 knots
Passengers: 221 first, 186 third (tourist from 1934)
Refrigerated space: 53,280 cubic feet (1928: 98,598 cubic feet)

1925: Launched: July 4 for the round Africa intermediate service. Smaller sized replacement for LLANDOVERY CASTLE (1). September: completed. Arrived Cape Town (via Suez): December 15. **1937**: February 25: during the Spanish Civil War, outbound for Marseilles, she hit a mine 2 miles south-east of Cabo Creus and with her two forward holds flooded, put into Port Vendres. After temporary repairs, she reached Genoa in May for major repairs. June 9: left Genoa for London. **1939**: Converted to oil fuel. **1940**: November 23: severely damaged at Southampton during air raid whilst being converted into a hospital ship. **1941**: Commissioned as 450-bed hospital ship HMHS LLANDOVERY CASTLE (No. 39). As such, she carried over 38,000 wounded personnel and operated in East Africa, the Mediterranean, Northern France and repatriated wounded service personnel to Canada. November: damaged in bombing attack at Suez. **1946**: October: sent for refit by Harland & Wolff Ltd. at Liverpool. **1947**: May: returned to round Africa service. Passenger capacity: 215 first, 198 tourist. **1952**: December: sold to the British Iron & Steel Corporation (BISCO) for scrap and arrived Inverkeithing, December 22 to be broken up by T. W. Ward.

LLANDAFF CASTLE Steel twin screw steamer (UC 1926-1942)
O.N. 149752
Builders: Workman, Clark & Co. Ltd., Belfast (yard no: 488)
Tonnage: 10,763 gross 6,538 net
Dimensions: 471.2 x 61.7 x 39.2 feet
Engines: Quadruple expansion by builder 1,058 h.p 5,500 i.h.p. 14 knots
Passengers: 213 first, 108 third (tourist from 1934)
Refrigerated space: 99,970 cubic feet

1926: Launched: August 10 for the round Africa intermediate service. Sister of LLANDOVERY CASTLE (2). **1927**: January: completed. Arrived Cape Town (via Suez): February 26. **1939**: Converted to oil fuel. December 26: requisitioned as a troop transport and used mainly in East and Southern African waters. **1942**: May: with WINCHESTER CASTLE, took part in the successful invasion of Madagascar. November 30: on voyage from Dar es Salaam to Durban, was torpedoed and sunk by German submarine U 177 off the northern coast of Zululand (27.20S-33.40E). Two lives were lost.

LLANDOVERY CASTLE (LD)

*The second LLANDOVERY CASTLE -
above (ML) hit a mine during the
Spanish Civil War. Right - seen here at
Port Vendres, Vernon Thomson removed
the story of this event from Marischal
Murray's Union-Castle Chronicle.*

LLANDAFF CASTLE

INTERMEDIATE MOTORSHIPS

LLANGIBBY CASTLE Steel twin screw motorship (UC 1929-1954)
O.N. 161329
Builders: Harland & Wolff Ltd., Glasgow (yard no: 841)
Tonnage: 11,951 gross 7,199 net
Dimensions: 485.6 x 66.2 x 39.2 feet
Engines: Burmeister & Wain design oil 4S SA 8-cyl. by builder 1,300 h.p. 8,500 b.h.p. 15 knots **Trials:** 17 knots
Passengers: 256 first, 198 third (tourist from 1934)
Refrigerated space: 123,970 cubic feet

1929: The first two funnelled intermediate ship and the first motorship ordered by Union-Castle (CARNARVON CASTLE was ordered as a steamship). Intended to be one of two sisters, her order with Harland & Wolff was planned for 1924 but was delayed for two years because of poor financial results. Launched: July 4 for the round Africa intermediate service. November: completed. **1930:** Arrived Cape Town (via Suez): January 19. **1940:** September 17: requisitioned as a troop transport. December 21: damaged with ROXBURGH CASTLE (1) in air raid at Liverpool. **1942:** January 16: rudder and part of stern blown away by torpedo from German submarine U 402 in North Atlantic (46.04N-19.06W) - 26 lives were lost. She undertook an epic journey to the Azores and then to Gibraltar where a temporary repair was made, eventually reaching the UK mid April. November 8: during the North Africa invasion at Oran, was hit by a shell which demolished the engineer's quarters and killed one man. **1944:** June: fitted with assault landing craft, took part in the D Day landings and during over sixty trips between Southampton and Normandy, carried in excess of 100,000 troops. **1945:** March: damaged in collision with Blue Funnel's ANTENOR (11,345/1925) in Solent. **1946:** For seven months, was engaged repatriating West African troops from India. With no stay in port longer than three day, her length of time away from Southampton was recorded as the longest voyage made by a company owned vessel. **1947:** January: sent to builders for refit. July: returned to round Africa service. Passenger capacity: 212 first, 198 tourist. **1954:** June: sold to the British Iron & Steel Corporation (BISCO) for scrap. July 12: arrived Newport, Monmouthshire to be broken up by John Cashmore Ltd.

DUNBAR CASTLE (2) Steel twin screw motorship (UC 1930-1940)
O.N. 161420
Builders: Harland & Wolff Ltd., Glasgow (yard no: 851)
Tonnage: 10,002 gross 5,985 net
Dimensions: 471.2 x 61.2 x 29.6 feet
Engines: Burmeister & Wain design oil 4S SA 6-cyl. by builder 977 h.p. 6,300 b.h.p. 14 knots **Trials:** 15.9 knots
Passengers: 193 first, 250 third
Refrigerated space: 97,050 cubic feet

1929: Launched: October 31 for the west coast intermediate service and a smaller version of LLANGIBBY CASTLE, but with combined bridge and poop deck. The names of the next group of intermediates all started with DU. **1930:** May: completed. Arrived Cape Town: July 1. **1938:** December: transferred to round Africa service. **1940:** January 9: hit a mine 2 miles north-east of Goodwin Sands (51.23N-01.34E) and sank with the loss of nine lives including her captain. The wreck with upper superstructure visible was demolished in August 1949.

LLANGIBBY CASTLE (LD)

DUNBAR CASTLE (FH)

During the Second World War
DUNBAR CASTLE hit a mine
and sank whilst LLANGIBBY
CASTLE took part in the D Day
landings - right.

DUNNOTTAR CASTLE Steel twin screw motorship (UC 1936-1958)
O.N. 164637
Builders: Harland & Wolff Ltd., Belfast (yard no: 959)
Tonnage: 15,002 gross 9,181 net
Dimensions: 540 x 71.9 x 37.8 feet
Engines: Burmeister & Wain design oil 2S DA 9-cyl. by builder 1,931 h.p.
9,500 b.h.p. 16 knots
Passengers: 258 first, 250 second
Refrigerated space: 200,819 cubic feet

1936: Launched: January 25 for the round Africa intermediate service.
The first of a new look single funnel intermediate design. June:
completed. Arrived Cape Town: July 21. October: during the mailship
rebuilding programme, transferred to mail service. **1938**: November:
returned to intermediate service. **1939**: August 30: requisitioned by
Admiralty and sent to Belfast for conversion into an armed merchant
cruiser HMS DUNNOTTAR CASTLE. Used on South Atlantic
patrols. **1942**: July 27: decommissioned and handed over to the
Ministry of War Transport for conversion into a troopship. Admiralty
considered buying her with CARNVARVON CASTLE and
PRETORIA CASTLE for conversion into an aircraft carrier - in end,
only the last mentioned was converted. **1947**: Continued to operate as
a troopship between Southampton and the Mediterranean. **1948**: April:
sent to her builders for a refit. **1949**: January: placed on round Africa
service. Passenger capacity: 207 first, 236 tourist (Post 1955: 105
first, 263 tourist). **1958**: July 16: final departure from Cape Town.
August: sold to Incres S. S. Co. Ltd., Monrovia and renamed
VICTORIA. **1959**: January: towed from London to Holland where
she was completely rebuilt by Dok-en-Werf Maatschappij Wilton-
Fijenoord, Schiedam into a cruise ship. With new Fiat C-757 diesel
engines (16,800 b.h.p. and 18 knots), her overall length was increased
by 12 feet. 14,917 gross tons and 600 one-class passengers. December:
undertook first cruise from Le Havre to Madeira and North Africa.
1964: Sold to Victoria S. S. Co. Ltd., Monrovia when Incres Line
were taken over by Clipper Lines. **1975**: November: with the

bankruptcy of her owners, bought by Victoria Shipping S.A. (A. J.
Chandris), Greek register, and towed from New York to Piraeus. **1976**:
June: after refit, recommenced cruising. **1977**: June: ownership
transferred to Phaidon Navegacion S.A. (A. J. Chandris), Panamanian
register, and renamed THE VICTORIA. **1993**: January: sold to the
Cyprus-based Princesa Victoria Co. Ltd., Louis Cruise Lines,
managers. Renamed PRINCESA VICTORIA. Passenger capacity:
750. **1997**: October 4: rescued passengers from the cruise ship
ROMANTICA (7,538/1939) which caught fire off the coast of Cyprus,
during a short cruise to Israel and Egypt. **1998**: Used as a hotel ship
during Expo 98 in Lisbon. **1999**: Still in service.

DUNVEGAN CASTLE (2) Steel twin screw motorship (UC 1936-1940)
O.N. 164702
Builders: Harland & Wolff Ltd., Belfast (yard no: 960)
Tonnage: 15,007 gross 9,179 net
Dimensions: 540 x 71.9 x 37.8 feet
Engines: Burmeister & Wain design oil 2S DA 9-cyl. by builder 1,931 h.p.
9,500 b.h.p. 16 knots
Passengers: 258 first, 250 second
Refrigerated space: 199,670 cubic feet

1936: Launched: March 26 for the round Africa intermediate service.
Sister of DUNNOTTAR CASTLE. August: completed. Arrived Cape
Town: October 6. **1937**: February: during the mailship rebuilding
programme, undertook voyages on mail service. **1938**: transferred to
round Africa service. **1939**: September 7: requisitioned by Admiralty
and sent to Belfast for conversion to an armed merchant cruiser HMS
DUNVEGAN CASTLE. **1940**: August 27: as escort for convoy to
Freetown, was torpedoed by German submarine U 46 west of Ireland
and sank the following day (54.50N-11.00W). 27 lives were lost.

DUNVEGAN CASTLE (LD)

Above - DUNNOTTAR CASTLE as built (LD). Converted into
a cruise ship, she is seen - below - off the coast of Turkey as
THE VICTORIA (PN).

DURBAN CASTLE Steel twin screw motorship (UC 1938-1962)
O.N. 166617
Builders: Harland & Wolff Ltd., Belfast (yard no: 987)
Tonnage: 17,388 gross 10,435 net
Dimensions: 570.7 x 76.4 x 39.5 feet
Engines: Burmeister & Wain design oil 2S DA 8-cyl. by builder 3,284 h.p. 16,000 b.h.p. 18 knots
Passengers: 220 first, 335 tourist
Refrigerated space: 178,850 cubic feet

1938: Launched: June 14 for the west coast intermediate service. Enlarged and more powerful version of DUNNOTTAR CASTLE. December: completed. She was one of three new ships named after South African cities - the others were CAPETOWN CASTLE and PRETORIA CASTLE. **1939**: Arrived Cape Town: January 18. September: requisitioned for one voyage as a troopship. **1940**: December: requisitioned as a full time troopship. **1942**: Took part in the North Africa invasion. **1943**: Fitted for carrying assault craft, transported marines for the landings at Sicily, Salerno and Anzio. **1944**: Landed troops for the invasion of Southern France and Italy. **1946**: November: sent to her builders for a refit. **1947**: July: reconditioned (183 first, 333 tourist), she was placed with her sister WARWICK CASTLE on the mail service until the mail fleet was back to full strength. **1950**: June: on the round Africa service. **1962**: March: sold to German breakers. April 13: arrived Hamburg for demolition by Eisen u. Metall A.G.

PRETORIA CASTLE (1)/**WARWICK CASTLE** (4) Steel twin screw motorship (UC 1939-1942 & 1946-1962)
O.N. 167220
Builders: Harland & Wolff Ltd., Belfast (yard no: 1006)
Tonnage: 17,392 gross 10,436 net
Dimensions: 570.7 x 76.4 x 39.5 feet
Engines: Burmeister & Wain design oil 2S DA 8-cyl. by builder 3,284 h.p. 16,000 b.h.p. 18 knots
Passengers: 220 first, 335 tourist
Refrigerated space: 178,680 cubic feet

1938: Launched: October 12 for the west coast intermediate service. Sister of DURBAN CASTLE. **1939**: March: completed. She was one of three new ships named after South African cities - the others were CAPETOWN CASTLE and DURBAN CASTLE. Arrived Cape Town: May 23. October 2: requisitioned by Admiralty and sent to Belfast for conversion into an armed merchant cruiser HMS PRETORIA CASTLE. **1942**: July: sold to the Admiralty with first option buy-back clause. August: decommissioned as an armed merchant cruiser and sent to Swan, Hunter & Wigham Richardson Ltd., Wallsend for conversion into an aircraft carrier, HMS PRETORIA CASTLE. **1943**: April 9: commissioned as the largest escort carrier in the Royal Navy. With 21 aircraft, used primarily as a training carrier. **1946**: January: repurchased by Union-Castle Line and rebuilt as a passenger ship. **1947**: March: reconditioned (205 first, 335 tourist), she was placed with her sister DURBAN CASTLE on the mail service until the mail fleet was back to full strength. Renamed WARWICK CASTLE. Her former name was given to the new flagship of the fleet, which was launched in August. **1950**: September: on the round Africa service. **1962**: June: sold to Industrias Siderurgicas S.A., Barcelona for scrap, and resold to Pedro Alberich, Barcelona. July 26: arrived Barcelona for demolition.

WARWICK CASTLE (LD)

DURBAN CASTLE (LD)

The aircraft carrier HMS PRETORIA CASTLE which after the war became WARWICK CASTLE.

POST-WAR INTERMEDIATES

BLOEMFONTEIN CASTLE Steel twin screw motorship (UC 1950-1959)
O.N. 183205
Builders: Harland & Wolff Ltd., Belfast (yard no: 1421)
Tonnage: 18,400 gross 10,473 net
Dimensions: 570.7 x 76.4 x 39.5 feet
Engines: Burmeister & Wain design oil 2S DA 8-cyl. by builder 4,000 h.p.
20,000 b.h.p. 18 knots
Passengers: 727 cabin class
Refrigerated space: 186,000 cubic feet

1949: Launched: August 25. Originally designed as an emigrant ship,
with the election of the Afrikaner-led Nationalist Party in 1948, and
the subsequent abolition of the assisted passage scheme for migrants,
her plans were modified and she was completed as a one-class (the
first) west coast intermediate ship. Her original plan featured a well
deck forward similar to the pre-war intermediates. She was also the
first Union-Castle passenger ship without tall masts and the last Union-
Castle diesel-powered passenger liner. **1950**: March: completed. Now
each provincial capital in the Union was featured in the fleet names.
Arrived Cape Town: April 24 and although her maiden voyage
continued round Africa, she operated subsequently on the west coast
intermediate routing, terminating at Beira. **1953**: January 8: rescued
passengers from the Holland Africa liner KLIPFONTEIN (10,544/
1939) which sank after hitting rocks five miles from Cape Barra, near
Inhambane, Moçambique. **1959**: November: sold to the National Greek
Australian Line Co. Ltd. (principals - Chandris Bros.), Piraeus and
after a brief refit on the Tyne, emerged as a 36 first class and 1,000
tourist class emigrant ship - renamed PATRIS. December: first voyage
from Piraeus to Australia and the start of the first liner service for
Chandris Lines. **1963**: With the removal of her refrigerated space, her
passenger accommodation was increased to 1,400 tourist. **1969**:
Service reduced to Djibouti-Australia to save time and fuel - passengers
were flown to Djibouti to join the ship. **1973**: Journey time reduced
further by operating the ship Singapore-Australia. She was also used
as a cruise ship out of Australia. **1975**: Between February 14 and
November 13, used as a floating accommodation ship at Darwin after
the city was badly hit by a cyclone. **1976**: Converted at Perama into a
side-loading, 300-car ferry - 1,000 passengers. June: first service on
the Ancona-Patras route. **1979**: Sold to Consolidated Ocean Transports
(principal - Karageorgis Lines), Piraeus, and renamed
MEDITERRANEAN ISLAND. **1981**: Renamed MEDITERRANEAN
STAR. Owners restyled Star Navigation Corp. **1986**: September:
laid up at Piraeus. **1987**: August: sold for scrap to St. Vincent flag
owners and then to Pakistani breakers. October 11: under the temporary
name TERRA, arrived at Gadani Beach for demolition by Golden
Pickers & Leather Industries.

RHODESIA CASTLE Steel twin screw steamer (UC 1951-1967)
O.N. 184515
Builders: Harland & Wolff Ltd., Belfast (yard no: 1431)
Tonnage: 17,041 gross 9,435 net
Dimensions: 556.4 x 74.4 x 40.2 feet
Engines: Parsons' designed double reduction steam turbines by builder
2,880 h.p. 14,400 s.h.p. 18 knots
Passengers: 526 cabin class
Refrigerated space: 131,300 cubic feet

1951: Launched: April 5 as round Africa intermediate ship. First of
three smaller versions of the DURBAN CASTLE. October: completed.
Arrived Cape Town: November 4. **1960**: August: withdrawn for major
refit. Passenger accommodation reduced to 442; partial air conditioning
fitted; funnel raised by 12 feet and given domed top. **1967**: May: laid
up in the River Blackwater with KENYA CASTLE. September: sold
to Taiwanese breakers. October 29: arrived at Kaohsiung for demolition
by Chin Ho Fa Steel & Iron Co. Ltd.

PATRIS (ex BLOEMFONTEIN CASTLE at Sydney (PN)

BLOEMFONTEIN CASTLE (LD)

RHODESIA CASTLE

KENYA CASTLE Steel twin screw steamer (UC 1952-1967)
O.N. 184572
Builders: Harland & Wolff Ltd., Belfast (yard no: 1432)
Tonnage: 17,041 gross 9,435 net
Dimensions: 556.4 x 74.4 x 40.2 feet
Engines: Parson design double reduction steam turbines by builder 2,880 h.p.
14,400 s.h.p. 18 knots
Passengers: 526 cabin class
Refrigerated space: 130,800 cubic feet

1951: Launched: June 21 as round Africa intermediate ship. **1952**:
February: completed. Maiden voyage was two week cruise to Las
Palmas and North Africa. Arrived Cape Town (via Suez): May 23.
1961: May: withdrawn for major refit. Passenger accommodation
reduced to 446; partial air conditioning fitted; funnel raised by 12 feet
and given domed top. **1967**: April: laid up in the River Blackwater
with RHODESIA CASTLE. July: sold to National Hellenic American
Line S.A. (principal - Chandris Bros.), Piraeus. Renamed
AMERIKANIS. August: arrived Piraeus. **1968**: August: completion
of refit at Piraeus into a 19,904 gross ton, 920 one-class liner. Operated
Piraeus-New York-Piraeus in the summer and cruising in the winter.
1970: Full time cruise ship. **1980**: Owners restyled Chandris American
Line S.A., Monrovia - chartered to Costa Line. **1984**: May: returned
to Chandris - owners restyled Fifth Transoceanic Shipping Co. Ltd.,
Panama. **1993**: Replaced THE VICTORIA (ex DUNNOTTAR
CASTLE) for Mediterranean cruises. **1996**: October: laid up at Eleusis,
Greece. **1999**: Still laid up.

BRAEMAR CASTLE (3) Steel twin screw steamer (UC 1952-1966)
O.N. 184728
Builders: Harland & Wolff Ltd., Belfast (yard no: 1459)
Tonnage: 17,029 gross 9,490 net
Dimensions: 556.4 x 74.4 x 40.2 feet
Engines: Parson design double reduction steam turbines by builder 2,880 h.p.
14,400 s.h.p. 18 knots
Passengers: 552 cabin class
Refrigerated space: 145,000 cubic feet

1952: Launched: April 24 as round Africa intermediate ship.
November: completed. Arrived Cape Town: December 7. **1955**: June:
during temporary replacement of STIRLING CASTLE on mail service,
set a record for an intermediate ship: Southampton-Cape Town in 13
days 17 hours 45 minutes. **1959**: December 1: ran aground on a
sandbank near Gibraltar during a gale. Refloated the following day
by three Admiralty tugs. **1960**: October: placed on the mail run whilst
CAPETOWN CASTLE was repaired after engine room explosion.
Major refit: passenger accommodation reduced to 445; partial air
conditioning fitted; funnel raised by 12 feet and given domed top.
1962: From June, operated London-Durban via Suez only. **1965**:
November: laid up at London. **1966**: January: sold for scrap. January
6: arrived at Faslane for demolition by Shipbreaking Industries Ltd.

KENYA CASTLE after her 1961 refit (FF)

BRAEMAR CASTLE (FF)

AMERIKANIS ex KENYA CASTLE (LMC)

THE ONLY UNION-CASTLE CRUISE SHIP

REINA DEL MAR Steel twin screw steamer (UC chartered 1964-1973: UC owned 1973-1975)
O.N. 187132
Builders: Harland & Wolff Ltd., Belfast (yard no: 1533)
Tonnage: 20,234 gross 11,211 net
Dimensions: 560 x 78.5 x 30.1 feet
Engines: Parson design double reduction steam turbines by builder
17,000 s.h.p. 18 knots
Passengers: 207 first, 216 cabin, 343 tourist
Refrigerated space: 19,780 cubic feet

1955: Launched: June 7 for Pacific Steam Navigation Co. Ltd., Liverpool. **1956**: April: completed for Liverpool-Valparaiso route. **1964**: March: end of South American service. Converted by Harland & Wolff Ltd. into a 1,047 two-class cruise ship and chartered to the Travel Savings Association Ltd. which was jointly owned by Union-Castle Line, Canadian Pacific, Royal Mail Lines and the founder, Max Wilson. June: first voyage in new role with T.S.A. logo on yellow funnel. October: Union-Castle who managed the ship, became sole owners of T.S.A. but not the owners of the ship. November: converted into 1,026 one-class cruise ship (during cruises, capacity was restricted to 998), and painted in Union-Castle colours. **1969**: Ownership transferred, within the Furness Withy group to Royal Mail Lines Ltd. Charter to Union-Castle extended for five years. **1973**: October: sold to Union-Castle Mail S.S. Co. Ltd. **1975**: May: transferred to Travel Savings Ltd. (Cayzer, Irvine & Co. Ltd., managers). Sold to Mitsui & Co. Ltd. and resold to Taiwanese breakers. July 30: arrived at Kaohsiung for demolition by Tung Cheng Steel Manufacturing Co. December 10: demolition commenced.

Chapter Three
CARGO SHIPS

SOUTHAMPTON CASTLE (LD)

Cargo had always played an important role in the development of the mail services to South Africa. The earliest mailships were of course cargo ships, which were adapted to carry passengers. As passenger facilities evolved so did the cargo carrying capabilities of the mailships. The intermediate ships were also cargo carriers with the Union Line "G" class specially designed with a shallow draft to enter ports like Durban and East London which had sandbars at their harbour entrances.

Delagoa Bay Railway

For most of the 19th century the imbalance between exports and imports was always a problem for the ship owners who operated to South Africa. Without a manufacturing infrastructure of its own, South Africa had to be import many goods, whilst export opportunities were limited to hides, elephant tusks, ostrich feathers, wool and other agricultural products. The great breakthrough in the freight business came after the discovery of gold in the Transvaal in 1886 when there was a great demand for mining equipment in South Africa. This was also the time of expansion in railways and in 1888 the Nederlandsche Zuid-Afrikaansche Spoorweg-Maatshappij (N.Z.A.S.M.) was granted a concession to build a railway linking Johannesburg with Delagoa Bay (Lourenço Marques). Not only was this a shorter route than to Durban (349 miles compared with 482 miles), it freed the Transvaal Republic from a reliance on the British colonies.

USA-South Africa services

The British & Colonial Steam Navigation Company (Bucknall Brothers) won the contract to transport material from the Netherlands for the construction of the new railway and in 1893, Donald Currie surprised his rivals by setting up a joint service with Bucknalls between South Africa and the United States called the American and African Line. At almost the same time, Union Line and Clan Line announced the formation of a similar joint service known as Union and Clan Line. Both companies used chartered ships with WORCESTER (2,908/1887) taking the first sailing from New York for the American and African Line in May, 1893 followed by the first Union and Clan Line service the following month - ARROYO (3,564/1890) which carried 18,000 cases of oil from New York. With limited cargo to pick up in South Africa, the ships would proceed beyond South Africa to load sugar in Mauritius or goods in India for the return voyage.

In 1894 Currie persuaded the Union and Clan Line to introduce the rebate system onto the United States-South Africa route so that sailing schedules could be co-ordinated and freight rates controlled. The following year, Union Line bought their first cargo ship for the North America service from Elder Dempster. The 5,305 gross ton RUTHENIA was to have been renamed GASCON but unfortunately she was lost on her delivery voyage. In 1898, three second-hand ships were purchased and given American names instead of the usual Union nomenclatures – SABINE, SUSQUEHANNA and SANDUSKY. The last mentioned was considerably larger than her running mates and as she was probably not profitable, was sold to Harland & Wolff after only a year's service.

Soon after amalgamation, the Union-Castle Line took delivery of four new cargo ships for the North American trade. These three-island type vessels were all different and ranged between 4,408 and 5,310 gross tons. From 1906 to 1908 SABINE and SUSQUEHANNA were transferred to the South African coast and carried Natal coal between Durban and Cape Town.

World War I standard ships

Between 1901 and 1915 the six-ship cargo fleet remained unchanged. During World War I, however, four second-hand vessels were purchased including the 7,486 gross ton CHEPSTOW CASTLE, the largest cargo ship owned by the company to that time. After the war, in 1919 the chairman of the Royal Mail Group Sir Owen Philipps came to an agreement with Lord Inchcape, head of P. & O., to take-over jointly 137 World War I British standard type cargo ships with the intention of selling them to other buyers. Unfortunately the

downturn in freight rates forced them to absorb these vessels into their own fleets. Philipps took over seventy-five "WAR" ships and spread them across the Royal Mail Group with Union-Castle taking seven. These unattractive vessels, with the three pre-war cargo ship survivors, were mainly employed on the United States and East Africa services. The combination of the recession of the late 1920s and the increase in round Africa intermediate sailing from 1931, however, resulted in the disposal of all but two of these ships by the early 1930s.

In addition to the standard ships, Union-Castle ordered two large cargo vessels from the Short Brothers yard at Sunderland based on the design of the CHEPSTOW CASTLE. These 7,600 gross shelter deck vessels, the SANDOWN CASTLE and SANDGATE CASTLE of 1921 and 1922, were also the first turbine-driven ships in the Union-Castle fleet and the last new dry cargo ships built for Union-Castle until TANTALLON CASTLE in 1954. Together with the final pair of World War I standard ships, they operated the USA service until the outbreak of war in 1939, although SANDGATE CASTLE was lost by fire in 1937. The USA route resumed spasmodically after the war but faded out by the mid-1950s.

South African fruit trade

From the first decade of the 20th century, Union-Castle worked closely with South African exporters to develop the seasonal fruit trade from South Africa. The mailships were ideal for the carriage of perishables as they were not only fast but also had priority over other vessels entering port. Before World War I a number of the passenger ships had their cargo areas modified to increase the available refrigerated space. In 1928, the new freight contract saw a significant rise in the amount of reefer space on the mailships and by 1930, deciduous fruit exports from South Africa had increased from two hundred thousand packages in 1910 to 2.5 million packages.

For the 1933 freight agreement, the South African Government requested even greater provision for the carriage of fruit and out of this came the order for STIRLING CASTLE and ATHLONE CASTLE and two fast fully refrigerated cargo ships. The ROSLIN CASTLE and ROTHESAY CASTLE of 1935 were the first cargo ships specially designed for the South Africa-UK fruit trade. In 1937 and 1939 four slightly larger versions were completed. For the fruit seasons from 1931 until the new reefer fleet was completed, Union-Castle chartered five of the "M" class refrigerated cargo ships originally built for Lamport & Holt (see Chapter Seven Sail, Currie family and chartered ships). By 1938 South African fruit exports had almost doubled compared with those for 1930.

The "R" class vessels were a great success and during the war, they were the only Union-Castle ships, according to the official Service List, which were not requisitioned by the government apart from some convoy duty. Because of their speed they were able to operate on their own and were used principally to carry meat from the River Plate to the UK. Their importance to the war effort was emphasised by the fact that the three which were lost during enemy attack were soon replaced by new "R" ships. After the war, two larger and final versions in the class were built and given South African names, RIEBEECK CASTLE and RUSTENBURG CASTLE - the latter was named after the citrus growing area in the Transvaal.

Post World War II

SANDOWN CASTLE was the only survivor of the pre-war dry cargo fleet and the company purchased four standard EMPIRE cargo ships consisting of two steam turbine ships, one motorship, and the BRAEMAR CASTLE, which was also the last Union-Castle coal fired vessel. The purchase of BRAEMAR CASTLE was something of an afterthought after three years charter. The company had also tried unsuccessfully in 1945-6 to buy a couple of C2 or C3 or Victory US standard ships.

In 1954 the first general cargo ships to be built for the company since SANDGATE CASTLE in 1922 were completed. The TANTALLON CASTLE and TINTAGEL CASTLE, a handsome pair of motorships, were not only the final Union-Castle cargo ships built by Harland and Wolff but also the last to enter service before the Cayzer take-over of the company in 1956.

The Clan Line take-over

The first cargo ships ordered by the new owners came from the Greenock Dockyard Company, a subsidiary of British and Commonwealth. These were the fast refrigerated ships, ROTHERWICK CASTLE and ROTHESAY CASTLE, which were built after pressure from the fruit exporters to increase capacity. When they appeared in 1959 and 1960 respectively, the Union-Castle cargo operation had become for all intents and purposes, Clan Line. From 1957-8 Union-Castle sailings were increasingly taken by Clan Line who introduced a number of new vessels during these years and this resulted in the turbine-driven DRAKENSBERG CASTLE and GOOD HOPE CASTLE being sold for scrap after only thirteen years service.

In 1962, two 1950s-built ex CLANs joined the fleet apparently after shippers had complained that when they booked Union-Castle, they were served by Clan. These ships were followed by a group of four CLAN reefers, three of which were Union-Castle owned. Designed for the South African fruit trade, these vessels originally employed cheaper Zulu crew but after political pressure for equal pay for all crew, regardless of origin, these vessels converted to all white crew in the mid 1970s and were renamed with Union-Castle names.

The highlight of the post-war cargo years was undoubtedly the Swan Hunter-built pair of fast cargo mailships, SOUTHAMPTON CASTLE and GOOD HOPE CASTLE, which also had significant reefer space. With a service speed of 25 knots, they were then the world's most powerful cargo liners. The latter was also the last ship to be built for Union-Castle Line.

The final fruit ships

After the closure of the mail service in 1977, the four remaining reefers continued to operate in Union-Castle colours but in 1979, they were transferred to the Safmarine/Union-Castle consortium Universal Reefers and given UNIVERSAL names, grey hulls and an unattractive red funnel with a large white "U." By 1981 WINCHESTER UNIVERSAL and DOVER UNIVERSAL had been sold and they were replaced by two second-hand leased vessels, EDINBURGH UNIVERSAL and STIRLING UNIVERSAL.

The Union-Castle name disappeared from the Lloyds Confidential Index in 1984 and in 1988, after the sale of the Cayzer interest in British and Commonwealth, STIRLING UNIVERSAL was sold. Although a leased ship, she was not only the last for British and Commonwealth, but also the final Union-Castle ship.

A taste of things to come. DRAKENSBERG CASTLE stranded in London's Victoria Docks during a strike in April 1947. (LD)

UNION LINE USA-SA CARGO FLEET

(GASCON) (1) Steel twin screw steamer (Union – sank before delivery 1895)
O.N. 99308
Builders: Armstrong, Mitchell & Co., Newcastle (yard no: 572)
Tonnage: 5,305 gross 3,428 net
Dimensions: 421 x 48 x 29.2 feet
Engines: Triple expansion by R. & W. Hawthorn Leslie & Co. Newcastle
600 h.p. 3,000 i.h.p. 12 knots

1891: Launched: June 20 as cargo ship RUTHENIA for City of Liverpool Steam Nav. Co. Ltd., (D. & C. Maciver, managers). August: completed. **1892**: November: bought by Ocean Transport Co. Ltd. (Elder, Dempster & Co., managers) with the company and renamed MARIPOSA. Chartered to Atlantic Transport Co. for their Liverpool-Canada service. **1895**: Sold, subject to delivery to Union Line but on September 24 she was wrecked on Forteau Point, Labrador whilst on voyage Montreal-Liverpool with general cargo and cattle. She was to be named GASCON.

SABINE Steel screw steamer (Union 1898-1900: UC 1900-1921)
O.N. 104458
Builders: Harland & Wolff Ltd., Belfast (yard no: 290)
Tonnage: 3,819 gross 3,002 net
Dimensions: 371 x 43.2 x 27.5 feet
Engines: Triple expansion by Muir & Houston Ltd., Glasgow 268 h.p.
1,800 i.h.p. 8.5 knots

1894: Launched: November 10 as MARINO for Ocean Transport Co. Ltd (Elder, Dempster & Co., managers). Used on Liverpool-Canada run. **1895**: March: completed. **1898**: Bought by Union Line for joint freight service with Clan Line between South Africa and USA. **1906**: From 1906 to 1909 carried Natal coal between Durban and Cape Town. **1909**: September: was chartered by the Australian Government and the owners of the WARATAH to search for the new Lund's Blue Anchor liner which had disappeared off the South African coast. In December, she returned to the Cape after an unsuccessful search. **1921**: Transferred within the group to the Union-Castle subsidiary Bullard King & Co. Ltd. (Natal Line), London and renamed UMZINTO - at some point prior to this, her funnel was heightened. **1925**: June: sold to Dutch breakers but resold in November for scrap in Venice - arrived December.

SUSQUEHANNA Steel screw steamer (Union 1898-1900: UC 1900-1921)
O.N. 106000
Builders: Barclay, Curle & Co. Ltd., Glasgow (yard no: 403)
Tonnage: 3,711 gross 2,395 net
Dimensions: 350 x 45.3 x 17.9 feet
Engines: Triple expansion by builder 344 h.p. 2,200 i.h.p. 10 knots

1896: Launched: April 14 as MOUNT SEPHAR, she was jointly owned by Barclay, Curle & Co. and Smith & Service, Glasgow, the latter being the managing owner. May: completed. She had an identical sister (yard no: 404), GUYANA (3,669/1896), built for Caw, Prentice, Clapperton & Co., Glasgow, which was sold in 1898 to George Smith & Sons (City Line) as CITY OF LUCKNOW. **1898**: Bought by Union Line for joint freight service with Clan Line between South Africa and USA. **1906**: From 1906 to 1909 carried Natal coal between Durban and Cape Town. **1917**: February 21: requisitioned as a transport - that year, carried munitions from USA to UK and to Northern Russia, sugar from Cuba and stores to Basra. **1921**: Sold to Denaby Shipping & Commercial Co. Ltd. (H. J. Tremellen, manager), London. Remained

registered at Southampton - name unchanged. **1922**: Reduced to a coal hulk at Brixham, Devon and renamed LONDON CITY. Replaced another LONDON CITY (ex CLAN FORBES 2,441/1882). **1923**: Parent company, Denaby & Cadeby Main Collieries, Ltd., taken over by Wm. France Fenwick & Co. Ltd. **1924**: Owners restyled The Denaby & Cadeby Main Collieries, Ltd., Southampton. **1930**: Ownership transferred to the Torbay & Brixham Coaling Co., Ltd., London - deleted from Lloyds Register. **1940**: July 15: bombed and sunk in air raid at Brixham but raised and repaired. **1942**: March 27: partially sunk in another air raid. Wreck was demolished after the war.

SANDUSKY Steel twin screw steamer (Union 1898-1899)
O.N. 99359
Builders: Harland & Wolff Ltd., Belfast (yard no: 242)
Tonnage: 5,504 gross 3,574 net
Dimensions: 430 x 47 x 22.4 feet
Engines: Triple expansion by Muir & Houston Ltd., Glasgow 268 h.p.
2,200 i.h.p. 11 knots

1891: Launched: October 31 as IONIA for City of Liverpool Steam Nav. Co. (D. & C. Maciver, managers). **1892**: January: completed. October: management transferred to Elder, Dempster & Co., following purchase of the owners by Ocean Transport Co. Ltd., Belfast - renamed MONTEZUMA. Chartered to Atlantic Transport Co. for their Liverpool-Canada service. **1898**: July: bought by Union Line for joint freight service with Clan Line between South Africa and USA. Renamed SANDUSKY. **1899**: Sold to Harland & Wolff and later resold to Mississippi & Dominion Steam Ship Co. Ltd. (Richard Mills & Co., managers) of Liverpool, renamed ENGLISHMAN. October 17: chartered as Boer War cavalry and infantry Transport No. 60. This lasted until November 3, 1902. **1916**: March 24: captured by German submarine U 43, and sunk after she had been abandoned, 30 miles north-east of Malin Head on voyage from Avonmouth to Portland, Maine. Ten lives were lost.

SABINE (ML)

LONDON CITY ex SUSQUEHANNA as a coal hulk at Brixham

ENGLISHMAN was SANDUSKY for a year

FIRST UNION-CASTLE CARGO SHIPS

Soon after amalgamation, Union-Castle took delivery of four new cargo ships for the USA-SA trade.

YORK CASTLE Steel screw steamer (UC 1901-1924)
O.N. 112849
Builders: Sir James Laing & Sons Ltd., Sunderland (yard no: 582)
Tonnage: 5,310 gross 3,467 net 8,400 deadweight
Dimensions: 408 x 50.3 x 29.2 feet
Engines: Triple expansion by G. Clark Ltd., Sunderland 487 h.p. 2,400 i.h.p. 9.5 knots

1901: Launched: March 5. Completed: May as a cargo ship for the South Africa-USA service. **1925**: January: sold to G. B. Bibolini, Genoa, renamed SAN TERENZO. **1932**: Sold for scrap while laid up at Genoa. Broken up 4th quarter.

GORDON CASTLE Steel screw steamer (UC 1901-1924)
O.N. 114677
Builders: Chas. Connell & Co. Ltd., Glasgow (yard no: 260)
Tonnage: 4,408 gross 2,824 net 7,010 deadweight
Dimensions: 385 x 50.2 x 26.5 feet
Engines: Triple expansion by Dunsmuir & Jackson Ltd., Glasgow 484 h.p. 2,200 i.h.p. 9.5 knots

1901: Laid down for John Warrack & Co., Leith as GORDON but bought on the stocks by Union-Castle Mail S.S. Co. Ltd. Launched: May 1 as a cargo ship for the South Africa-USA service. June: completed. **1918**: May 15: damaged in air attack on Calais. **1924**: May: sold for demolition. September 9: sailed from London for demolition in Germany.

AROS CASTLE Steel screw steamer (UC 1901-1917)
O.N. 114732
Builders: Barclay, Curle & Co. Ltd., Whiteinch (yard no: 427)
Tonnage: 4,460 gross 2,869 net
Dimensions: 392.4 x 48.6 x 27 feet
Engines: Triple expansion by builder 475 h.p. 2,500 i.h.p. 9.5 knots

1901: Launched: July 4 as a cargo ship, used primarily for the South Africa-USA service. August: completed. **1917**: November 21: torpedoed and sunk in Atlantic by German submarine U 90, 300 miles south-west of Bishop Rock (47.19N-12.45W) on voyage from London to Baltimore, Maryland in ballast. Three lives were lost.

CORFE CASTLE Steel screw steamer (UC 1901-1927)
O.N. 114773
Builders: Barclay, Curle & Co. Ltd., Whiteinch (yard no: 428)
Tonnage: 4,592 gross 2,958 net 7,230 deadweight
Dimensions: 401.7 x 48.6 x 27 feet
Engines: Triple expansion by builder 462 h.p. 2,400 i.h.p. 9.5 knots

1901: Launched: September 12 as a cargo ship, used primarily for the South Africa-USA service.. October: completed. **1927**: September: sold to W. Schuchmann, Geestemunde. Renamed OSTSEE. **1932**: Sold for scrap. November 3: arrived at Lübeck for demolition by Flenderwerke A.G. **1933**: January: demolition commenced.

YORK CASTLE (FH)

GORDON CASTLE (AD)

AROS CASTLE (JC)

CORFE CASTLE (TH)

SECOND-HAND PURCHASES 1915-1917

CHEPSTOW CASTLE Steel screw steamer (UC 1915-1932)
O.N. 135294
Builders: Short Bros. Ltd., Sunderland (yard no: 381)
Tonnage: 7,486 gross 4,668 net 11,300 deadweight
Dimensions: 425.5 x 56.3 x 28.3 feet
Engines: Quadruple expansion by North Eastern Marine Engineering Co. Ltd., Newcastle 607 h.p. 3,400 i.h.p. 11 knots
Passengers: 12

1913: Launched: October 2 as ANGLO-BRAZILIAN for Nitrate Producers' S.S. Co. Ltd. (Lawther, Latta & Co., managers), London. December: completed. **1915**: Bought by Union-Castle Mail S.S. Co. Ltd. and renamed CHEPSTOW CASTLE. **1927**: The first ship to berth at the new harbour at Walvis Bay, South-West Africa. **1931**: December: because of the Depression, laid up at Rothesay Bay. **1932**: April 7: dragged anchors and ran ashore at Toward Point. April 20: refloated and sold to Smith & Houston Ltd. for scrap. May 10: arrived Port Glasgow.

CARLISLE CASTLE Steel screw steamer (UC 1916-1918)
O.N. 135264
Builders: Northumberland S.B. Co. Ltd., Newcastle (yard no: 209)
Tonnage: 4,325 gross 2,709 net
Dimensions: 400 x 53 x 23.8 feet
Engines: Triple expansion by Blair & Co. Ltd., Stockton 421 h.p. 2,000 i.h.p. 8.5 knots

1913: Launched: July 19 as HOLTYE for F. S. Holland, London. September: completed. One notable feature was the relatively high 'tween deck space designed to carry troops, horses or emigrants. **1916**: January: bought by Union-Castle Mail S.S. Co. Ltd. and renamed CARLISLE CASTLE. **1918**: February 14: torpedoed and sunk in the English Channel by German submarine UB 57, 8 miles east by north from the Royal Sovereign Light-vessel on voyage from Portland, Maine to London with general cargo and grain. One life was lost.

CRAWFORD CASTLE Steel screw steamer (UC 1917-1930)
O.N. 129150
Builders: Northumberland S.B. Co. Ltd., Newcastle (yard no: 175)
Tonnage: 4,383 gross 2,823 net 7,525 deadweight
Dimensions: 380 x 49 x 26.45 feet
Engines: Triple expansion by North Eastern Marine Engineering Co. Ltd., Newcastle 367 h.p. 1,800 i.h.p. 8 knots

1910: Completed: November as HOVA for F. S. Holland, London. **1917**: November: bought by Union-Castle Mail S.S. Co. Ltd. F. S. Holland ceased trading that year. **1920**: February: renamed CRAWFORD CASTLE. **1926**: October: first Union-Castle ship to dock alongside the new deep-water quay at Kilindini. **1930**: February: sold to W. Kunstmann, Stettin and renamed VICTORIA W. KUNSTMANN. **1936**: Sold to Emder Dampfer Kompanie A.G. (Wilh. Nübel), Emden, and renamed RADBOD. **1944**: December 5: sank during Allied air raid at Selbervik, near Ålesund, Norway.

CARLOW CASTLE Steel screw steamer (UC 1917-1930)
O.N. 139199
Builders: Northumberland S.B. Co. Ltd., Newcastle (yard no: 230)
Tonnage: 5,833 gross 3,708 net 9,150 deadweight
Dimensions: 400 x 53 x 32.8 feet
Engines: Triple expansion by Richardson, Westgarth & Co. Ltd., Sunderland 465 h.p. 3,650 i.h.p. 11.5 knots

1916: June: cargo ship purchased on the stocks. Launched: November 9. **1917**: February: completed. **1930**: April: sold to Sun Shipping Co. Ltd. (Mitchell Cotts & Co., managers), London and renamed CAPE ST. COLUMBA. **1935**: February: sold to Carras Bros., Chios, and renamed ADELFOTIS. **1939**: Transferred to Michael Carras, Chios. **1943**: May 1: torpedoed, shelled and sunk in South Atlantic (03.32S-21.33W) by German submarine U 182 on voyage from San Lorenzo and Buenos Aires to UK with cargo of linseed.

CHEPSTOW CASTLE (TH)

CARLISLE CASTLE as HOLTYE (JC)

CRAWFORD CASTLE (AD)

CARLOW CASTLE (JC)

WORLD WAR ONE STANDARD SHIPS

DROMORE CASTLE Steel screw steamer (UC 1919-1942)
O.N. 143836
Builders: Harland & Wolff Ltd., Greenock (formally Caird & Co. Ltd.)
(H. & W. yard no: 539; Caird yard no: 359)
Tonnage: 5,242 gross 3,199 net 7,930 deadweight
Dimensions: 400.3 x 52.3 x 28.5 feet
Engines: Triple expansion by builder 517 h.p. 2,500 i.h.p. 10 knots
Passengers: 4

1919: Laid down as a modified "B" type standard ship WAR POPLAR
(2). Launched: August 28. November: completed as DROMORE
CASTLE. **1941**: December 12: mined and sunk 20 miles south, south-
east of Humber (53.29N-00.52E) on voyage in ballast between London
and Leith. No lives were lost.

DUNDRUM CASTLE Steel screw steamer (UC 1919-1943)
O.N. 144207
Builders: Harland & Wolff Ltd., Greenock (formally Caird & Co. Ltd.)
(H. & W. yard no: 572; Caird yard no: 357)
Tonnage: 5,259 gross 3,199 net 7,930 deadweight
Dimensions: 400.3 x 52.3 x 28.5 feet
Engines: Triple expansion by J. G. Kincaid & Co. Ltd., Greenock 517 h.p.
2,500 i.h.p. 11 knots
Passengers: 4

1919: Laid down as a modified "B" type standard ship WAR OAK.
Launched: October 23. December: completed as DUNDRUM
CASTLE. **1940**: June 17: during the evacuation of troops from St.
Nazaire after the fall of France, she assisted in the rescue of survivors
from the Cunard liner LANCASTRIA (16,243/1922) which was sunk
during an air raid with the loss of over 3,000 lives - the worst British
merchant marine loss of the war. **1943**: April 2: caught fire in the Red
Sea and sank (14.37N-42.23E) on voyage from Liverpool to Aden
with general cargo. No lives were lost.

RIPLEY CASTLE Steel twin screw steamer (UC 1919-1931)
O.N. 140379
Builders: Kawasaki Dockyard Co. Ltd., Kobe (yard no: 389)
Tonnage: 7,591 gross 4,636 net 10,449 deadweight
Dimensions: 445.5 x 58.4 x 31.3 feet
Engines: Triple expansion by builder 659 h.p. 3,200 i.h.p. 11 knots
Passengers: 6

1917: Completed: June as a Japanese-built standard ship (recognisable
by the triangular shaped crosstrees) WAR SOLDIER for the Shipping
Controller - managed by Furness, Withy & Co. Ltd. **1919**: December:
bought by Union-Castle Mail S.S. Co. Ltd. **1920**: June: renamed
RIPLEY CASTLE. **1931**: December: sold for scrap to Italian breakers.
1932: January 7: Arrived Genoa, and reported later that month as
waiting demolition at Savona.

DROMORE CASTLE (HAN 163/331)

DUNDRUM CASTLE (AD)

RIPLEY CASTLE (LD)

ROSYTH CASTLE Steel screw steamer (UC 1919-1921)
O.N. 142724
Builders: Canadian Vickers Ltd., Montreal (yard no: 19)
Tonnage: 4,328 gross 2,580 net 7,211 deadweight
Dimensions: 380.4 x 49.2 x 26.7 feet
Engines: Triple expansion by builder 474 h.p. 2,400 i.h.p. 10 knots

1918: Completed: August as a Canadian built standard ship WAR EARL for the Shipping Controller. Her managers were Harris & Dixon Ltd. **1919**: November: bought by Union-Castle Mail S.S. Co. Ltd. **1920**: February: renamed ROSYTH CASTLE. **1921**: April: sold to Union-Castle subsidiary Bullard King & Co. Ltd. (Natal Line), London and renamed UMLAZI. **1936**: June: sold to Campden Hill S.S. Co. Ltd. (Counties Ship Management, managers), London and renamed CAMPDEN HILL. **1937**: November: sold to Kitagawa Sangyo Kaiun K.K., Osaka and renamed HOKUJU MARU. **1938**: Because of new Japanese Government transliteration system, the rendering of her name into Roman letters changed to HOKUZYU MARU. After the war, the transliterated name reverted to HOKUJU MARU. **1955**: Sold to Osaka Zosen-sho K.K., Tokyo. **1966**: Reported scrapped at Osaka.

BRATTON CASTLE Steel screw steamer (UC 1920-1931)
O.N. 144539
Builders: Armstrong Whitworth & Co. Ltd., Newcastle (yard no: 951)
Tonnage: 6,696 gross 4,154 net 10,840 deadweight
Dimensions: 412.2 x 55.8 x 34.4 feet
Engines: Triple expansion by builder 517 h.p. 2,500 i.h.p. 9 knots
Passengers: 4

1919: Laid down as a modified prefabricated "N" (National) standard ship WAR FERVOUR or WAR DUTY. Launched: December 8. **1920**: May: completed as BRATTON CASTLE. **1931**: December: sold to Rethymnis & Kulukundis, Piraeus and renamed PROTEUS. **1932**: Registered in Panama to Atlanticos S.S. Co. Ltd. Name changed to MOUNT TAURUS. **1936**: Owners became Atlanticos S.S. Co. Ltd. & Tramp Shipping Development Co. Ltd. (Kulukundis Bros., managers), Syra. **1942**: November 17: torpedoed and sunk in Atlantic (54.30N-37.30W) by German submarine U 264 on voyage from London to Halifax, Nova Scotia.

BAMPTON CASTLE Steel screw steamer (UC 1920-1932)
O.N. 144603
Builders: Armstrong Whitworth & Co. Ltd., Newcastle (yard no: 957)
Tonnage: 6,698 gross 4,154 net 10,840 deadweight
Dimensions: 412.2 x 55.8 x 34.45 feet
Engines: Triple expansion by builder 517 h.p. 2,500 i.h.p. 11 knots
Passengers: 4

1920: Laid down as a modified prefabricated "N" (National) standard ship WAR FERVOUR or WAR DUTY. Launched: March 4 as BAMPTON CASTLE (sister to BRATTON CASTLE). July: completed. **1931**: May: laid up at Netley. **1932**: January: sold to Rethymnis & Kulukundis, Piraeus and renamed ATLANTIS. Later that year, registered in Panama to Atlanticos S.S. Co. Ltd., and name changed to MOUNT TAYGETUS. **1933**: December 23: stranded on Memphis Rock, English Narrows, Chile on voyage from San Antonio, Chile to London with cargo of oats, barley, etc. **1934**: January 1: refloated. Abandoned to salvors as constructive total loss. Taken to the New Waterway and in July, sold to Metal Industries Ltd. for scrap. July 19: Arrived Rosyth. September: demolition commenced.

UMLAZI ex ROSYTH CASTLE (LD)

BRATTON CASTLE

BAMPTON CASTLE (JM)

BANBURY CASTLE Steel screw steamer (UC 1920-1931)
O.N. 142647
Builders: Swan Hunter & Wigham Richardson Ltd., Newcastle (yard no: 1089)
Tonnage: 6,429 gross 4,002 net 11,750 deadweight
Dimensions: 412.4 x 55.8 x 34.4 feet
Engines: Triple expansion by builder 517 h.p. 2,500 i.h.p. 9 knots
Passengers: 4

1918: Launched: August 8. September completed as a modified prefabricated "N" (National) standard ship WAR CLIMAX for the Shipping Controller. Her managers were Lowden, Connell & Co. **1919**: September: sold to Glen Line and renamed GLENSTRAE. **1920**: August: bought by Union-Castle Mail S.S. Co. Ltd. and renamed BANBURY CASTLE. **1931**: Sold to G. Vergottis, Piraeus and renamed ROKOS. **1935**: Registered with Ionian S.S. Co. Ltd, Argostoli. **1941**: May 26: bombed by German aircraft at Suda Bay, subsequently drove ashore and wrecked.

FIRST UNION-CASTLE TURBINE SHIPS

SANDOWN CASTLE Steel screw steamer (UC 1921-1950)
O.N. 146167
Builders: Short Bros. Ltd., Sunderland (yard no: 407)
Tonnage: 7,607 gross 4,707 net 11,500 deadweight
Dimensions: 425.5 x 56.3 x 36.4 feet
Engines: Geared turbines by North Eastern Marine Engineering Co. Ltd., Newcastle 642 h.p. 3,200 s.h.p. 12 knots
Passengers: 12

1920: Launched: October 12 as cargo ship. **1921**: Completed: April. The first Union-Castle turbine ship, her design was largely based on the earlier Short Bros.' CHEPSTOW CASTLE. Funnel was later heightened. **1924**: Delivered 330 head of South African cattle to Birkenhead in a venture to rival River Plate imports but failed because

costs were too high. **1930**: April: converted to oil firing and fitted with Oertz streamlined rudder. **1950**: June: laid-up at Sunderland requiring repairs costing £80,000. August: sold to the British Iron & Steel Corporation (BISCO) for £17,000. Scrapped at Dunston by Clayton & Davie Ltd.

SANDGATE CASTLE Steel screw steamer (UC 1922-1937)
O.N. 146633
Builders: Short Bros. Ltd., Sunderland (yard no: 408)
Tonnage: 7,634 gross 4,725 net 11,500 deadweight
Dimensions: 425.5 x 56.3 x 36.4 feet
Engines: Geared turbines by North Eastern Marine Engineering Co. Ltd., Newcastle 642 h.p. 3,200 s.h.p. 12 knots
Passengers: 12

1920: Launched: December 23 as a cargo ship primarily for the South Africa-USA service. Sister of SANDGATE CASTLE. **1921**: Because of the economic recession, work ceased and she was laid up in the Tyne. **1922**: February: towed back to Sunderland. Engines fitted on the Tyne May-August. Completed: September. **1926**: October: outbound for Mauritius, collided in the Thames with the Pelton S.S. Co. Ltd.'s STESSO (2,290/1922) and Wilh. Wilhelmsen's MEXICANO (3,694/1912). **1929**: December: the first Union-Castle coal burner to be converted to oil firing. Fitted with Oertz streamlined rudder. **1937**: June 26: on voyage New York-Cape Town caught fire and was abandoned 350 miles north-east of Bermuda (36.51N-60.05W). Crew rescued by Dollar Line's PRESIDENT PIERCE (14,123/1921). June 30: last sighting by Italia's CONTE DI SAVOIA (48,502/1932).

BANBURY CASTLE (FH)

SANDOWN CASTLE as built (TH)

SANDOWN CASTLE after her funnel was heightened (TH)

SANDGATE CASTLE (LD)

"R" CLASS REFRIGERATED MOTORSHIPS

ROSLIN CASTLE (3) Steel screw motorship (UC 1935-1967)
O.N. 164448
Builders: Harland & Wolff Ltd., Belfast (yard no: 943)
Tonnage: 7,016 gross 4,260 net 8,510 deadweight
Dimensions: 426.5 x 61.3 x 32 feet
Engines: Burmeister & Wain design oil 2S DA 8-cyl. by builder 1,643 h.p.
8,000 b.h.p. 16 knots
Passengers: 4 (from 1946 to 1955)
Refrigerated space: 362,738 cubic feet

1934: Launched: December 20 as the first of the fast "R" class fully refrigerated cargo ships designed primarily for the South African fruit trade. Also the first cargo motorship in the fleet. **1935**: April: completed. **1940**: March 31: ran aground briefly at the entrance to Perim harbour and was refloated undamaged with aid of Danish tug PROTECTOR. **1967**: Sold for scrap. December 3: arrived Kaohsiung, Taiwan.

ROTHESAY CASTLE (1) Steel screw motorship (UC 1935-1940)
O.N. 164453
Builders: Harland & Wolff Ltd., Belfast (yard no: 944)
Tonnage: 7,016 gross 4,260 net 8,510 deadweight
Dimensions: 426.5 x 61.3 x 32 feet
Engines: Burmeister & Wain design oil 2S DA 8-cyl. by builder 1,643 h.p.
8,000 b.h.p. 16 knots **Trials**: 18.1 knots
Refrigerated space: 362,738 cubic feet

1935: Launched: February 21 as one of the first generation fast "R" class fully refrigerated cargo ships designed primarily for the South African fruit trade. May: completed. **1940**: January 4: wrecked at Sanaig Point, Isle of Islay (55.53N-6.21W) at the end of voyage from New York to Glasgow with cargo of meat.

ROCHESTER CASTLE (1) Steel screw motorship (UC 1937-1970)
O.N. 165455
Builders: Harland & Wolff Ltd., Belfast (yard no: 992)
Tonnage: 7,795 gross 4,736 net 9,258 deadweight
Dimensions: 457.1 x 63.3 x 34.3 feet
Engines: Burmeister & Wain design oil 2S DA 8-cyl. by builder 1,642 h.p.
8,000 b.h.p. 16 knots
Passengers: 12 (from 1946 to 1955)
Refrigerated space: 409,795 cubic feet

1937: Launched: February 11 as the first of a slightly larger second generation "R" class fully refrigerated fruit ships. April: completed. **1942**: August: took part in Operation Pedestal, the relief of Malta. Among the five survivors of a fifteen ship convoy, she reached Valetta August 13 badly damaged by torpedoes from German E-boats. December: left Malta with temporary repairs for New York, via Suez and the Cape for full repair work. **1970**: Sold to the Castle Shipping Co. Ltd., Cyprus, and renamed GLENDA. Resold to Chinese Mainland ship-breakers. November 13: arrived Whampoa.

ROSLIN CASTLE (RP)

ROTHESAY CASTLE (LD)

ROCHESTER CASTLE (LD)

ROXBURGH CASTLE (1) Steel screw motorship (UC 1937-1943)
O.N. 165481
Builders: Harland & Wolff Ltd., Belfast (yard no: 993)
Tonnage: 7,801 gross 4,738 net 9,250 deadweight
Dimensions: 457.1 x 63.3 x 34.3 feet
Engines: Burmeister & Wain design oil 2S DA 8-cyl. by builder 1,642 h.p.
8,000 b.h.p. 16 knots
Refrigerated space: 410,397 cubic feet

1937: Launched: March 25 as a second generation "R" class fully
refrigerated fruit ship. June: completed. **1940**: December 21: damaged
with LLANGIBBY CASTLE in air raid on Liverpool. **1941**: May 4:
damaged again in air raid on Liverpool. **1943**: February 22: torpedoed
and sunk in North Atlantic (38.12N-26.22W), off Ferraria Point, Azores
by German submarine U 107 on voyage from Glasgow to Buenos
Aires with chemicals and mails.

RICHMOND CASTLE (1) Steel screw motorship (UC 1939-1942)
O.N. 167169
Builders: Harland & Wolff Ltd., Belfast (yard no: 1012)
Tonnage: 7,798 gross 4,728 net 9,258 deadweight
Dimensions: 457.4 x 63.3 x 34.3 feet
Engines: Burmeister & Wain design oil 2S DA 8-cyl. by builder 1,642 h.p.
8,000 b.h.p. 16 knots
Refrigerated space: 403,161 cubic feet

1938: Launched: November 8 as a second generation "R" class fully
refrigerated fruit ship. **1939**: February: completed. **1942**: August 4:
torpedoed and sunk in North Atlantic (50.25N-35.05W) by German
submarine U 176 on voyage from Buenos Aires & Montevideo-
Avonmouth with frozen meat.

ROWALLAN CASTLE (1) Steel screw motorship (UC 1939-1942)
O.N. 167199
Builders: Harland & Wolff Ltd., Belfast (yard no: 1013)
Tonnage: 7,801 gross 4,738 net 9,258 deadweight
Dimensions: 457.4 x 63.3 x 34.3 feet
Engines: Burmeister & Wain design oil 2S DA 8-cyl. by builder 1,642 h.p.
8,000 b.h.p. 16 knots
Refrigerated space: 402,780 cubic feet

1938: Launched: December 8 as a second generation "R" class fully
refrigerated fruit ship. **1939**: March: completed. **1942**: February 14:
bombed by German aircraft in convoy from Alexandria to Malta
(34.54N-19.40E). Taken in tow by HMS ZULU, she was too badly
damaged and was sunk.

ROXBURGH CASTLE in Cape Town 1940 (JM)

RICHMOND CASTLE

ROWALLAN CASTLE

ROWALLAN CASTLE (2) Steel screw motorship (UC 1943-1971)
O.N. 168422
Builders: Harland & Wolff Ltd., Belfast (yard no: 1150)
Tonnage: 7,950 gross 4,728 net 9,275 deadweight
Dimensions: 457.4 x 63.3 x 34.3 feet
Engines: Burmeister & Wain design oil 2S DA 8-cyl. by builder 1,647 h.p. 8,000 b.h.p. 16 knots
Passengers: 12 (from 1947 to 1957)
Refrigerated space: 418,234 cubic feet

1942: Launched: December 23 as a second generation "R" class fully refrigerated fruit ship. Replaced recently lost ROWALLAN CASTLE (1). **1943**: April: completed October. Carried the largest shipment of fruit exported from South Africa - 155,000 cases of citrus. **1971**: August: sold to Taiwanese breakers, Sheyh Sheng Huat Steel & Iron Works Co. Ltd. September 2: arrived Kaohsiung.

RICHMOND CASTLE (2) Steel screw motorship (UC 1944-1971)
O.N. 169963
Builders: Harland & Wolff Ltd., Belfast (yard no: 1178)
Tonnage: 7,971 gross 4,740 net 9,275 deadweight
Dimensions: 457.4 x 63.3 x 34.3 feet
Engines: Burmeister & Wain design oil 2S DA 8-cyl. by builder 1,647 h.p. 8,000 b.h.p. 16 knots
Passengers: 12 (from 1947 to 1957)
Refrigerated space: 418,532 cubic feet

1944: Launched: March 23 as a second generation "R" class fully refrigerated fruit ship. Replaced lost RICHMOND CASTLE (1). September: completed. **1956**: April: towed disabled Greek GEORGE D GRATSOS (7,171/1944) 1,191 miles from north of Walvis Bay to Cape Town. **1971**: Sold to Chinese breakers, China National Machinery Import & Export Corporation. August 27: arrived Shanghai.

ROXBURGH CASTLE (2) Steel screw motorship (UC 1945-1971)
O.N. 180491
Builders: Harland & Wolff Ltd., Belfast (yard no: 1187)
Tonnage: 8,003 gross 4,746 net 9,275 deadweight
Dimensions: 457.4 x 63.3 x 34.3 feet
Engines: Burmeister & Wain design oil 2S DA 8-cyl. by builder 1,647 h.p. 8,000 b.h.p. 16 knots
Passengers: 12 (from 1947 to 1957)
Refrigerated space: 418,131 cubic feet

1944: Launched: October 31 as a second generation "R" class fully refrigerated fruit ship. Replaced lost ROXBURGH CASTLE (1). **1945**: February: completed. **1947**: January 2: left Southampton on the first post-war Union-Castle mail sailing to South Africa. **1971**: Sold to Chinese breakers, China National Machinery Import & Export Corporation. July 19: arrived Shanghai.

ROWALLAN CASTLE in wartime guise

RICHMOND CASTLE (BI)

ROXBURGH CASTLE (BI)

RIEBEECK CASTLE (2) Steel screw motorship (UC 1946-1971)
O.N. 180830
Builders: Harland & Wolff Ltd., Belfast (yard no: 1277)
Tonnage: 8,322 gross 4,923 net 9,198 deadweight
Dimensions: 457.3 x 63.3 x 35.5 feet
Engines: Burmeister & Wain design oil 2S DA 8-cyl. by builder 1,938 h.p.
8,000 b.h.p. 16 knots
Passengers: 7 (until 1957)
Refrigerated space: 424,788 cubic feet

1945: Launched: October 23 as the first of the third generation "R" class fully refrigerated fruit ships. Original plans included accommodation for 36 passengers. RAKAIA (ex EMPIRE ABERCON) of the New Zealand Shipping Company Ltd. was built to the same plan. **1946**: March: completed. **1971**: Sold to Taiwanese breakers, China Steel Corporation. September 2: arrived Kaohsiung.

RUSTENBURG CASTLE Steel screw motorship (UC 1946-1971)
O.N. 180893

Builders: Harland & Wolff Ltd., Belfast (yard no: 1278)
Tonnage: 8,322 gross 4,923 net 9,198 deadweight
Dimensions: 457.3 x 63.3 x 35.5 feet
Engines: Burmeister & Wain design oil 2S DA 8-cyl. by builder 1,938 h.p.
8,000 b.h.p. 16 knots
Passengers: 7 (until 1957)
Refrigerated space: 424,788 cubic feet

1946: Launched: March 5 as third generation "R" class fully refrigerated fruit ship. Original plans included accommodation for 36 passengers along the lines of the similar size RAKAIA (ex EMPIRE ABERCON) of the New Zealand Shipping Company Ltd. June: completed. **1955**: May: replaced STIRLING CASTLE for a northbound mail voyage following an engine breakdown on the mailship. **1971**: Sold to Chinese breakers, China National Machinery Import & Export Corporation. September: arrived Shanghai.

WORLD WAR TWO STANDARD SHIPS

DRAKENSBERG CASTLE Steel screw steamer (UC 1946-1959)
O.N. 180157
Builders: J. L. Thompson & Sons Ltd., Sunderland (yard no: 633)
Tonnage: 9,905 gross 7,186 net 12,058 deadweight
Dimensions: 475.4 x 64.1 x 40 feet
Engines: 2 double reduction steam turbines by Charles A. Parsons & Co. Ltd., Newcastle 1,226 h.p. 6,800 s.h.p. 15.5 knots
Passengers: 36

1944: Launched: October 18 for Ministry of War Transport as the fast standard dry-cargo ship EMPIRE ALLENBY. **1945**: June: completed. Managers were Prince Line Ltd. **1946**: March: sold to Union-Castle Mail S.S. Co. Ltd. and renamed DRAKENSBERG CASTLE. June: registered in Cape Town. **1952**: Passenger accommodation reduced to 12. **1954**: Given new hull colours - black with white band. **1957**: Passenger accommodation removed. **1959**: Sold with GOOD HOPE CASTLE to Hong Kong breakers Hong Kong Salvage & Towage Ltd. August 5: arrived Hong Kong.

RIEBEECK CASTLE (RP)

RUSTENBURG CASTLE (LD)

DRAKENSBERG CASTLE post 1954 - right
and pre 1954 - below (LD)

GOOD HOPE CASTLE (1) Steel screw steamer (UC 1946-1959) **O . N .** 166220
Builders: Caledon S.B. & Engineering Co. Ltd., Dundee (yard no: 407)
Tonnage: 9,879 gross 7,054 net 11,755 deadweight
Dimensions: 475.8 x 64.4 x 40 feet
Engines: 2 double reduction steam turbines by Richardsons, Westgarth & Co. Ltd., Hartlepool 1,226 h.p. 6,800 s.h.p. 15.5 knots
Passengers: 54

1945: Launched: January 12 for Ministry of War Transport as a fast standard dry-cargo ship EMPIRE LIFE. May: completed. Managers were T. & J. Harrison. **1946**: March: sold to Union-Castle Mail S.S. Co. Ltd. and renamed GOOD HOPE CASTLE. July 14: registered in Cape Town. **1950**: March: funnel heightened. **1952**: Passenger accommodation reduced to 12. **1954**: Given new hull colours - black with white band. **1957**: Passenger accommodation removed. **1959**: January: on charter to Springbok Line with her funnel repainted in Springbok Line colours. Sold with DRAKENSBERG CASTLE to Hong Kong breakers, Hong Kong Salvage & Towage Ltd. July 14: arrived Hong Kong. September: demolition commenced.

KENILWORTH CASTLE (3) Steel screw motorship (UC 1946-1967)
O.N. 169418
Builders: Chas. Connell & Co. Ltd., Glasgow. (yard no: 446)
Tonnage: 9,916 gross 7,118 net 11,943 deadweight
Dimensions: 475.4 x 64.3 x 40 feet
Engines: Doxford design oil 2S DA 6-cyl. by Barclay, Curle & Co. Ltd., Whiteinch 1,291 h.p. 6,800 s.h.p. 15.5 knots
Passengers: 36

1944: Launched: August 18 for Ministry of War Transport as the fast standard dry-cargo ship EMPIRE WILSON. Completed: December. Managers were Stanley & John Thompson Ltd. **1946**: Sold to Union-Castle Mail S.S. Co. Ltd. and renamed KENILWORTH CASTLE. **1952**: Passenger accommodation reduced to 12. **1954**: Given new hull colours - black with white band. **1957**: Passenger accommodation removed. **1967**: April: sold to the Hong Kong Chiap Hua Manufactory Co. Ltd. for demolition. June 4: arrived Hong Kong. Resold to Taiwanese breakers. July 31: arrived in tow at Kaohsiung. December: demolition commenced.

BRAEMAR CASTLE (2) Steel screw steamer (UC chartered 1946-1949: UC 1949-1950)
O.N. 180051
Builders: Short Bros. Ltd., Sunderland (yard no: 478)
Tonnage: 7,067 gross 4,879 net 10,080 deadweight
Dimensions: 431 x 56.3 x 35.2 feet
Engines: Triple expansion by J. Dickinson & Sons Ltd., Sunderland 510 h.p. 2,500 i.h.p. 10 knots

1943: Launched: August 14 for Ministry of War Transport as the standard dry-cargo tramp EMPIRE DUCHESS. December: completed and placed under H. Hogarth & Sons Ltd., management. **1946**: August: chartered to Union-Castle Mail S.S. Co. Ltd. as a supplementary cargo vessel. **1949**: May: sold to Union-Castle Mail S.S. Co. Ltd. and renamed BRAEMAR CASTLE. The last Union-Castle coal burner. **1950**: Sold to King Line Ltd., London and renamed KING JAMES - converted to oil fuel. **1958**: Sold to Cambay Prince S.S. Co. Ltd. (John Manners & Co. Ltd., managers), Hong Kong, renamed TYNE BREEZE. **1963**: Sold to Cathay Trader S.S. Co. Ltd., Hong Kong. Renamed CATHAY TRADER. **1964**: Sold to Pacific Pearl Nav. Co. Ltd., Hong Kong. Renamed PEARL LIGHT. **1966**: Sold to Marikar Nav. & Agencies Ltd., Hong Kong. Renamed HABIB MARIKAR. **1967**: November 4: after an engine breakdown on voyage from Hong Kong to Chittagong with cement, ran aground on Lincoln Island (in the Paracels), 400 miles south, south-west of Hong Kong (16.38N-112.45E) - constructive total loss. One life was lost.

KENILWORTH CASTLE (LD)

GOOD HOPE CASTLE as built - left (FH) and - above - after her funnel was heightened (LMC)

BRAEMAR CASTLE

NEW CARGO SHIPS 1953-1966

TANTALLON CASTLE (3) Steel screw motorship (UC 1954-1971)
O.N. 186029
Builders: Harland & Wolff Ltd., Belfast (yard no: 1499)
Tonnage: 7,448 gross 4,369 net 10,835 deadweight
Dimensions: 477.2 x 65.1 x 27.8 feet
Engines: Burmeister & Wain design oil 2S DA 8-cyl. by builder
8,500 b.h.p. 16 knots
Passengers: 12 (to 1964)

1953: Launched: October 22 as a fast dry-cargo ship - the first to be
built specially for Union-Castle since SANDGATE CASTLE in 1922.
1954: March: completed. **1963**: No longer carrying passengers. **1971**:
Sold with TINTAGEL CASTLE (2) to Pateras Bros. Ltd., Piraeus and
registered under Aria Shipping Co. Ltd., Famagusta. Renamed ARIS
II. **1972**: Name changed to ARIS. **1978**: Sold to Japanese breakers,
Ishikawajima Kogyo K.K. Arrived Aioi prior to August 3.

TINTAGEL CASTLE (2) Steel screw motorship (UC 1954-1971)
O.N. 186074
Builders: Harland & Wolff Ltd., Belfast (yard no: 1500)
Tonnage: 7,447 gross 4,368 net 10,854 deadweight
Dimensions: 477.2 x 65.8 x 29.2 feet
Engines: Burmeister & Wain design oil 2S DA 8-cyl. by builder
8,500 b.h.p. 16 knots
Passengers: 12 (to 1964)

1954: Launched: February 4 as a fast dry-cargo ship. June: completed.
1963: No longer carrying passengers. **1971**: Sold with TANTALLON
CASTLE (3) to Pateras Bros. Ltd., Piraeus and registered under to
Armar Shipping Co., Cyprus. Renamed ARMAR. **1978**: Sold to
Taiwanese breakers, Nan Eng Steel Enterprise Co. Ltd. June 27: arrived
Kaohsiung. Demolition began: August 2.

TINTAGEL CASTLE (JC)

TANTALLON CASTLE at the start of her career whilst LLANGIBBY CASTLE - right - was nearing the end of hers. (LD)

TANTALLON CASTLE

ROTHERWICK CASTLE Steel screw motorship (UC 1959-1975)
O.N. 301038
Builders: Greenock Dockyard Co. Ltd, Greenock (yard no: 494)
Tonnage: 9,650 gross 5,244 net 10,240 deadweight
Dimensions: 480 x 66.1 x 28 feet
Engines: Burmeister & Wain design oil 2S SA 6-cyl. by J. G. Kincaid & Co. Ltd., Greenock 9,500 b.h.p. 16.5 knots
Refrigerated space: 453,320 cubic feet

1959: Launched: August 19 as a fast refrigerated fruit ship. December: completed. **1975**: Sold to Sea Fortune Shipping Co., Monrovia (principals, Trans Globe Maritime Ltd.), and renamed SEA FORTUNE. **1978**: Ownership transferred to Barbridge Shipping Ltd., Monrovia (same principals). **1980**: Sold to Jersey Shipping Ltd., Panama (managing operator, Wallem Shipmanagement Ltd.). Renamed SILVER RAYS. **1982**: Sold to Bangladesh breakers, Lucky Trading Co. Ltd. August 28: arrived Chittagong Roads. October 8: arrived Chittagong. **1983**: January: demolition commenced.

ROTHESAY CASTLE (2) Steel screw motorship (UC 1960-1975)
O.N. 301158
Builders: Greenock Dockyard Co. Ltd, Greenock (yard no: 495)
Tonnage: 9,650 gross 5,244 net 10,210 deadweight
Dimensions: 480 x 66.1 x 28 feet
Engines: Burmeister & Wain design oil 2S SA 6-cyl. by J. G. Kincaid & Co. Ltd., Greenock 9,500 b.h.p. 16.5 knots **Trials**: 18.9 knots
Refrigerated space: 449,520 cubic feet

1959: Launched: December 30 as a fast refrigerated fruit ship. **1960**: June: completed. **1975**: Sold to Lloyd Uruguayo S.A., Montevideo, and renamed LAURA. **1980**: September: arrived Gadani Beach for demolition by S. Z. Enterprises Ltd. Demolition work commenced: October 5.

ROTHERWICK CASTLE (LD)

ROTHERWICK CASTLE (RP)

ROTHESAY CASTLE (LD)

SOUTHAMPTON CASTLE Steel twin screw motorship (UC 1965-1978)
O.N. 307788
Builders: Swan, Hunter & Wigham Richardson Ltd., Wallsend (yard no: 2010)
Tonnage: 10,538 gross 4,235 net 11,211 deadweight
Dimensions: 545 x 77.4 x 31.1 feet
Engines: Sulzer design oil 2S SA 8-cyl. by Wallsend Slipway and Engineering Co. Ltd. (port) and Barclay, Curle & Co. Ltd., Glasgow (starboard) 34,720 b.h.p. 25 knots
Refrigerated space: 380,310 cubic feet

1964: Launched: October 20 as a fast refrigerated fruit and mail ship. **1965**: May: completed. At the time, she and her sister GOOD HOPE CASTLE (2) were the world's most powerful cargo liners. **1967**: For calls at St. Helena and Ascension, accommodation was added for 12 passengers by Cammell Laird (Shipbuilders) Ltd., Birkenhead. **1977**: October 11: left Cape Town on the final sailing of the mail contract. October 20: arrived Southampton. **1978**: February: sold to Costa Armatori S.p.A., Genoa and renamed FRANCA C., she and her sister departed from Southampton still in Union-Castle hull colours because of a painters' strike. Used on the Italy-South America fruit run. **1983**: Sold for scrap to Court Shipping Ltd., Valletta, and renamed FRANCA. Resold to Chinese breakers China National Metals and Minerals. **1984**: January 19: arrived Dalian for demolition.

GOOD HOPE CASTLE (2) Steel twin screw motorship (UC 1966-1978)
O.N. 307986
Builders: Swan, Hunter & Wigham Richardson Ltd., Wallsend (yard no: 2011)
Tonnage: 10,538 gross 4,235 net 11,211 deadweight
Dimensions: 545 x 77.4 x 31.1 feet
Engines: Sulzer design oil 2S SA 8-cyl. by Wallsend Slipway and Engineering Co. Ltd. (port) and Barclay, Curle & Co. Ltd., Glasgow (starboard) 34,720 b.h.p. 25 knots
Refrigerated space: 380,313 cubic feet

1966: Launched: February 16 as a fast refrigerated fruit and mail ship. December: completed. Delivery was three and a half months late and CAPE TOWN CASTLE was given a brief reprieve as her replacement. **1967**: For calls at St. Helena and Ascension, accommodation was added for 12 passengers by Cammell Laird (Shipbuilders) Ltd., Birkenhead. **1973**: June 29: on voyage from Ascension to Cape Town, was abandoned after major fire 35 miles south-east of Ascension. Towed by the German tug ALBATROS to Antwerp for damage assessment, arriving August 18. October: towed by HEROS to Bilbao for extensive repairs by Astilleros Espanoles S.A. **1974**: May: returned to service. **1978**: February: sold to Costa Armatori S.p.A. Genoa and renamed PAOLO C. Used on the Italy-South America fruit run. **1984**: Sold for scrap to Court Shipping Ltd., Valletta, and renamed PAOLO. Resold to Chinese breakers China National Metals and Minerals. July 27: arrived Shanghai for demolition.

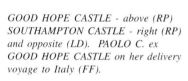

GOOD HOPE CASTLE - above (RP)
SOUTHAMPTON CASTLE - right (RP)
and opposite (LD). PAOLO C. ex
GOOD HOPE CASTLE on her delivery
voyage to Italy (FF).

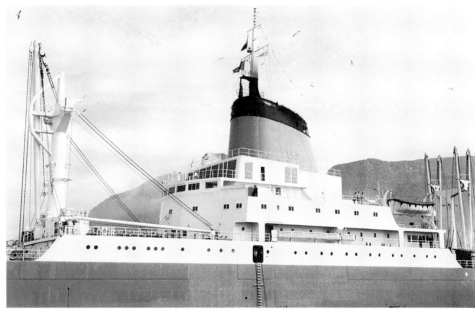

CLAN LINE DRY CARGO SHIPS & REEFERS

KINPURNIE CASTLE (1) Steel screw steamer (B. & C. transfer 1962-1967)
O.N. 185001
Builders: Greenock Dockyard Co. Ltd., Greenock (yard no: 481)
Tonnage: 8,163 gross 4,587 net 11,070 deadweight
Dimensions: 488.9 x 66.4 x 29.6 feet
Engines: Double reduction geared steam turbines by Parsons Marine Turbine Co. Ltd., Wallsend 10,340 s.h.p. 17 knots

1953: Launched: October 22 as CLAN STEWART for Clan Line Steamers Ltd., Glasgow. **1954**: February: completed. **1961**: July: register changed to London and management transferred to South African Marine Corp. Ltd. (Safmarine) Renamed SOUTH AFRICAN SCULPTOR. **1962**: Transferred to Union-Castle Mail S.S. Co. Ltd. and renamed KINPURNIE CASTLE. Still owned by Clan Line. **1967**: Sold to Astro Firme Cia. Nav. S.A. (principal: D. Th. Petropoulis), Panama and renamed HELLENIC MED. Greek flag. **1978**: March 15: arrived Gadani Beach, Pakistan for scrap.

KINNAIRD CASTLE Steel screw steamer (B. & C. transfer 1962-1969)
O.N. 185040
Builders: Greenock Dockyard Co. Ltd., Greenock (yard no: 487)
Tonnage: 7,737 gross 3,512 net 10,075 deadweight
Dimensions: 465 x 65.9 x 27.3 feet
Engines: Double reduction geared steam turbines by Parsons Marine Turbine Co. Ltd., Wallsend 9,400 s.h.p. 16.5 knots

1956: Launched: January 17 as CLAN ROSS for Clan Line Steamers Ltd., Glasgow. April: completed. **1961**: July: register changed to London and management transferred to South African Marine Corp. Ltd. (Safmarine) Renamed SOUTH AFRICAN SCIENTIST. **1962**: Transferred to Union-Castle Mail S.S. Co. Ltd. and renamed KINNAIRD CASTLE. Still owned by Clan Line. **1967**: Ownership transferred to King Line Ltd. **1975**: Sold to Monnoo Overseas Ltd., Dubai and registered under Dasonab Cia. Nav. S.A., Panama. Renamed NAZEER. **1978**: April 26: arrived Gadani Beach, Pakistan for scrap.

WINCHESTER CASTLE (2)/**WINCHESTER UNIVERSAL**
Steel screw motorship (UC 1965-1980)
O.N. 304194
Builders: Greenock Dockyard Co. Ltd., Greenock (yard no: 506)
Tonnage: 7,955 gross 4,272 net 11,738 deadweight
Dimensions: 485.4 x 68.1 x 28.2 feet
Engines: Burmeister & Wain design oil 2S SA 7-cyl. by J. G. Kincaid & Co. Ltd., Greenock 10,350 b.h.p. 17.5 knots
Refrigerated space: 506,864 cubic feet

1964: Launched: August 26 as CLAN RAMSAY for Union-Castle Mail S.S. Co. Ltd. (Cayzer, Irvine & Co. Ltd., managers). **1965**: March: completed as a refrigerated cargo ship designed primarily for the South African fruit trade. **1977**: Renamed WINCHESTER CASTLE. **1979**: Renamed WINCHESTER UNIVERSAL when transferred to the joint Union-Castle/Safmarine consortium Universal Reefers. **1980**: Sold to Kappa Maritime Ltd. and registered under Braganza Bay Shipping Corp., Monrovia (Greek flag), and renamed LADY MADONNA. **1985**: April 25: arrived Gadani Beach, Pakistan for scrap.

KINPURNIE CASTLE

KINNAIRD CASTLE (LMC)

KINPURNIE CASTLE

WINCHESTER CASTLE (IS)

DOVER CASTLE (3)/DOVER UNIVERSAL
Steel screw motorship (UC 1965-1981)
O.N. 307627
Builders: Greenock Dockyard Co. Ltd., Greenock (yard no: 507)
Tonnage: 7,955 gross 4,272 net 11,730 deadweight
Dimensions: 485.4 x 68.1 x 28.3 feet
Engines: Burmeister & Wain design oil 2S SA 7-cyl. by J. G. Kincaid & Co. Ltd., Greenock 10,350 b.h.p. 17.5 knots
Refrigerated space: 506,864 cubic feet

1964: Launched: December 21 as CLAN RANALD for Union-Castle Mail S.S. Co. Ltd. (Cayzer, Irvine & Co. Ltd., managers). **1965**: June: completed as a refrigerated cargo ship designed primarily for the South African fruit trade. **1977**: January: renamed DOVER CASTLE. **1979**: Renamed DOVER UNIVERSAL when transferred to the joint Union-Castle/Safmarine consortium Universal Reefers. **1981**: June: sold to Kappa Maritime Ltd and registered under Invergordon Shipping Co., Monrovia (Greek flag), and renamed GOLDEN SEA. **1985**: May 9: arrived Karachi prior to delivery at Gadani Beach for scrap by Noor Mohammad & Co.

BALMORAL CASTLE (3)/BALMORAL UNIVERSAL
Steel screw motorship (UC 1965-1982)
O.N. 307638
Builders: Greenock Dockyard Co. Ltd., Greenock (yard no: 508)
Tonnage: 7,955 gross 4,272 net 11,730 deadweight
Dimensions: 485.4 x 68.1 x 28.3 feet
Engines: Burmeister & Wain design oil 2S SA 7-cyl. by J. G. Kincaid & Co. Ltd., Greenock 10,350 b.h.p. 17.5 knots
Refrigerated space: 506,864 cubic feet

1965: Launched: May 3 as CLAN ROBERTSON for Union-Castle Mail S.S. Co. Ltd. (Cayzer, Irvine & Co. Ltd., managers). November: completed as a refrigerated cargo ship designed primarily for the South African fruit trade. **1976**: November: renamed BALMORAL CASTLE. **1979**: Renamed BALMORAL UNIVERSAL when transferred to the joint Union-Castle/Safmarine consortium Universal Reefers. **1980**: Modified to carry frozen produce such as meat or fish. **1982**: December: sold with KINPURNIE UNIVERSAL to Comninos Bros. Shipping Co. S.A., Piraeus and registered under National History Cia. Nav. S.A., Panama (Greek flag), and renamed PSARA REEFER. **1984**: June 19: arrived Chittagong for scrap by Saleh Steel Industries Ltd.

KINPURNIE CASTLE (2)/KINPURNIE UNIVERSAL
Steel screw motorship (UC 1976-1982)
O.N. 307645
Builders: Greenock Dockyard Co. Ltd., Greenock (yard no: 509) The last ship built by the yard.
Tonnage: 7,955 gross 4,272 net 11,918 deadweight
Dimensions: 485.4 x 68.1 x 28.3 feet
Engines: Burmeister & Wain design oil 2S SA 7-cyl. by J. G. Kincaid & Co. Ltd., Greenock 10,350 b.h.p. 17.5 knots
Refrigerated space: 506,864 cubic feet

1965: Launched: September 24 for Houston Line Ltd. (Cayzer, Irvine & Co. Ltd., managers) as CLAN ROSS. **1966**: March: completed as a refrigerated cargo ship designed primarily for the South African fruit trade. **1976**: December: transferred to Union-Castle Mail S.S. Co. Ltd. and renamed KINPURNIE CASTLE. **1979**: Renamed KINPURNIE UNIVERSAL when transferred to the joint Union-Castle/Safmarine consortium Universal Reefers. **1980**: Modified to carry frozen produce such as meat or fish. **1982**: December: sold with BALMORAL UNIVERSAL to Comninos Bros Shipping Co. S.A., Piraeus and registered under National Heritage Cia. Nav. S.A., Panama (Greek flag), and renamed SYROS REEFER. **1984**: February 5: ran aground at Grave Point, 14 miles north-west of Port Stanley, Falkland Islands during gale. Refloated unaided. July 31: arrived Chittagong for scrap by National Shipbreakers.

DOVER CASTLE (AG)

BALMORAL CASTLE (AG)

KINPURNIE UNIVERSAL (FF)

FINAL LEASED SHIPS

EDINBURGH UNIVERAL Steel screw motorship (UC leased 1981-1984)
O.N. 390785
Builders: Lübecker Flenderwerke A.G., Lübeck (yard no: 619)
Tonnage: 9,996 gross 5,465 net 10,873 deadweight
Dimensions: 472.5 x 70.5 x 30.8 feet
Engines: oil 2S SA 7-cyl. by Masch. Augsburg-Nürnberg (M.A.N.), Hamburg 18,660 h.p. 22 knots
Refrigerated space: 482,671 cubic feet

1978: Launched: August 26 as POLAR HONDURAS for Hamburg-Südamerikanische Dampfschifffahrts-Gesellschaft. **1979**: January: completed as a fast refrigerated ship for world-wide reefer services.. **1981**: January: sold to Barclays Mercantile Industrial Finance Ltd., London. Renamed EDINBURGH UNIVERSAL and leased to Union-Castle Mail S.S. Co. Ltd. (George F. Cullen Ltd., managers). **1984**: Transferred to Hong Kong register and renamed CASPIAN UNIVERSAL. Lease now with Bridgeworth Ltd., Hong Kong (Cayzer Irvine Shipping Ltd., managers). **1985**: December: sold to Easterly Ltd. (Enterprises Shipping & Trading S.A., managers), Nassau. **1989**: Renamed CASPIAN. Owners restyled Caspian Marine Enterprises S.A. (Enterprises Shipping & Trading S.A., managers), Nassau. **1994**: Sold to Kingfisher Maritime Ltd. (Principal: Lomar Shipping Ltd. London), Nassau. Reverted to POLAR HONDURAS. **1997**: Transferred to the Cypriot flag and operated by Lagoa Shipping Corp., Piraeus. **1999**: Still in service.

STIRLING UNIVERAL Steel screw motorship (UC leased 1981-1984)
O.N. 391161
Builders: A/S Framnæs Mek. Verks., Sandefjord (yard no: 192)
Tonnage: 9,065 gross 4,907 net 12,475 deadweight
Dimensions: 475.7 x 75.6 x 31.2 feet
Engines: Sulzer design oil 2S SA 6-cyl. by A/S Horten Verft, Horten 20,100 b. h.p. 22 knots
Refrigerated space: 541,671 cubic feet

1979: Launched: March 9 as HILCO SPEEDSTER for Irgens Larsen A/S, Oslo. December: completed as a fast refrigerated ship. **1981**: January: sold to Lombard Facilities Ltd., London. Renamed STIRLING UNIVERSAL and leased to Union-Castle Mail S.S. Co. Ltd. (George F. Cullen Ltd., managers). **1984**: Transferred to Hong Kong register and renamed SPEEDSTER UNIVERSAL. Lease now with Bridgeworth Ltd., Hong Kong (Cayzer Irvine Shipping Ltd., managers). **1986**: October: nominal ownership transferred to South Eastern Ltd., Nassau (Cayzer Irvine Shipping Ltd., managers). **1987**: After sale of Cayzer interest in British & Commonwealth, managers renamed C.I. Shipping Ltd. The last British & Commonwealth ship. **1988**: April: sold to Irano-Hind Shipping Co. Ltd, Teheran (part of the Islamic Republic of Iran Shipping Lines) and renamed SHAMS. **1989**: Transferred to Islamic Republic of Iran Shipping Lines, Bandar Abbas. Renamed IRAN DAMAVAND and then IRAN MOFID. **1999**: Still in service.

Top - STIRLING UNIVERSAL(FF)
Right - EDINBURGH UNIVERSAL

Chapter Four
COASTERS & FEEDERSHIPS

AFRICAN COASTAL SERVICES

At the start of the Union Line mail service to the Cape in 1857, goods and passengers bound for other South African ports were trans-shipped and transferred at Cape Town onto local coasters. Two of these, MADAGASCAR (321/1855) and WALDENSIAN (285/1855) were owned by John T. Rennie who had the Cape-Natal mail contract. After the loss of both his ships, Rennie abandoned the coastal service and Union Line stepped in with their own Intercolonial Service linking Cape Town with Algoa Bay (Port Elizabeth) and Port Natal (Durban). Occasional calls were also made at East London. NORMAN inaugurated the new route in February 1863 and later that year she was joined by DANE.

In the late 1850s the regular mail service between South Africa and England was only monthly with a two-day gap between the arrival of the mailship at Cape Town and the departure of the England-bound vessel. This meant that for those living in the Eastern Cape and Natal, replies to letters received from abroad would have to wait a further month until the next mailship sailing. In November 1864, Union Line decided to extend the Intercolonial Service to Mauritius so that mail could be transferred to P. & O. ships carrying the Australian mail on the "overland" mail service via the Suez Isthmus. ATHENS took the first sailing of this alternative mail service which was further extended to Ceylon in 1866. These ships would leave Cape Town eight days after the arrival of the mailship and pick up mail at Port Elizabeth and Durban en route for Mauritius

ANGLIAN of 1864 was the first purpose-built Union Line coastal ship and was designed with a shallow draft to cross the sand bar at the entrance to Durban harbour. She was followed by MAURITIUS (a second-hand replacement for ATHENS) and NATAL in 1865 and DANE in 1866. In January 1868, Union introduced a twice-monthly England-Cape mail service which meant that the Mauritius-Ceylon extension to the Intercolonial Service was no longer necessary and MAURITIUS and ANGLIAN were sold the following year.

After the opening of the Suez Canal in 1869 the British Government took a keen interest in ending the slave trade which was still prevalent along the East Coast of Africa and controlled to a great extent by the Sultan of Zanzibar. It was felt that if there was a greater British presence in the region, this vile traffic could be stopped for once and for all. Proposals were put forward for the establishment of two regular steamship services, one from Aden to Zanzibar and the other from Cape Town to Zanzibar. In June 1872 a joint Union Line and British India Steam Navigation Company bid was put forward and confident about the outcome, Union placed orders for new ships. At the end of October the Treasury confirmed the eight-year contract but the subsequent outcry caused great problems for Union Line and ultimately paved the way for the western mail contract to be shared with Donald Currie in 1876 (see Chapter One Passenger Mailships).

Painted buff instead of the company black, NATAL inaugurated the new Cape Town-Zanzibar line on February 12, 1873. Three new ships were built for the service and were appropriately given "African" names, ZULU, BASUTO and KAFIR. Also in 1873, Union introduced NAMAQUA a specially built coaster for the Cape Town-Port Nolloth, Namaqualand copper trade. In 1880 some of the older mail ships were placed on the Zanzibar run including NYANZA which was bought by the Sultan. The Zanzibar contract ceased in 1881 and Union Line did not consider it worthwhile renewing it. Thus, the British India Steam Navigation Company extended its service southwards to Lourenço Marques.

Donald Currie also operated a small fleet of coasters. In 1873, a year after the start of his Colonial Mail Line Cape mail service, he transferred the 1865-built FLORENCE from the North Sea to the Cape-Natal coastal run. The only clipper stemmed steamer in the Donald Currie South Africa fleet, she remained a regular caller at South African ports for sixteen years. With the arrival of his purpose-built Cape mail ships, in 1879, two of the Currie "family" North Sea ships were switched to the South African coastal run – these were COURLAND and ELIZABETH MARTIN. In July 1879, ELIZABETH MARTIN took the first sailing of a new Currie service between Durban and Mauritius. Because of the confusion of ownership of the various Currie "family" North Sea ships, the histories of these ships are featured in Chapter Seven Sail, Currie family and chartered ships.

By 1878, the only Union Line coaster in South Africa was NATAL. In the same year, Currie had three new coasters on the South African service, MELROSE, DUNKELD and VENICE. Because of the recession during the early 1880s Union Line built no new coasters until 1886 when AFRICAN was completed as the first in the fleet to be built with triple expansion engines. She was followed in 1887 by a much smaller, SAXON, which was used mainly on the Cape Town-Knysna run. The final pair of coasters NORSEMAN and TYRIAN were built in 1890 but with the arrival of the first shallow draft "G" class intermediates in 1893, the three largest Union coasters were sold, leaving only SAXON in service. The Currie coastal fleet followed suit soon afterwards with VENICE, the final Currie South African coastal passenger vessel until her sale in 1898.

During the Anglo-Boer war, there was severe congestion at all the South African ports and Union-Castle bought three small second-hand coasters to help with the discharge of cargo. LOCHGAIR and MACHRIE were used at Port Elizabeth whilst BELLONA operated in Table Bay. In 1904, MACHRIE was transferred to Teneriffe where, under the Spanish flag, she carried bananas from outlying islands and trans-shipped them onto the Union-Castle intermediate ships.

The final Union-Castle African coastal service operated out of Beira, Moçambique the port at the end of the railway line linking Rhodesia and the coast. The first coaster based here was a former Brazilian vessel IPU. From 1915, she was used to carry cargo and passengers between Beira and Chinde which was then the main port for Nyasaland. IPU was replaced in 1924 by INCOMATI whose place was later taken by the purpose-built ROVUMA of 1927 which remained with the company until 1949.

SOUTHAMPTON FEEDER SERVICES

The first use of feederships in the history of Union Line occurred in January 1857 when SAXON arrived at Southampton with 40 tons of French goods for Brazil to be trans-shipped onto NORMAN. The first purpose-built Union feedership, however, was NORSEMAN of 1890 which was transferred on completion to the South African coastal run.

In 1906, Union-Castle started a fortnightly feeder service between Southampton, Hamburg and Bremen using Donald Currie's Liverpool and Hamburg Line HANSA which was bought the following year. Apart from the disruption of World War I, HANSA and a Royal Mail Steam Packet charter EIDER (bought by Union-Castle in 1927) operated this feeder service from 1907 until 1936 when both were replaced by the 14-knot motorship WALMER CASTLE but with her loss during the war, the service was discontinued.

UNION LINE COASTERS 1864-1873

ANGLIAN (1) Iron screw steamer (Union 1864-1869)
O.N. 47988
Builders: Charles Lungley & Co., Deptford, London
Tonnage: 661 gross 532 net
Dimensions: 204.9 x 26.3 x 15.9 feet
Engines: 2-cyl. horizontal direct-acting by C. A. Day & Co., Southampton 80 h.p. 8 knots
Passengers: not known

1864: Registered: October 10. Specially designed for use on Cape-Natal mail service. Shallow draft enabled her to cross the bar at Durban. Arrived Cape Town: November 24. Also operated to Mauritius. **1868**: Surplus due to closure of Mauritius route. **1869**: November: sold with MAURITIUS to Palgrave, Murphy & Co., Dublin. **1876**: Given new 98 h.p. compound engine and boilers by T. Richardson & Sons, Hartlepool. **1883**: January: renamed CITY OF LISBON and used on Dublin-Iberian Peninsular route. **1903**: November 6: on voyage from Malaga to Liverpool, sunk in collision with Isle of Man Steam Packet's DOUGLAS off New Brighton, River Mersey. Subsequent attempts to raise her failed and she was blown up.

MAURITIUS Iron screw steamer (Union 1865-1869)
O.N. 51284
Builders: John Key & Son, Kinghorn, Fife (yard no: 2)
Tonnage: 587 gross 442 net
Dimensions: 210 x 26.4 x 15 feet
Engines: 2-cyl. horizontal direct-acting from builder's works at Kirkcaldy 120 h.p. 8 knots
Passengers: not known

1864: August 18: launched for George Duncan & Co., London, as PRINCESS HELENA. **1865**: Bought by Union as a replacement for ATHENS on Cape-Mauritius service. Registered: August 15. Arrived Cape Town: September 26. **1866/7**: Out of service for six months because of a problem on the patent slipway in Cape Town. All her machinery had to be removed before she could be released. **1868**: Surplus due to closure of route. **1869**: November: sold with ANGLIAN to Palgrave, Murphy & Co., Dublin - name unchanged. **1872**: November 6: lost off Portpatrick.

NATAL (1) Iron screw steamer (Union 1865-1883)
O.N. 51288
Builders: C. A. Day & Co. Southampton (yard no: 25)
Tonnage: 618 gross 487 net
Dimensions: 205.9 x 27.8 x 15.5 feet
Engines: 2-cyl. simple by C. A. Day & Co., Southampton 100 h.p. 8 knots
Passengers: 50 saloon

1865: Built for South African coastal service. Registered: November 20. **1866**: Arrived Cape Town: January 29. **1873**: February 12: after service on Mauritius and Ceylon run and a refit in Cape Town, she inaugurated the new Zanzibar line. Her colour scheme was changed to buff instead of the company black. **1874**: Given new 2-cyl. 120 h.p. compound engine by builder. Speed increased to 10 knots. **1879**: Chartered as a transport during Zulu War. **1881**: February: Zanzibar contract ceased. **1883**: September: sold to Trinder Anderson & Co., London for use on a new service between Fremantle and Singapore. **1884**: January 4: left London for Fremantle. New route was very successful and resulted in the formation of the West Australian S.N. Co. in 1886. **1887**: March: with the arrival of the newly built AUSTRALIND, sold to Goh Siam Swee, Bangkok - name unchanged. **1890**: Bought by Ang Ing Tjo & Co., Bandjermassin - renamed SRIE BANDJAR. **1899**: Sold twice: firstly to A. Elizalde fu A as LIBERTAS and then to Mendezona & Cia., Manila as ALAVA. **1901**: Sold to G. Urrutia & Cia., Manila - name unchanged. **1905**: September 26: constructive total loss after running ashore at Cavite (Manila Bay) in the Philippines.

CITY OF LISBON ex ANGLIAN (AA)

MAURITIUS (SAL)

NATAL (AG)

DANE (2) Iron screw steamer (Union 1866-1871)
O.N. 56124
Builders: John Key & Son, Kinghorn, Fife (yard no: 6)
Tonnage: 788 gross 536 net
Dimensions: 227 x 28.2 x 16.5 feet
Engines: 2-cyl. simple from builder's works at Kirkcaldy 160 h.p. 10 knots
Passengers: 50 first, 20 second, 40 third

1866: Launched: June 28 for Cape-Mauritius service (extended to Ceylon in 1866). Registered: August 23. Arrived Cape Town: October 1. **1868**: Surplus with MAURITIUS and ANGLIAN due to closure of route. **1869**: Operated on Cape mail service, probably as an "extra" steamer. **1870**: Between July and August undertook one round voyage from Southampton to Azores, probably on charter to carry oranges. December: returned to Cape mail route. **1871**: September: bought by Baron de Fonte Bella of Ponta Delgada, Azores for his newly formed Empreza Insulana de Navegação, Lisbon. Renamed ATLANTICO, she was their first ship - the last liner built for this company was the FUNCHAL of 1961. October 15: first sailing Lisbon-Azores. **1872**: operated St Michael's- Southampton with oranges. **1873**: November: refit at Leith. **1877**: May 14: dragged her anchor in the River Tagus and foundered after colliding with the Portuguese warship VASCO DA GAMA.

ZANZIBAR/ZULU Iron screw steamer (Union 1872-1877)
O.N. 62238
Builders: Oswald & Co., Sunderland (yard no: 134)
Tonnage: 944 gross 679 net
Dimensions: 224.7 x 29.1 x 17.1 feet
Engines: 2-cyl. compound by builder 110 h.p. 9 knots
Passengers: not known

1872: Launched: August 17 as ZANZIBAR but completed as ZULU for the Natal-Zanzibar Line. Registered: November 16. Arrived Cape Town: December 31 (via Natal). **1877**: July: bought by Solomon Ezekiel. July 31: on first voyage from Cardiff to Bombay for new owners was wrecked 20 miles north of Peniche, Portugal - no fatalities.

NAMAQUA Iron screw steamer (Union 1873-1876)
O.N. 68813
Builders: Thomas Ridley Oswald & Co., Sunderland (yard no: 135)
Tonnage: 352 gross 203 net
Dimensions: 163.5 x 22.2 x 11.0 feet
Engines: 2-cyl. compound by builder 70 h.p. 7 knots
Passengers: 20

1872: Launched November for the Port Nolloth, Namaqualand-Cape Town copper trade run. **1873**: Registered: February 26. Arrived Cape Town: April 10. **1876**: March 29: ran aground at Island Point near the Groen River, south of Hondeklip Bay on a voyage from Cape Town to Port Nolloth. All were saved but ship was a total loss. Her engines, shaft and propeller are reportedly still visible on the rocks.

BASUTO Iron screw steamer (Union 1873-1876)
O.N. 68816
Builders: R. Thompson Jnr., Sunderland (yard no: 62)
Tonnage: 1,034 gross 651 net
Dimensions: 220 x 30.4 x 15.6 feet
Engines: 2-cyl. compound by George Clark, Sunderland 130 h.p.
Passengers: not known

1873: Launched: January 11 for the Natal-Zanzibar line as running mate for ZULU. Registered: March 12. Arrived Cape Town: April 21. **1875**: April 29: first Union Line to call at Port Alfred, Cape Colony. **1876**: August: returned to Southampton with full cargo of wool and no passengers. September: sold to an unknown French company. October: 11: abandoned by her crew in a gale off La Coruña, Spain.

KAFIR Iron screw steamer (Union 1873-1878)
O.N. 68825
Builders: John Key & Son Kinghorn, Fife, (yard no: 19)
Tonnage: 982 gross 613 net
Dimensions: 249.6 x 28.8 x 15.9 feet
Engines: 2-cyl. compound from builder's works at Kirkcaldy 130 h.p. 10 knots
Passengers: not known

1873: Launched: September 23 for the coastal service. Registered: November 8. Arrived Cape Town: December 18. **1875**: February: first Union Line ship to visit Delagoa Bay (Lourenço Marques). **1878**: February 14: on a voyage from Cape Town to East Africa, after striking Albatross Rock near Olifantsbos Point (just north-west of Cape Point), she was beached and four men drowned in the subsequent rescue.

DANE (SAL)

KAFIR (AG)

CASTLE LINE COASTERS 1877-1878

MELROSE Iron screw steamer (Castle 1877-1894)
O.N. 76948
Builders: Robert Steele & Co., Greenock (yard no: 100)
Tonnage: 839 gross 518 net
Dimensions: 229.6 x 29.1 x 16.4 feet
Engines: 2-cyl. compound by builder 113 h.p. 9 knots
Passengers: 25 first, 25 second

1877: Laid down as MARITZBURG but launched in February as MELROSE for Cape-Natal coastal service. Registered: April 19. Arrived Cape Town: June 23. Broke down on first coastal voyage and had to be towed from Mossel Bay to Cape Town by TAYMOUTH CASTLE also on her maiden voyage. October: shaft broke near East London. **1883**: July: soon after leaving Cape Town for Port Elizabeth, James Carey a Fenian who was travelling under an assumed name, after turning Queen's evidence following the Phoenix Park murders, was shot dead in second class by a fellow Fenian Patrick O'Donnell - O'Donnell was later executed for this crime. **1887**: Took Donald Currie to Knysna to visit the Millwood gold workings. **1891**: September 9: struck a reef on voyage Delagoa Bay-Inhambane. Later repaired at Cape Town. **1892**: Ownership transferred to James B. Smith, Liverpool and James Currie, Leith. **1894**: June: sold to Samuel Hough Liverpool for his Liverpool-London coastal service. **1897**: June: renamed ANNIE HOUGH. **1902**: June: bought by Bermond, Hector-Hee & Co., Bordeaux - renamed EMYRNE. **1906/7**: New owners: Moinard & Rouxel, Bordeaux - later her port of registration was Diego Suarez, Madagascar (French flag). **1911**: May 10: wrecked on Diego Island, eight miles north north-east of Diego Suarez whilst on a voyage from Diego Suarez to Majunga with cargo of salt.

DUNKELD Iron screw steamer (Castle 1878-1893)
O.N. 79638
Builders: Robert Napier & Sons, Glasgow (yard no: 368)
Tonnage: 1,158 gross 742 net
Dimensions: 240.8 x 32.3 x 18.8 feet
Engines: 2-cyl. compound by builder 150 h.p. 900 i.h.p. 9 knots
Trials: 11.2 knots
Passengers: not known

1878: Launched: August for Cape-Natal coastal service. Registered: October 9. Arrived Cape Town: December 12. **1893**: May: taken over by Fairfield in part payment for new ships. August: sold to J. Clark, Glasgow, name unchanged. **1897**: October: sold to Compañía Valenciana de Vap. Correos de Africa, Valencia and renamed ALCIRA. **1914**: September 7: on voyage from Barcelona to Almeria, sunk after collision with the Italian steamship AVVENIRE (900/1872) off Cape Gata near Almeria, Spain.

VENICE Iron screw steamer (Castle 1878-1898)
O.N. 77096
Builders: Robert Steele & Co., Greenock (yard no: 106)
Tonnage: 511 gross 311 net
Dimensions: 173.7 x 24.6 x 13.2 feet
Engines: 2-cyl. compound by builder 70 h.p.
Passengers: not known

1878: April: completed for Cape-Natal coastal service. Registered: May 9. Arrived Cape Town: July 26. Replaced the chartered STETTIN. **1888**: July 14: arrived at Port Elizabeth with the dismasted TWEED in tow. **1898**: May: sold to Donaldson & Sievewright, London, name unchanged. **1900**: August: bought by A. Borges, Lourenço Marques and renamed LUSITANA. **1902**: Sold to J. Montezuma, Chinde - became a hulk.

MELROSE (AG)

Above - Knysna in the 1890s with
MELROSE alongside SAXON (MP)
Right - DUNKELD
Below - VENICE leaving Durban

FINAL UNION LINE COASTERS

AFRICAN (2) Steel screw steamer (Union 1886-1893)
O.N. 92034
Builders: Raylton Dixon & Co. Middlesborough (yard no: 266)
Tonnage: 1,372 gross 866 net
Dimensions: 244.2 x 33.3 x 23.6 feet
Engines: Triple expansion by T. Richardson & Sons, Hartlepool
200 h.p. 12 knots
Passengers: 112

1886: Launched: March 3 for South African coastal service, with shallow draft and first in Union's fleet to be built with triple expansion engines. Registered: May 20. Arrived Cape Town: July 11. **1893**: December: sold to F. H. Powell & Co., Liverpool, renamed GRACEFUL - used on Liverpool-London route. **1902**: Bought by Østlandske Lloyd (R. Andvord, Manager), Christiania, Norway. Fitted with taller funnel and renamed SOVEREIGN, she was placed on the Oslo-Newcastle run. **1906**: Sold with the service to Fred. Olsen, Christiania and registered in the ownership of A/S Ganger Rolf (Fred. Olsen, manager) - name unchanged. **1912**: November: purchased by Det Bergenske D/S, Bergen (Bergen Line), renamed ZETA. Bergen-Continental service. **1931**: August: broken up at Stavanger by Brødrene Anda.

SAXON (3) Iron screw steamer (Union 1887-1896)
O.N. 94503
Builders: Oswald, Mordaunt & Co., Southampton (yard no: 246)
Tonnage: 469 gross 296 net
Dimensions: 145.7 x 24.7 x 16.6 feet
Engines: Triple expansion by builder 75 h.p. 450 i.h.p. 10.5 knots
Passengers: 17 first, 30 second

1887: Launched: November 19 for South African coastal service. Registered: December 24. **1888**: Arrived Cape Town: February 6. **1892**: Spent the rest of her career mainly on the Cape Town-Knysna run. **1896**: January: sold to Empresa Africana de Navegação, Lourenço Marques who intended to name her LOURENÇO MARQUES. January 28: on her delivery voyage from Durban, she was wrecked on a reef off Kosi Bay near the Moçambique border. All her passengers were transferred to lifeboats and landed safely at Delagoa Bay. Today the wreck is popular among divers and is the most northerly on the South African coast.

NORSEMAN (2) Steel screw steamer (Union 1890-1893)
O.N. 97211
Builders: Day, Summers & Co., Southampton (yard no: 85)
Tonnage: 938 gross 557 net
Dimensions: 230.1 x 30 x 12.4 feet
Engines: Triple expansion by builder 125 h.p. 700 i.h.p. **Trials**: 11.4 knots
Passengers: 30 first, 20 second

1890: Launched: March 22 as Southampton-Hamburg feedership, she was used instead on the South African coastal service between Durban and Beira. Registered: July 10. Arrived Cape Town: September 15 after two-month voyage from England. **1893**: November: sold to Walter S. Bailey (Bailey & Leetham), Hull, name unchanged. **1896**: May: bought by L. Ballande, fils ainé, Nouméa as SAINT-ANTOINE for service between New Caledonia and Australia. **1902**: New owners: Union Commerciale et de Navigation Calédonienne - name unchanged. **1925**: Sold to Soc. du Tour des Côtes, Nouméa. **1928**: May 26: wrecked 30 miles south-west of Nouméa, bound for Nouméa with copra and coffee.

TYRIAN Steel screw steamer (Union 1890-1894)
O.N. 97207
Builders: Day, Summers & Co. Southampton (yard no: 84)
Tonnage: 1,455 gross 886 net
Dimensions: 260.3 x 33.1 x 23.3 feet
Engines: Triple expansion by builder 200 h.p. 1,100 i.h.p. **Trials**: 12.9 knots
Passengers: 36 first, 22 second, 45 third

1890: Launched: January 22 for South African coastal service. Union's first steel hull ship. May: completed. Arrived Cape Town: July 22 (via coast). **1894**: Sold to W. H. Smith & Son, Pty. Ltd., Melbourne, name unchanged. Used on Melbourne-Queensland run. **1901**: Company restyled as Howard Smith & Co., Ltd. **1913**: Company restyled again as Australian Steamships Pty. Ltd. (Howard Smith Ltd., managers). **1915**: May: bought by Kiodo Kisen Goshi Kaisha, Dairen as KIODO MARU NO 16. **1938**: November 14: on voyage Tsingtao-Dairen, caught fire 36N-122E. Towed into Tsingtao, beached and broken up.

SAXON at Knysna (MP)

AFRICAN at Knysna (MP)

ZETA ex AFRICAN (TH)

TYRIAN (AG)

POST BOER WAR & BEIRA

MACHRIE Steel screw steamer (UC 1901-1918)
O.N. 113913
Builders: Scott & Sons, Bowling, Glasgow (yard no: 145)
Tonnage: 251 gross 41 net
Dimensions: 116.8 x 21.5 x 9.4 feet
Engines: 2-cyl. compound by Muir & Houston Ltd., Glasgow 35 n.h.p.

1900: Completed: October for Glasgow Steam Coasters Co., Ltd., (Paton & Hendry, managers), Glasgow. **1901**: July: sold to Union-Castle Mail S.S. Co. Ltd. to relieve congestion at South African ports. Name unchanged. **1904**: Transferred to Teneriffe, she was registered under the name of C. J. Rufino Hamilton of Santa Cruz de Teneriffe (Hamilton & Co. were the local agents for Union-Castle) and operated with a Spanish crew for the Teneriffe Fruit Agency. In this role, she carried bananas from outlying islands and transhipped them onto the Union-Castle intermediate ships. **1918**: March: sold to Ramon de Otalde, Bilbao, and renamed MARGARITA. **1924**: Transferred to Teneriffe register - same owners, renamed ANSELMI. **1932**: Sold to A. Alvarez S. en C., Bilbao Reverted to MARGARITA. **1937**: October 22: bound for Santander, captured by Nationalist transport MARUJA Y AURORA in the Bay of Biscay with 400 refugees from Gijon. **1939**: Renamed ANSELMI - same owners. **1942**: Registered Aviles. June: lengthened to 135.9 feet overall - 381 gross tons. **1965**: Scrapped.

LOCH GAIR Steel screw steamer (UC 1901-1902)
O.N. 96006
Builders: Scott & Co. Bowling, Glasgow (yard no: 69)
Tonnage: 77 gross 34 net
Dimensions: 65.8 x 18.1 x 8.1 feet
Engines: 2-cyl. compound by Muir & Houston Ltd., Glasgow 17 h.p. 150 i.h.p.

1888: Completed for John G.Stewart, Glasgow as LOCH GAIR. **1897**: Lengthened to 81.6 feet, tonnages becoming 111 gross and 46 net. **1901**: July: sold to Union-Castle Mail S.S. Co. Ltd. to relieve congestion at Port Elizabeth. **1902**: December: Sold to the Port Elizabeth Harbour Board, Port Elizabeth. **1911**: Sold to Seychelles Trading Co., Port Elizabeth. Name unchanged. **1915**: Deleted from the Mercantile Navy List. **1926**: Broken up.

BELLONA Steel screw steamer (UC 1901-1912)
O.N. 114759
Builders: J. Kievits & van Riede & Co., Papendrecht, Netherlands
Tonnage: 117 gross 56 net
Dimensions: 85.2 x 20.2 x 7.3 feet
Engines: 2-cyl. compound by builder 35 h.p. 7 knots

1901: Completed for Joseph Constant, London and immediately sold to Union-Castle Mail S.S. Co. Ltd. to relieve congestion at Port Elizabeth. **1912**: June 10: stranded near Cape Hangklip whilst on a voyage from Cape Town to Stoney Bay with a cargo of whaling stores. Later declared a constructive total loss.

IPU Steel screw steamer (UC 1915-1924)
O.N. 138991
Builders: A/S Fredriksstad Mek. Verksted, Fredrikstad, Norway (yard no: 99)
Tonnage: 712 gross 417 net
Dimensions: 191.1 x 33.1 x 11 feet
Engines: Triple expansion by builder 36 h.p. 8.5 knots
Passengers: 12

1905: June: completed for Empreza de Nav. L. Lorentzen, Para, Brazil as a Brazilian coastal trader. **1915**: February: sold to Union-Castle Mail S.S. Co. Ltd. as a coaster based in Beira. Name unchanged, she was used mainly to carry cargo and passengers between Beira and Chinde, which was then the main port for Nyasaland. **1917**: Chartered by the Admiralty for two years as a troop/cargo transport on the East African coast. **1924**: January: sold to Glendenning S.S. Co. Ltd., London, and renamed CHYKO. Continued to operate on East African run. Replaced by INCOMATI. **1925**: February 2: struck a reef at Fungu Miza and beached at Kutami, 20 miles south of Dar es Salaam. Declared a constructive total loss.

INCOMATI Steel twin screw steam tug (UC 1924-1928)
O.N. not applicable
Builders: Gebr. Sachsenberg A.G., Rosslau, Germany
Tonnage: 340 gross 118 net
Dimensions: 129.6 x 25.6 x 12 feet
Engines: 2-cyl. compound by builder 43 h.p. 10 knots
Passengers: 26

1912: Completed: October for Deutsche Ost-Afrika-Linie, Hamburg as an East African tender and sea-going tug LEUTNANT. **1914**: August: at the outbreak of war, sought refuge at Beira. **1916**: March: taken over by the Portuguese Government and renamed INCOMATI, registered at Beira. **1924**: Sold to Union-Castle Mail S.S. Co. Ltd. and based at Beira, remained under the Portuguese flag. Replaced IPU. **1928**: February: following the arrival of ROVUMA, sold to Cia Nacional de Nav., Lisbon, name unchanged, and used on Moçambique coast, towing barges Beira-Chinde. **1930**: Transferred to Loanda, Portuguese West Africa. **1931**: June: arrived Lisbon for the service as company harbour tug. **1933**: Converted into a lighter. **1969**: Transferred to SOCARMAR, Lisbon and registered at Barreiro for River Tagus service - sold to Portuguese interests during late 1980s/early 1990s.

ROVUMA Steel twin screw steamer (UC 1927-1949)
O.N. 149901
Builders: Ardrossan Dockyard Ltd., Ardrossan (yard no: 338)
Tonnage: 1,289 gross 739 net
Dimensions: 211.8 x 35.1 x 19.1 feet
Engines: Triple expansion by William Beardmore & Co. Ltd., Glasgow 125 h.p. 750 i.h.p. 11 knots

1927: Launched: July 12 as a coaster to be based in Beira. September: completed. On maiden voyage, towed the new company tug ULUNDI to Port Elizabeth. Arrived Beira: December 8. **1949**: Sold to Colonial Steamships Ltd. (Rogers & Co., managers), Mauritius. Registered at St. Louis and renamed FLOREAL. **1955**: February: sold to African Coasters Pty. Ltd. (Grindrod, Gersigny & Co. Pty. Ltd., managers), Durban, and renamed BOUNDARY. **1962**: October: sold for scrap to K. Nathan (Pty.) Ltd., Durban. Demolition delayed so that she could be used in film *Sanders of the River* starring Richard Todd. December: demolition commenced. **1963**: Demolition complete.

IPU (TH)

INCOMATI (FH)

ROVUMA (AD)

SOUTHAMPTON FEEDERSHIPS

HANSA Steel screw steamer (UC 1907-1937)
O.N. 118477
Builders: A.G. "Neptun" Rostock, Germany (yard no: 230)
Tonnage: 880 gross 516 net 1,260 deadweight
Dimensions: 215 x 30.6 x 14.1 feet
Engines: Triple expansion by builder 98 h.p. 620 i.h.p. 8 knots

1904: Completed: August as BORKUM for Nord-Ostsee Rhederei, Hamburg and sold to Liverpool and Hamburg Line (Donald Currie & Co.), Liverpool as a North Sea trader. **1907**: January: transferred to Union-Castle Mail S.S. Co. Ltd. as a cargo feedership between Southampton-Hamburg and Bremen. **1937**: May: sold to Stanhope S.S. Co. Ltd. (J. A. Billmeir & Co. Ltd., manager), London for use supplying Republican held ports during the Spanish Civil War, and renamed STANRAY. October: just after the end of the war in Northern Spain, she was captured by an armed trawler in international waters near Aviles but was released after the arrival of the Royal Navy. **1938**: September: sold for scrap to Van Heyghen Frères and broken up at Ghent.

EIDER Steel screw steamer (UC chartered 1907-1927: 1927-1936)
O.N. 113912
Builders: Campbeltown S.B. Co. Ltd. (yard no: 60)
Tonnage: 1,236 gross 779 net
Dimensions: 230.5 x 32.7 x 16.4 feet
Engines: Triple expansion by Hutson & Sons Ltd., Glasgow
120 h.p. 650 i.h.p. 8 knots

1900: Launched: September 8 for Royal Mail Steam Packet Co. as a feedership between Southampton-Hamburg and Bremen. October: completed. **1907**: chartered to Union-Castle for same service. **1927**: February: sold to Union-Castle Mail S.S. Co. Ltd. - name and service unchanged. **1936**: December: sold to the Stanhope S.S. Co. Ltd. (J. A. Billmeir & Co. Ltd., manager), London for use supplying Republican-held ports during the Spanish Civil War - renamed STANHILL. **1937**: July: sold to J. Stavrou & Co. Ltd., London. Reverted to EIDER. **1938**: April: sold to Adriatico Tirreno Jonio Ligure (A. T. J. L.) S.A. (Alberto Ravano, manager), Genoa and renamed DOCILITAS. **1943**: September: seized by the Germans. **1944**: May 4: sunk at Genoa in air raid. **1946**: September: raised for scrap. **1947**: August: demolition complete.

WALMER CASTLE (3) Steel screw motorship (UC 1936-1941)
O.N. 165337
Builders: Harland & Wolff Ltd., Belfast (yard no: 983)
Tonnage: 906 gross 350 net
Dimensions: 236.2 x 39.3 x 12.5 feet
Engines: Oil 2S DA 8-cyl. by builder 539 h.p. 1,800 b.h.p. 14 knots

1936: Launched: September 17 as a feedership between Southampton-Hamburg and Bremen. November: completed. Replaced HANSA and EIDER. **1940**: Requisitioned as a convoy rescue ship based at Scapa Flow. **1941**: September 21: bombed by German aircraft in convoy from Glasgow to Gibraltar (47.16N-22.25W). She caught fire and, badly damaged, was subsequently sunk by gunfire from escort. Thirteen lives were lost.

HANSA

EIDER (TH)

WALMER CASTLE (LD)

BRITON (TH)

STIRLING CASTLE at Southampton (AG)

RHODESIA CASTLE on her way to the breakers (IS)

KENYA CASTLE (IS)

DUNNOTTAR CASTLE (IS)

ROWALLAN CASTLE (IS)

ROCHESTER CASTLE (IS)

RUSTENBURG CASTLE (IS)

RUSTENBURG CASTLE (IS)

RIEBEECK CASTLE final sailing in 1971 (IS)

ROTHESAY CASTLE (IS)

KINNAIRD CASTLE leaving Durban (IS)

TINTAGEL CASTLE (IS)

SOUTHAMPTON CASTLE taking the final sailing of the mail contract in October 1977 (IS)

DOVER CASTLE at Southampton (AG)

REINA DEL MAR final voyage to Taiwan for scrap (IS)

WINCHESTER UNIVERSAL (IS)

Chapter Five
TUGS & TENDERS

Both Union Line and Castle Packets operated their own tugs and tenders at the various key ports, especially in South Africa.

Southampton

At Southampton, FALCON was with Union Line and subsequently Union-Castle Line, for forty-three years and acted as a general purpose tender, often serving the ships laid up at Netley.

In the 19th century, Cape Town's Alfred Dock, completed in 1870, was the only man made harbour in South Africa capable of receiving large ocean going ships. With locally owned tugs and tenders, there was little need for the mailship companies to operate their own vessels. At East London and Durban, however, sandbars and shallow waters were major constraints on the size of ship able to enter these ports, whilst at Port Elizabeth ships had to anchor in the bay. This meant that cargo had to be offloaded into barges and passengers placed into large wicker baskets which were lowered into tenders.

Port Elizabeth

Although Donald Currie initially had his own tug KOODOO based at Port Elizabeth, much of the landing activity was undertaken by two brothers William and Rosario Messina who operated from the 1881-built North Jetty, a small construction only suitable for lighters. The Messina Brothers' company, later known as Messina Brothers, Coles and Searle Ltd. was bought by Union-Castle Line in January 1922 for £55,000. Union-Castle subsequently ordered two new tugs from the Henry Robb shipyard at Leith to replace the ageing COLONIST and ULUNDI - the 1925 WILLIAM MESSINA and 1927 ULUNDI. Following the opening of the deep water Charles Malan Quay in October 1933, the role of the passenger tenders was over and Union-Castle soon disposed of all but one of the tugs, WILLIAM MESSINA. ULUNDI is now a permanent exhibit at the Durban Maritime Museum.

East London

East London is South Africa's only river port. Unlike the practice at Port Elizabeth, the two mailship companies operated their own passenger tenders and this continued after the merger, with Union-Castle introducing STORK in 1905 and KOODOO in 1924. At East London, passengers were loaded into baskets right up to 1937 when the entry into the enlarged port by ATHLONE CASTLE on November 5 finally brought this era to an end.

Durban

In Durban, both companies operated not only passenger tenders but also tugs and barges. UNION was Union Line's first tug and was completed in 1878. She was designed for easy access over sandbars and had a propeller on her bow and stern. At the same time, the company built a number of 50-ton barges to carry cargo from ships anchored in the roadstead. In 1884, another Union ship with propellers at either end, CARNARVON, arrived in South Africa. Although a small coaster, CARNARVON was also designed to tow barges and was later used to carry sugar from the various river mouths along the Natal coast. Union Line also ran two handsome tenders at Durban - the 1892 Denny-built NATAL and TITAN which was completed by Day, Summers at Southampton in 1898.

In 1882, Donald Currie and his business associates purchased a Durban shipping and loading agency, the Towage & Lighterage Company (Messrs. James & Hitchins Bros.) and formed a new company, the Natal Shipping Company Ltd. which was registered on August 30, 1882. Two years later, another Durban company was bought, Morrison & Company, and the purchase included nine lighters. As a result of this deal, the Natal Shipping Co. Ltd. was restructured as The African Boating Company Ltd. and registered on August 12, 1884. Although the company owned some interesting ships, under the management of the Hitchins brothers and J. Morrison it became the leading landing agent at Durban especially after winning the Imperial Government contract. After the Union-Castle merger, The African Boating Company took over the local assets of Union Line including TITAN, NATAL and eleven barges. To give some idea of the scale of their operation, in 1901 they landed and shipped 61,000 men, 812,000 tons of Imperial stores and 76,000 head of cattle and horses.

Everything changed for The African Boating Company after the depth of water at the bar was increased by dredging to 26 feet. On June 26, 1904 ARMADALE CASTLE was the first mailship to enter Durban harbour and land her cargo alongside. In May 1912, following the take-over by Royal Mail Line, Union-Castle purchased most of the remaining shares in The African Boating Company and by now owned 97% of the stock. In 1918 The African Boating Company was formally liquidated.

Moçambique and East Africa

With the completion in 1894 of the Delagoa Bay railway linking the Transvaal with Lourenço Marques, Donald Currie had attempted to gain control over the railway and the port facilities. When this came to nought, he turned his attention to Beira 528 miles to the north. The Beira Railway Company Limited had recently built a railway which provided the shortest route from the sea to Mashonaland (Rhodesia). Because of swamps, the new railway stopped forty miles from Beira and goods and passengers were carried in riverboats run by Frank Johnson. Currie bought Johnson's business but this appears to have been a raw deal, as the anticipated demand for goods and passengers at Beira did not materialise. The railway was extended to Beira in 1896 and the following year the Beira Boating Company was established with Currie a major shareholder.

After a period of relative inactivity, Union-Castle took a greater interest in Beira after the start of the Royal East African Service in 1910. The railway had been extended to the copperbelt town of N'dola and to Elisabethville, and Union-Castle transferred the tug and tender TITAN to the Beira Boating Company in 1912. By the late 1920s the Union-Castle operation at Beira was greatly extended with the introduction of new intermediate liners and the first purpose-built coaster, ROVUMA, which was based at Beira. The Beira Boating Company also ordered two new tugs from Henry Robb & Co. who also built twenty lighters, pontoons and barges for the company. The Beira Boating Company eventually became a wholly owned subsidiary of British and Commonwealth but by 1977 the company had ceased to exist.

At Mombasa, in 1917 Union-Castle also acquired a share in the newly formed African Wharfage Company which became jointly controlled by Union-Castle and the British India Steam Navigation Company with Smith Mackenzie the general managers. In 1963 the East African Railways and Harbour Corporation established the East African Landing and Lighterage Company to handle all cargo at ports in Kenya and Tanganyika and The African Wharfage Company was absorbed into this new company.

⚓ ⚓ ⚓ ⚓ ⚓ ⚓ ⚓ ⚓ ⚓ ⚓ ⚓ ⚓

SOUTHAMPTON

UNION LINE

SEAGULL Screw steam launch (Union 1885-1898)
O.N. not known
Builders: probably Day, Summers & Co., Southampton
Tonnage: 24 gross
Dimensions: not known
Engines: 2-cyl. compound probably by Day, Summers & Co. as they built her boiler

1885: Mooring and dispatch launch at Southampton. **1898**: Sold locally to become harbour ferry.

FALCON Steel screw steam tender (Union 1896-1900: UC 1900-1942)
O.N. 105511
Builders: Day, Summers & Co., Southampton (yard no: 103)
Tonnage: 41 gross 28 net
Dimensions: 69.9 x 12.5 x 7 feet
Engines: 2-cyl. by builder 30 h.p. **Trials**: 10.3 knots

1896: Launched: February 1 as tender at Southampton - replaced SEAGULL. **1922**: Converted to oil fire. **1939**: September 4: requisitioned by Admiralty. Used by the Stores & Transport Office and based at Cowes. **1940**: September 3: released from service and laid up. **1942**: December 5: sold to Admiralty with buy back option. **1944**: February: allocated to Dartmouth for special service. July: replaced LADY BEATRICE at Plymouth. **1945**: January: laid up at Chadder Yard, Salcombe. **1946**: Placed on surplus list for disposal.

PORT ELIZABETH

CASTLE LINE

KOODOO (1) Iron screw steam tug (Castle 1875-1884)
O.N. 73555
Builders: Barclay, Curle & Co., Whiteinch (yard no: 254)
Tonnage: 53 gross 13 net
Dimensions: 65.8 x 16 x 8 feet
Engines: 2-cyl. simple by builder 21 h.p.

1875: Launched: June 13 for Algoa Bay Steam Towing Co. (Donald Currie & Co., managers) as tug for Algoa Bay (Port Elizabeth). Registered: August 31. Arrived Cape Town: December 18 after three month journey from Glasgow. **1876**: January 21: arrived Algoa Bay. Was also used to carry stores to Bird Island Lighthouse. **1881**: Used to ferry troops in Natal During the Zulu War. **1884**: February: sold to the Port Elizabeth Boating Co. Ltd., Port Elizabeth. Remained registered at London. **1895**: October 4: transferred to Port Elizabeth register. December: sold to Portuguese owners.

MESSINA BROS., COLES & SEARLE
(Bought by Union-Castle January 1, 1922)

COLONIST Wooden screw stem tug (MBCS 1922-1927)
O.N. 95212
Builders: J. Mackenzie & Co., Leith (yard no: 24)
Tonnage: 33 gross 15 net
Dimensions: 57 x 14.5 x 7.2 feet
Engines: 2-cyl. compound by Hawthorns & Co., Leith 19 h.p.

1889: Completed as tug for Port Elizabeth for William & Rosario Messina, Port Elizabeth. Registered at Leith. **1927**: June 13: scuttled off Cape Recife.

KOODOO (DR)

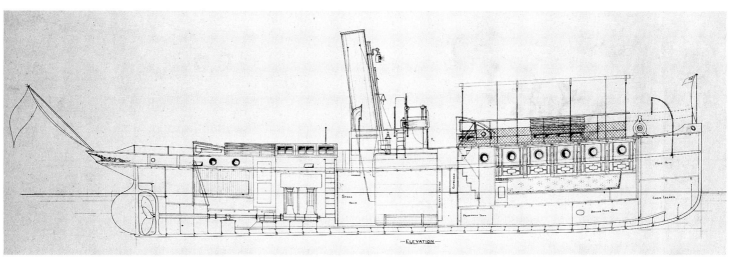

Top - builders plan for FALCON (SOU). Right - FALCON in the 1930s (LD)

COLONIST (DR)

ULUNDI (2) Composite screw steam tug (MBCS 1922-1927)
O.N. 88208
Builders: J.Mackenzie & Co., Leith (yard no: 70)
Tonnage: 63 gross 8 net
Dimensions: 70 x 16.2 x 8.3 feet
Engines: 2-cyl. compound by Hawthorns & Co., Leith 38 h.p.

1899: Launched: October 17 as Port Elizabeth tug for Messina Bros., Port Elizabeth. The second with this name. December: completed. March: arrived Port Elizabeth. **1927**: May 6: scuttled south-west of Cape Recife.

TALANA Composite screw steam tug (MBCS 1922-1934)
O.N. 88209
Builders: Hawthorns & Co., Leith (yard no: 86),
Tonnage: 103 gross 19 net
Dimensions: 81 x 18.1 x 10.5 feet
Engines: 2-cyl. compound by builder 50 h.p. 350 i.h.p. 11 knots

1901: Launched: January 24 as Port Elizabeth tug for Messina Bros. (Coles & Searle, managers), Port Elizabeth. March: completed. **1931**: September: sold to Ocean Industries Ltd., Durban and converted into a fishing vessel. **1934**: May 3: wrecked 70 miles north of East London, near Cape Morgan.

ITALA Steel screw steam tug (MBCS 1922-1935)
O.N. 153844
Builders: Cox & Co., Falmouth (yard no: 90),
Tonnage: 54 gross 21 net
Dimensions: 65 x 12.2 x 8 feet
Engines: 2-cyl. compound by builder 210 i.h.p. 9 knots

1902: Launched: April 9 as Port Elizabeth tug for Messina Bros. (Coles & Searle, managers), Port Elizabeth. **1932**: Only registered July 1. **1935**: February: sold to Harald Smedsvick, Port Elizabeth. July: sold to Elnar Kristian Brakke, Port Elizabeth. Name unchanged. **1940**: April: bought by Irvin & Johnson (South Africa) Ltd., Cape Town as tug and trawler, presumably because so many of their fleet had been requisitioned for war service**.** Name unchanged. **1945**: Scuttled "as

Soldiers boarding TALANA in rough weather during World War One

188

Messina Bros. were based at North Jetty, Port Elizabeth (DR)

*ULUNDI - right (DR) and ITALA - below
both gave long service to Messina Bros.*

WILLIAM MESSINA Steel screw steam tug (MBCS 1925-1941)
O.N. 148573
Builders: Henry Robb Ltd., Leith (yard no: 21),
Tonnage: 120 gross 39 net
Dimensions: 90.2 x 20.1 x 9.9 feet
Engines: 2-cyl. compound by Ross & Duncan, Govan 59 h.p.
350 i.h.p. 11 knots

1925: Ordered by Union-Castle Mail S.S. Co. Ltd. for Messina Bros. (Coles & Searle, managers), Port Elizabeth. Launched: March 12 as tug for Port Elizabeth. April: completed. Took 58 days to reach Port Elizabeth on delivery voyage. **1939**: After the outbreak of war, chartered by the South African Defence Department as an examination vessel at Port Elizabeth. **1942**: June: as the last privately owned tug to operate at Port Elizabeth, bought by the South African Defence Department for use as an examination ship in Table Bay. **1946**: Laid up at Saldanha Bay. Sold by the War Disposal Board to Gelcer & Co., Cape Town and converted into a fishing vessel. **1947**: Sold to the South African Railways & Harbours Administration and reconverted into a tug based at Mossel Bay. Name unchanged. **1959**: Transferred to East London. **1964**: Taken out of service and laid up. **1967**: December: sold to K. Nathan (Pty.) Ltd., Durban for scrap.

ULUNDI (3) Steel screw steam tug (MBCS 1927-1935)
O.N. 149911
Builders: Henry Robb & Co., Leith (yard no: 78)
Tonnage: 97 gross 9 net
Dimensions: 75 x 18 x 10.6 feet
Engines: 2-cyl. compound by William Beardmore & Co. Ltd., Coatbridge 54 h.p. 10.5 knots

1927: Ordered by Union-Castle Mail S.S. Co. Ltd. for Messina Bros. (Coles & Searle, managers), Port Elizabeth. Launched: September 16 as tug for Port Elizabeth. October: completed. Towed to Port Elizabeth by the brand new Union-Castle coaster ROVUMA. Arrived: November 27. **1935** Sold to the South African Railways & Harbours Administration for use as a tug based at Durban. Name unchanged. **1939**: Requisitioned for war service as an examination vessel by the South African Seaward Defence Force at Durban. **1982**: November 17: decommissioned as a S.A.R. & H. tug. **1984**: Transferred to the Durban Museum Trust. **1988**: Durban Museum Trust assets taken over by the City of Durban. **1993**: September 4: formally opened to the public as permanent exhibit for Durban Maritime Museum.

JOAN Screw motor launch (MBCS 1932-1941)

1932: Built at Durban for Messina Bros. (Coles & Searle, managers), Port Elizabeth. Licensed to carry 100 passengers and named after the daughter of Captain H. Sorensen, manager and director of Messina Bros. **1933**: After the completion of the Port Elizabeth Harbour was kept on standby and used at weekends for trips around the bay and fishing parties. **1941**: Sold to the South African Government and shipped to Suez where she was used as a tender. **1945**: Trace lost.

WILLIAM MESSINA at Leith prior to her two-month delivery voyage to Port Elizabeth

The 1927 ULUNDI remained a working tug right up to 1982. She now belongs to the Durban Maritime Museum (DR)

EAST LONDON

UNION LINE

MIDGE Steel screw steam tender (Union 1889-1900: UC 1900-1908)
O.N. 84609
Builders: Day, Summers & Co., Southampton (yard no: 83)
Tonnage: 65 gross 36 net
Dimensions: 78.7 x 15.1 x 7.8 feet
Engines: 2-cyl. compound by builder 21 h.p. **Trials**: 9 knots

1889: Completed: July for Union S.S. Co. Ltd. as a single screw tender for East London where passengers had to disembark in large baskets. Registered: May 1 at Cape Town. **1907**: February: sold to African Fisheries, East London. **1909**: March: sold first to Salvino Infroud, then to Nangle Hallett & Jackson and finally to Jacob Rittenberg, trading as Perks & Co., East London. **1910**: October: bought by Irvin & Johnson, Cape Town. **1918**: February: damaged near mouth of Bushman's River but later refloated and reconditioned. **1922**: December: owners restyled Irvin & Johnson (South Africa) Ltd. **1927**: December: scrapped East London. **1928**: January 11: register closed.

LIZZIE Iron screw steam tender (Union 1879-1885)
O.N. 51648
Builders: Day, Summers & Co., Southampton
Tonnage: 19 gross 14 net
Dimensions: 52 x 12.5 x 4.9 feet
Engines: not known 16 h.p.

1879: Completed for Union S.S. Co. Ltd. as a single screw tender for service in South Africa. **1881**: March 1: Arrived at Algoa Bay. Registered at Cape Town: April 12. **1885**: May 14: wrecked on Buffalo River Bar, East London, inbound with mails from NORHAM CASTLE.

CASTLE LINE

PENGUIN Steel twin screw steam tender (Castle 1899-1900: UC 1900-1924)
O.N. 110187
Builders: Cox & Co., Falmouth (yard no: 69)
Tonnage: 123 gross 56 net
Dimensions: 90.2 x 19.3 x 7.45 feet
Engines: not known 36 h.p. 240 i.h.p. 9 knots

1899: Launched: June 8 for Donald Currie & Co. London as a tender for East London where passengers had to disembark in large baskets. September: completed. **1924**: Sold to the African Wharfage & Lighterage Co., Mombasa, which was jointly owned by Union-Castle and the British India Steam Navigation Co. Renamed NYATI. **1928**: Broken up locally.

DOLPHIN Steel screw steam tender (Castle 1883-1900: UC 1900-1901)
O.N. 87103
Builders: Thames Iron Works & Shipbuilding Co., Blackwall
Tonnage: 49 gross 34 net
Dimensions: 76.2 x 16.9 x 4.9 feet
Engines: 2-cyl. compound by John Stewart & Son, Blackwall 20 h.p.

1883: Completed as for Donald Currie & Co., London a single screw tender for East London. Registered: May 22 in name of F. J. Mirrielees (Donald Curries' son-in-law). July: arrived in East London as counterpart to Union's tender LIZZIE. **1901**: Sold to Clifford E. Knight, Cape Town. Port of registry changed to Cape Town. **190?**: Sold to Owen R. Vaggers. **1910**: New owner Cecil Govey. **1911**: Sold to Olga Elli Co. Ltd., Cape Town. **1947**: No longer in Mercantile Navy List.

DOLPHIN (BG)

PENGUIN at the East London landing jetty

PENGUIN (left) and MIDGE (right) (DR)

UNION-CASTLE LINE

STORK Steel twin screw steam tender (UC 1905-1942)
O.N. 120633
Builders: Hawthorns & Co. Ltd., Leith, (yard no: 107)
Tonnage: 278 gross 107 net
Dimensions: 115.5 x 24.1 x 10.4 feet
Engines: Triple expansion by builder 70 h.p. 8 knots

1905: Launched: October for Union-Castle Mail S.S. Co. Ltd. as a twin screw tender for East London. **1914**: Took part in the invasion of German South-West Africa. **1917**: Chartered by the Admiralty for use as a naval tug. **1919**: Returned from war service. **1939**: At the outbreak of war, was requisitioned by the South African Seaward Defence Force. Used initially as an examination vessel at East London, she was later stationed at Durban. **1942**: June: sold to the South African Defence Department. **1945**: Surplus to requirements at the end of the war, sold to Stork S.S. Co. (Pty.) Ltd. as a tug and registered at Durban. **1958**: After a period as a pleasure steamer in Durban Bay, was scuttled locally.

KOODOO (2) Steel twin screw steam tender (UC 1924-1938)
O.N. 147697
Builders: J. I. Thornycroft & Co. Ltd., Southampton (yard no: 1029)
Tonnage: 119 gross 55 net
Dimensions: 90.6 x 19.1 x 7.6 feet
Engines: 2-cyl. compound by builder 40 h.p. 240 i.h.p. 8 knots

1924: Launched: June 3 for Union-Castle Mail S.S. Co. Ltd. as a twin screw tender for East London. August: completed. **1938**: May: sold to the South African Railways & Harbour Administration and used as a pilot tug based at East London **1960**: February 27: towed out to sea with another local East London tug MARY and scuttled near the Hood Point lighthouse.

STORK - top (LD) and opposite - passengers landing in the basket

MARY (left) and KOODOO (right) in 1960 being towed out to sea for scuttling (EL)

DURBAN

UNION LINE

UNION (2) Iron twin screw steam tug (Union 1878-1894)
O.N. 76845
Builders: Aitken & Mansel, Whiteinch (yard no:100)
Tonnage: 113 gross 49 net
Dimensions: 90.5 x 20 x 8.7 feet
Engines: 2-cyl. compound vertical by James Howden & Co., Glasgow 50 h.p.

1878: Union Line's first tug. Launched: October: as a fore-and-aft-screw lighter tug (i.e. with propeller on her bow and stern) for use at Durban. Union also built a number of 50 ton iron barges to carry cargo loaded from ships anchored in the roadstead. Registered: December 3. **1879**: Delivery voyage to the Cape took 38 days. Arrived Durban: February 14 and four days later was in service ferrying passengers across the bar to NYANZA in the bay. August: carried troops to Port St. Johns. **1880s**: Used for local coastal service and at some point was transferred to Delagoa Bay (Lourenço Marques). **1894**: September 1: wrecked at Chinde Bar near the mouth of the Zambezi River.

CARNARVON Iron twin screw steamer (Union 1884-1896)
O.N. 90411
Builders: Day, Summers & Co., Southampton (yard no: 70)
Tonnage: 104 gross 47 net
Dimensions: 90.1 x 17.1 x 8 feet
Engines: 2-cyl. compound by builder 40 h.p. **Trials**: 8.5 knots

1884: Launched: June for Union S.S. Co. Ltd. as a coaster for the small river ports of South Africa. With a screw at either end for easy access over the sandbars, she was also designed to tow barges. Registered: August 30. Chartered by the Grahamstown & Port Alfred Railway Co. for use at Port Alfred, South Africa. Arrived Cape Town: October 25 after a seven-week journey from Southampton rigged as a schooner. Arrived Port Alfred: November 2, a month after the completion of the Grahamstown-Port Alfred railway. Registered at Port Alfred. **1886**: Following the collapse of the Grahamstown & Port Alfred Railway Co., she was chartered by the Umzinto Shipping Co. to tow barges with sugar from the mouth of the Umzinto River, Natal to Durban. **1892**: The Umzinto Shipping Co. went bankrupt. **1894**: Transferred to Delagoa Bay (Lourenço Marques) as replacement for the wrecked UNION (2). **1896**: Sold to Silva Vianna & Cia., Lourenço Marques. Name unchanged. **1902**: November: reported missing with all hands after sailing from the Limpopo River for Lourenço Marques on November 1.

UNION (DUR)

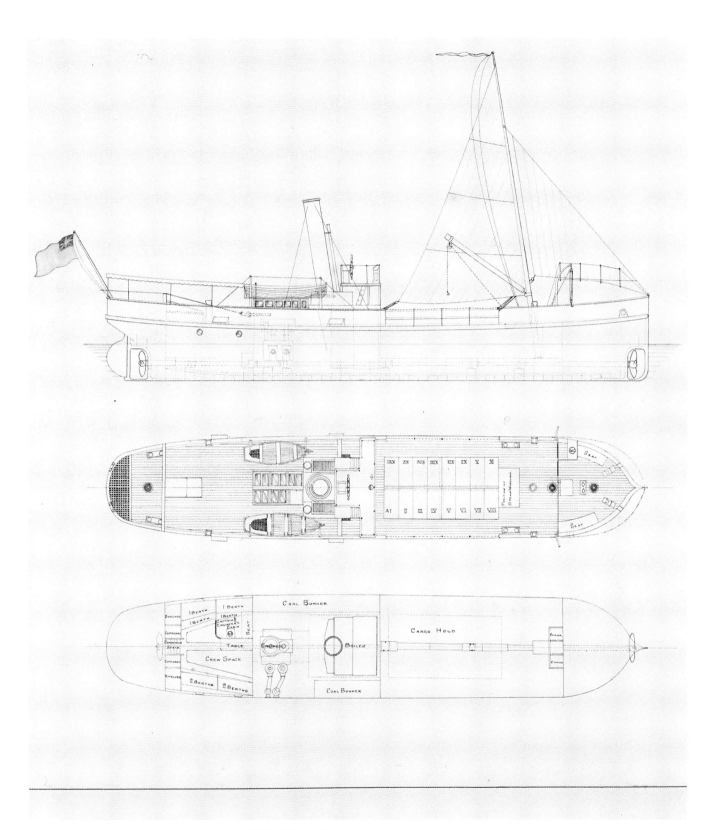

Builders plan of the unusual fore-and-aft propeller CARNARVON (SOU)

NATAL (2) Steel twin screw steam tender (Union 1892-1900: UC 1900-1901: ABC 1901-1913)
O.N. 98854
Builders: William Denny & Bros., Dumbarton (yard no: 471)
Tonnage: 158 gross 59 net
Dimensions: 110 x 23.6 x 10 feet
Engines: 2-cyl. compound by builder 50 h.p.

1892: Launched: April 21 for Union S.S. Co. Ltd. May: completed as passenger tender and tug for Durban. Prior to 1904 passengers had to disembark on tenders because of the sand bar at the entrance to Durban harbour. **1894**: Operated joint feeder service with the Castle Line carrying mail between Durban and East London. **1900**: Because of congestion during the Boer War in Cape Town, NATAL was used to ferry goods and passengers from the intermediate ships which were compelled to anchor in the bay. **1901**: July: transferred by Union-Castle S.S. Co. Ltd. with TITAN to the African Boating Co. Ltd., Durban. **1913**: November: sold to Cape Town City Steamers Ltd., (W. Gowan & Co., managers) for use as a pleasure steamer serving the newly opened Municipal Pier. Renamed SIR FRED. **1915**: Sold to Alfred James Parker, Cape Town as a fishing vessel, name reverted to NATAL. **1916**: May 7: was wrecked at Stoney Bay, off Cape Hangklip.

TITAN Steel twin screw steam tender (Union 1898-1900: UC 1900-1912: BBC 1912-1930)
O.N. 109287
Builders: Day, Summers & Co., Southampton (yard no: 117)
Tonnage: 151 gross
Dimensions: 100 x 21.1 x 8.5 feet
Engines: 2-cyl. compound by builder 52 h.p. **Trials**: 10.7

1898: Launched: July 21 for Union S.S. Co. Ltd. as a tug and tender for Durban. **1901**: July: transferred by Union-Castle S.S. Co. Ltd. with NATAL to the African Boating Co. Ltd., Durban. **1911**: November: transferred to the Beira Boating Co. Ltd., London. **1930**: September: broken up locally at Beira.

CASTLE LINE

FOX Iron screw steam tug (Castle 1877-1900: UC 1900-1912)
O.N. 79602
Builders: Thames Iron Works & Shipbuilding Co., Blackwall
Tonnage: 55 gross 25 net
Dimensions: 76 x 14.5 x 8.4 feet
Engines: 2-cyl. compound by John Stewart & Son, Blackwall 35 h.p.

1877: Completed for Donald Currie & Co., London as passenger tender and tug for Durban. Registered: July 3. **1878**: Delivery voyage London-Cape Town took 41 days. September: arrived Durban. She appears to have been operated by the Towage & Lighterage Company (Messrs. James & Hitchins Bros.), Durban. **1882**: When Messrs. James & Hitchins Bros. were taken over to form the Natal Shipping Company Ltd. (later African Boating Company Ltd.), ownership was transferred to Sir Thomas Brassey (later Lord Brassey), London (business associate of Donald Currie). **1912**: March: a month before Union-Castle was taken over by Royal Mail, ownership was transferred to African Boating Co. Ltd. June: sold to Charles Ocean Johnson. Name unchanged, port of registry changed to Port Natal (Durban). **1913**: January: ownership transferred to Irvin & Johnson Ltd., Cape Town. **1922**: December: owners restyled Irvin & Johnson (South Africa) Ltd. **1927**: August: broken up.

NATAL on the left side of the Alfred Dock entrance, Cape Town in the early 1900s (CA AG 9947)

NATAL alongside MOOR in Durban Bay (BG)

TITAN at the Durban landing wharf (CA C5897)

THE NATAL SHIPPING COMPANY LTD.

(established August 30, 1882)

AFRICAN BOATING COMPANY LTD.

(established August 12, 1884)

LION Iron twin screw steamer (ABC 1882-1904)
O.N. 87018
Builders: Thames Iron Works & Shipbuilding Co., Blackwall (yard no:17h)
Tonnage: 141 gross 78 net
Dimensions: 101.6 x 19.6 x 8.5 feet
Engines: 2-cyl compound by J. Stewart & Son, London 60 h.p. 270 i.h.p. 9 knots **Trials**: 9.6 knots

1882: Launched: October for the Natal Shipping Co. Ltd., London for use as a coaster and barge tow at Port Shepstone and other Natal minor ports. Registered: November 29 in the name of one of Donald Currie's business associates, Henry Johnson Houghton. **1884**: August: owners restyled African Boating Co. Ltd. **1904**: July 21: wrecked on the bar at Durban with the loss of six lives.

SOMTSEU Iron twin screw steamer (ABC 1883-1890)
O.N. 77075
Builders: Thames Iron Works & Shipbuilding Co. Ltd., Blackwall
Tonnage: 77 gross 47 net
Dimensions: 92.8 x 17.4 x 6.4 feet
Engines: 2-cyl. compound by T. Young & Sons, Blackwall 30 h.p.

1878: Launched: January as a Natal coaster for a local landing agent Thomas Nutter Price. SOMTSEU was named after a famous Xhosa hunter and was the African nickname for Sir Theophilus Shepstone, a key figure in the Natal Government, especially concerning African affairs. Registered: March 4 at London. Operated along the Natal coast, primarily between Durban and the mouths of the Umkomazi River, and the Umzimkulu River mouth (Port Shepstone), carrying sugar, and as far south as Port St. John on the Umzimvubu River, Cape Colony. **1880**: April: first ship to enter Port Shepstone after the completion of the breakwater. **1882**: October: grounded off the Umkomazi River, but later refloated. **1883**: August: sold to the Natal Shipping Co. Ltd., London. **1884**: August: owners restyled African Boating Co. Ltd. **1890**: September: sold to James E. Mills (Tom H.

Mills & Co., manager), Stockport. This company had a tie up with Charles (later Sir Charles) George Smith and he probably chartered the ship as a sugar carrier. Smith was a one of the leading lights in the Natal sugar trade, and his shipping interests were the basis of the well know South African coaster firm Smith's Coasters (Pty.) Ltd. formed in 1927. **1896**: Last ship to call at Port Grosvenor, Cape Colony. **1897**: April: sold to Portuguese owners and register closed.

PANTHER Steel twin screw steamer (ABC 1899-1918)
O.N. 112643
Builders: Ramage & Ferguson Ltd., Leith (yard no:167)
Tonnage: 236 gross 90 net
Dimensions: 110 x 23.1 x 10.9 feet
Engines: Triple expansion by builder 63 h.p. 450 i.h.p. 8 knots

1899: Launched: November 1 for African Boating Co. Ltd., London as a coaster and barge tow for the Natal minor ports - a larger version of LION. Completed: December. **1900**: February: arrived Durban under own steam. **1918**: African Boating Co. Ltd. liquidated. Sold to South African Railways & Harbours, Johannesburg as a Durban-based tug. Registered in Durban. **1933**: June: sold to a Durban marine engineer S. M. Patterson, Durban and was used for deep sea fishing trips and pleasure cruises. **1947**: July 4: towed out to sea off Durban and scuttled.

WHELP Composite screw steam launch (ABC 1902-19??)

1902: Arrived in Durban on board Bullard King's UMSINGA. No further information.

DURBAN BARGES

The African Boating Co. Ltd. also owned the following known barges:

1884: acquired from Morrison & Co., nine lighters:
DEE, DOON, LEA, ESK, TWEED, CLYDE, TRENT, AVON & YARE. These were probably given numbers in place of the names.

1901: acquired from Union S.S. Co. Ltd., eleven lighters:
Numbers: **30** (150 gross, 81 feet), **31** (100 gross, 72 feet), **32** (100 gross, 64 feet), **33** (100 gross, 64 feet), **34** (60 gross, 66 feet), **35** (60 gross, 66 feet), **36** (50 gross, 61 feet), **37** (50 gross, 50 feet), **38** (50 gross, 64 feet), **39 & 40** two new lighters.

LION (DR)

SOMTSEU loading sugar in 1881 on the north bank of the Umzimkulu River (ILL)

PANTHER (JM)

MOÇAMBIQUE & EAST AFRICA

LOURENÇO MARQUES

LOURENÇO MARQUES BARGES
Day, Summers & Co., Southampton built the following barges for Union S.S. Co. Ltd. These were acquired by The African Boating Co. Ltd. in 1901.

Yard no: 112-116 Five 75 gross ton cargo barges. 75 x 18 x 5.3 feet. Completed in 1898.

BEIRA

BEIRA BOATING CO LTD (established 1897)

BUSI Steel screw steam tug (BBC 1927-1967)
O.N. 149923
Builders: Henry Robb & Co., Leith (yard no: 76)
Tonnage: 97 gross
Dimensions: 75.4 x 18.1 x 8.3 feet
Engines: 2-cyl. compound by William Beardmore & Co. Ltd., Coatbridge 53 h.p. 10.5 knots

1927: Completed: October for the Beira Boating Company Ltd. (W. Barr, manager), London. **1968**: No longer in Mercantile Navy List.

MUDA Steel screw steam tug (BBC 1928-1977)
O.N. 160558
Builders: Henry Robb & Co., Leith (yard no: 109)
Tonnage: 82 gross
Dimensions: 77 x 18.1 x 8.3 feet
Engines: 2-cyl. compound by William Beardmore & Co. Ltd., Coatbridge 54 h.p. 10.5 knots

1928: Completed: September for the Beira Boating Company Ltd. (W. Barr, manager), London. **1976**: Still in Mercantile Navy List. **1977**: Beira Boating Company is no longer mentioned in the British & Commonwealth annual accounts.

JOYCE Launch (BBC 19??-1945)

1945: November: sold and replaced by ex-Admiralty launch from HMS PRETORIA CASTLE. No further information.

BEIRA LIGHTERS, PONTOONS & BARGES

Between 1928 and 1930, Henry Robb & Co., Leith built the following lighters, pontoons and barges for the Beira Boating Company Ltd.:

Yard no: 97-102 Six 75 gross ton cargo lighters. 73 x 18 x 7.6 feet. Completed in 1928.
Yard no: 130-131 Two 75 gross ton water carrying lighters. 73 x 18 x 7.6 feet. Completed in May,1929.
Yard no: 132-133 Two 85 gross ton cargo pontoons. 50 x 33 x 6 feet. Completed in February, 1929.
Yard no: 166 -175 Ten 105 gross ton cargo lighters. 75 x 20 x 9.6 feet. Completed in 1930.

EAST AFRICA

FIREFLY Launch (UC 1910-19?)

1910: Completed as tender for East African ports. Carried out on DUNLUCE CASTLE. No further information.

GLOWWORM Launch (UC 1910-1920)

1910: Completed as tender for East African ports. Used mainly at Mombasa. **1920**: Sold to unknown buyers.

BUSI

Chapter Six
WAR MANAGED SHIPS

EDUARD WOERMANN (ML)

WORLD WAR ONE

SALTA Steel twin screw steamer (UC managed 1915-1917)
O.N. 136744
Builders: Forges et Chantiers de la Méditerranée, La Seyne (yard no: 1048)
Tonnage: 7,284 gross 4,239 net
Dimensions: 449.4 x 53.3 x 31.7 feet
Engines: Triple expansion by builder 7,300 i.h.p. 16 knots
Passengers: 68 first, 45 second, 30 third, 1,500 steerage

1911: Launched: March 13 as passenger liner for Soc. Générale de Transports Maritimes à Vapeur, Marseilles. Designed for S.G.T.M.'s Marseilles-South America service and near sister of VALDIVIA. July: completed. **1914**: December 3: chartered by the Admiralty and converted in a 461-bed hospital ship. **1915**: January: placed under Union-Castle Mail S.S. Co. Ltd. management. **1917**: April 10: on voyage from Southampton-Le Havre with hospital stores and no patients, hit mine half a mile north of Whistle Buoy, Le Havre Roads. Mine was laid the previous day by UC 26. Sank with loss of 86 lives.

HUNTSEND Steel twin screw steamer (UC managed 1915-1923)
O.N. 136828
Builders: A.G. Weser, Bremen (yard no: 160)
Tonnage: 8,826 gross 5,116 net
Dimensions: 462.1 x 57.5 x 35.7 feet
Engines: Quadruple expansion by builder 756 h.p. 6,500 i.h.p. 14.5 knots
Passengers: 107 first, 113 second, 128 third

1907: Launched: December 17 as passenger liner LÜTZOW for Norddeutscher Lloyd, Bremen. **1908**: April: completed. Placed on Far East service. **1914**: August 4: captured by the British as war prize in the Mediterranean near the Suez Canal. Management was awarded to Harris & Dixon, London. **1915**. July 3: renamed HUNTSEND - Expeditionary Force Transport No. C6182. July: management changed to Union-Castle Mail S.S. Co. Ltd. Variety of duties, mainly trooping. **1923**: November: bought back by Norddeutscher Lloyd, and reverted to LÜTZOW. **1924**: Rebuilt as two-class liner for Bremen-New York route. **1932**: December: sold for scrap to Bremer Vulkan. Broken up at Vegesack.

POLGLASS CASTLE Steel screw steamer (UC managed 1915-1921)
O.N. 139080
Builders: Swan, Hunter & Wigham Richardson Ltd., Newcastle (yard no: 406)
Tonnage: 4,762 gross 2,968 net 7,023 deadweight
Dimensions: 390 x 51.5 x 27.5 feet
Engines: Quadruple expansion by builder 492 h.p. 2,400 i.h.p. 11 knots

1903: Launched: September 7 as cargo ship REICHENFELS for Deutsche Dampfschifffahrts-Gesellschaft "Hansa", Bremen. October:

completed. **1914**: August 5: taken as a war prize at Colombo. Requisitioned by the Admiralty, she was managed, name unchanged, by Grahams & Co. **1915**: August: Union-Castle Mail S.S. Co. Ltd. become managers and registered owners, as Crown nominees. Renamed POLGLASS CASTLE. Between September 2, 1915 and November 20, 1920 carried a variety of cargo including coal, wheat, sugar, as well as steel from the USA to France. **1918**: Ownership transferred to the Shipping Controller, still under Union-Castle management. **1921**: December: sold back to "Hansa". Name reverted to REICHENFELS. **1934**: 1st quarter broken up by A.G. "Weser", Bremen.

PROFESSOR Steel screw steamer (UC managed 1915-1921)
O.N. 143442
Builders: Reiherstieg Schiffswerft, Hamburg (yard no: 445) for
Tonnage: 6,061 gross 3,588 net 6,200 deadweight
Dimensions: 392.9 x 52.4 x 26.9 feet
Engines: Triple expansion by builder 484 h.p. 3,800 i.h.p. 12.5 knots
Passengers: 120 first, 94 second, 50 third

1912: Launched: June 27 as passenger liner PROFESSOR WOERMANN Woermann-Linie K.G., Hamburg. September: completed. Used on Hamburg-West Africa service. **1914**: August 21: captured by the cruiser HMS CARNARVON off the Cape Verde Islands while serving as a naval supply vessel. Taken as a war prize to Freetown. **1915**: Renamed PROFESSOR, she became an Admiralty troop transport, managed by Union-Castle Mail S.S. Co. Ltd. Between September 29, 1915 to May 10, 1919 used on South and East Africa service as troop carrier and depot ship. **1917**: March: ran aground at Beira and sustained serious damage which was only finally repaired at Durban in May 1919. **1919**: June 14 to July 22: carried passengers between South and East Africa for Union-Castle. September: arrived on Tyne for further repairs, which were completed in January 1920. **1920**: Transferred to the Shipping Controller, same managers. January 11 to August 22: carried troops between UK and China. **1921**: December: sold to Hugo Stinnes A.G. für Seeschiffahrt u. Überseehandel, Hamburg for their Hamburg-Brazil-River Plate service, and renamed EDMUND WAGENKNECHT. Reconditioned at Reiherstiegwerft. **1922**: Renamed GENERAL SAN MARTIN, same owners. **1924**: Following the death of Hugo Stinnes, the shares of Hugo Stinnes A.G. für Seeschiffahrt u. Überseehandel were transferred to the Deutsch-Austral & Kosmos Linie which had been controlled by Stinnes since the early 1920s. **1926**: Deutsch-Austral & Kosmos Linie taken over by Hamburg-Amerikanische-Packetfahrt-Actien-Gesellschaft (HAPAG.). Sold to Lloyd Brasileiro, Rio de Janeiro as ALMIRANTE JACEGUAY. **1958**: Broken up at Rio de Janeiro by Virgilio Martins Correa. July: work commenced.

SALTA (WSS)

PROFESSOR as PROFESSOR WOERMANN (ML)

POLGLASS CASTLE as REICHENFELS (TH)

HUNTSEND

HUNTSCASTLE Steel screw steamer (UC managed 1916-1921)
O.N. 139107
Builders: Flensburger Schiffbau-Gesellschaft, Flensburg (yard no: 214)
Tonnage: 5,528 gross 3,482 net
Dimensions: 403.2 x 49.4 x 27 feet
Engines: Quadruple expansion by builder 381 h.p. 2,400 i.h.p. 12 knots
Passengers: 40 first, 30 second, 62 third

1902: Launched: July 9 as cargo liner LOUISIANA for D.G. "Argo" A.G., Bremen. August: completed. **1905**: June: sold to Woermann-Linie A.G., Hamburg for use on their Hamburg-West Africa service. Rebuilt as a passenger cargo liner and renamed ERNA WOERMANN. **1914**: September 27: captured at Duala by HMS CUMBERLAND as war prize for the British government. Used in the German South-West Africa campaign to carry troops. **1915**: December: renamed HUNTSCASTLE and registered at London - Expeditionary Force Transport (No. 1260). **1916**: January: management awarded to Union-Castle Mail S.S. Co. Ltd. and carried stores to East Africa. **1917**: Between January 26, 1917 and January 16, 1921: transported troops and supplies to Egypt and Mesopotania. **1921**: August: sold to Deutsche Ost-Afrika-Linie, Hamburg for their round Africa service. Renamed SULTAN. **1932**: December: sold for scrap. **1933**: Broken up at Hamburg, 4th quarter by Blohm & Voss.

HUNTSCLIFF Steel screw steamer (UC managed 1916-1918)
O.N. 139110
Builders: Bremer Vulkan, Vegesack (yard no: 553)
Tonnage: 5,442 gross 3,393 net
Dimensions: 419.8 x 54.5 x 28.2 feet
Engines: Quadruple expansion by builder 3,500 i.h.p. 11.5 knots
Passengers: 12 first

1911: Launched: September 29 as cargo ship RUFIDJI for Deutsche Ost-Afrika-Linie, Hamburg. November: completed. Placed on Hamburg-East Africa service. **1914**: August 18: intercepted by HM Torpedo Boat 060 off Cape Point and escorted to Simon's Town as war prize for the British Government. **1916**: January: renamed HUNTSCLIFF, registered London and managed by Union-Castle Mail S.S. Co. Ltd. On East Africa duty as Expeditionary Force Transport No. G6128 until January 1918. **1918**: October 8: on voyage between Montreal and Bantry Bay, Ireland with cargo of oats, ship was abandoned after encountering rough weather and all crew were taken on board the White Star liner TEUTONIC (9,984/1889). October 14: After numerous attempts, a towline was attached to the U.S. Navy tug GENESEE. October 17: tow was abandoned after 280 miles because of deteriorating weather and she foundered 120 miles off the Irish coast.

ASSOUAN Steel screw steamer (UC managed 1916-1917)
O.N. 112771
Builders: Lloyd Austro-Ungarico, Trieste (yard no: 33)
Tonnage: 2,765 gross 1,780 net
Dimensions: 344 x 37.7 x 24.9 feet
Engines: 2-cyl. compound by builder 303 h.p. 800 i.h.p. 9 knots
Passengers: 107 first, 20 second

1882: Launched: June as PANDORA for Lloyd Austro-Ungarico's Trieste-Bombay route. She was also their first steel ship. **1891**: With the withdrawal of Hungary from the partnership, the company was restyled Österreichischer Lloyd (Lloyd Austriaco). **1900**: Sold to Khedivial Mail Steamship & Graving Dock Co. Ltd., London and renamed ASSOUAN. November 6: registered at London. **1914**: Between September 1, 1914 and May 15, 1915 used as an Indian Expeditionary Force Transport. **1915**: November: taken over by Admiralty for use as block ship but never used. **1916**: January: Union-Castle Mail S.S. Co. Ltd. appointed managers. **1917**: March 12: register closed "on sale to Admiralty." March 15: registered at Durban, name unchanged, with new owner: Cecil Platt, a sugar planter from Isipingo, Natal. Platt formed the Assouan Steamship Co. Ltd., Durban to manage

the ship. **1918**: January 14: after the failure of the Assouan Steamship Co. Ltd., she was sold to the newly formed Assouan Steamship Co. (Transvaal) Ltd. October: chartered by the Union Government to carry railway material from New York to South Africa. Because of engine problems and difficulties with her crew, the New York-Cape Town voyage only culminated on June 30, 1920. **1921**: Assouan Steamship Co. (Transvaal) Ltd. went into liquidation. June 13: sold to Stafford Mayer Co. South Africa Ltd., Durban. July 1: transferred to Port Louis, Mauritius register. November 12: sold to Mauritius Union Steam Nav. Co. Ltd., Port Louis, name unchanged. **1922**: January: laid up at Port Louis. July 8: sold to Alfred Lionel Hall, Port Louis for scrap. Broken up during 4th quarter.

FIELD-MARSHAL Steel twin screw steamer (UC managed 1916-1922)
O.N. 142385
Builders: Reiherstieg Schiffswerft, Hamburg (yard no: 410),
Tonnage: 6,142 gross 3,819 net
Dimensions: 415.8 x 50.4 x 28.1 feet
Engines: Triple expansion by builder 4,000 i.h.p. 13 knots
Passengers: 113 first, 75 second, 80 third, 120 soldiers 'tween decks

1903: Launched: February 21 as passenger liner FELDMARSCHALL for Deutsche Ost-Afrika-Linie, Hamburg. June: completed. Placed on round Africa service. **1914**: August 2: at the outbreak of war, took shelter at Dar es Salaam. **1915**: August 17: damaged by gunfire from HMS HYACINTH. **1916**: October: after the fall of Dar es Salaam, taken as war prize by the British Government. Renamed FIELD-MARSHAL, she became a troop transport, managed by Union-Castle Mail S.S. Co. Ltd. Expeditionary Force Transport No. D60. **1919**: Repatriated German colonists from East Africa to Hamburg. **1922**: October: sold to Chungwha Nav. Co. Ltd., Shanghai for China–Pacific trade, and renamed LING NAM. **1925**: July: seized by creditors. **1926**: November: sold by auction in Hong Kong to J. M. Brodeth. **1927**: Sold to Ling Nam S.S. Co. Ltd. (Williamson & Co. Ltd., managers), Hong Kong, and refitted for deck passenger trade. **1928**: August: new owners Ho Hong S.S. Co. Ltd., Singapore. Renamed HONG KHENG. **1942**: February: escaped from Singapore to Bombay, and allocated to Ministry of War Transport for Bombay-East Africa trade, British India S.N. Co. Ltd., managers. **1946**: Returned to owners. **1947**: July 19: on voyage from Rangoon to Swatow and Amoy in ballast with 1,800 deck passengers, stranded on Chilang Point near Hong Kong (22.39N-115.34E). No loss of life but constructive total loss.

HUNTSCLIFF as RUFIDJI (ML)

HUNTSCASTLE as ERNA WOERMANN (ML)

FIELD-MARSHAL

ASSOUAN (ML)

LEASOWE CASTLE Steel twin screw steamer (UC managed 1917-1918)
O.N. 140272
Builders: Cammell Laird & Co. Ltd., Birkenhead (yard no: 806)
Tonnage: 9,737 gross 5,381 net
Dimensions: 488.5 x 58.2 x 32.9 feet
Engines: Quadruple expansion by builder 1,759 h.p. 6,500 i.h.p. 17 knots
Passengers: 60 first, 450 second, 1,800 third

1914: Laid down as passenger liner VASILISSA SOPHIA (Queen Sofia) for The National Steam Navigation Co. Ltd. of Greece (Embiricos Bros., managers), Andros. Designed for Piraeus-New York route. Her sister, VASILEFS CONSTANTINOS (King Constantine) was completed in December. Because of war priorities, construction period was prolonged. **1915**: Launched: March 16. September: completed, but was laid up either because the British Government refused to let her sail (at the time, the Greek king was pro German) or because her owners were concerned about attack from submarines. **1917**: Chartered as a troop transport (Expeditionary Force Transport No. F8021). March: renamed LEASOWE CASTLE, Union-Castle Mail S.S. Co. Ltd. managers. April 20: torpedoed by German submarine U 35 west of Gibraltar but managed to reach Gibraltar for repairs. **1918**: May 27: 150 miles west of Alexandria, on voyage Alexandria-Marseilles with 3,000 troops, torpedoed and sunk by UB 51 at 1.30 a.m. 92 lives were lost.

HUNTSPILL Steel twin screw steamer (UC managed 1917-1920)
O.N. 139055
Builders: Lloyd Austriaco, Trieste (yard no: 70)
Tonnage: 5,440 gross 3,136 net
Dimensions: 399.7 x 49 x 23.8 feet
Engines: Triple expansion by builder 788 h.p. 5,800 i.h.p. 14.5 knots
Passengers: 107 first, 20 second

1904: Completed: January as passenger liner KOERBER for Österreichischer Lloyd (Lloyd Austriaco), Trieste. Placed on Trieste-Durban route. **1907**: February: Trieste-Durban route abandoned to Deutsche Ost-Afrika-Linie. KOERBER was transferred to Trieste-Bombay service. **1914**: August: detained at Port Said on voyage Shanghai-Trieste and taken by the British Government as war prize. **1915**: October 4: renamed HUNTSPILL. Between October 30, 1915 and February 26, 1921 used mainly in Mediterranean as a troopship - Expeditionary Force Transport (No. E80). **1917**: May: Union-Castle Mail S.S. Co. Ltd. become managers. **1919**: January: with Trieste in Italian hands after the war, Lloyd Austriaco was converted from an Austrian to an Italian firm, Lloyd Triestino. **1920**: Management changed to Anchor Line (Henderson Bros.). **1921**: Management changed to British India S.N. Co. Ltd. September: returned to Lloyd Triestino, Trieste, and renamed ASIA. **1929**: March 1: driven ashore in a gale at Trieste. March 6: refloated and docked. **1933**: 2nd quarter scrapped by Cantieri Riuniti dell'Adriatico at Monfalcone.

HUNTSGREEN Steel twin screw steamer (UC managed 1917-1919)
O.N. 139066
Builders: F. Schichau, Danzig (yard no: 801)
Tonnage: 9,144 gross 5,148 net
Dimensions: 463 x 57.7 x 35.8 feet
Engines: Quadruple expansion by builder 820 h.p. 6,500 i.h.p. 14.5 knots
Passengers: 107 first, 113 second, 132 third

1907: Laid down as HOHENLOHE for Norddeutscher Lloyd, Bremen but launched: November 9 as passenger liner DERFFLINGER for NDL's Far East service. **1908**: May: completed. **1914**: August 3: disabled by the British in the Suez Canal. October 13: taken by the Egyptian Government and handed over to HMS FOXHOUND. Renamed HUNTSGREEN and managed by F. Green & Co., London as an Expeditionary Force Transport No. C8260 - used mainly to carry troops. **1917**: May: management changed to Union-Castle Mail S.S. Co. Ltd. **1919**: Management changed to Orient Steam Navigation Co., London - this ceased in May 1921. **1922**: September: sold to Fisher Alimonda & Co. Ltd., London. **1923**: January: sold to Crete Shipping Co. Ltd. (Stelp & Leighton Ltd.), London. June: sold back to Norddeutscher Lloyd, and name reverted to DERFFLINGER. Rebuilt as two-class liner for Bremen-New York route. **1932**: May: sold to Stern & Co., Essen for scrap and broken up for them in December, by the Technical Service Department of NDL at Bremerhaven.

HUNTSCRAFT Steel screw steamer (UC managed 1917-1919)
O.N. 136793
Builders: W. Doxford & Sons Ltd., Sunderland (yard no: 455)
Tonnage: 5,113 gross 3,176 net
Dimensions: 420 x 54.1 x 26.3 feet
Engines: Triple expansion by builder 577 h.p. 1,864 i.h.p. 11.5 knots

1913: Launched: June 3 as cargo ship SÜDMARK for Hamburg-Amerikanische-Packetfahrt-Actien-Gesellschaft (HAPAG), Hamburg. July: completed. Placed on Far East service. **1914**: August 15: on voyage Colombo-Hamburg captured by HMS BLACK PRINCE in the Indian Ocean, and taken for the British Government as war prize. **1915**: September: renamed HUNTSCRAFT and managed by Harris & Dixon, London. Expeditionary Force Transport No. E216. **1917**: May: management taken over by Union-Castle Mail S.S. Co. Ltd. **1918**: July 6: torpedoed by submarine 10 miles south-east of St. Catherine's Point but towed to Netley and repaired. **1920**: January: sold to Clan Line Steamers Ltd., Glasgow. Renamed CLAN MACKAY. **1934**: October 19: on voyage from Cairns to Montreal, stranded on Carpenter Rock, Sierra Leone. Constructive total loss.

CLAN MACKAY ex HUNTSCRAFT

LEASOWE CASTLE (AG)

HUNTSPILL

HUNTSGREEN

HUNSLET Steel screw steamer (UC managed 1917-1921)
O.N. 137678
Builders: Wigham Richardson & Co. Ltd., Newcastle (yard no: 336)
Tonnage: 5,632 gross 3,567 net 8,000 deadweight
Dimensions: 418 x 54 x 20.1 feet
Engines: Quadruple expansion by builder 494 h.p. 2,900 i.h.p. 11 knots

1898: Launched: March 23 as cargo ship TANNENFELS for Deutsche Dampfschifffahrts-Gesellschaft "Hansa", Bremen. April: completed. **1914**: August: requisitioned by the German Navy as a collier. September 14: captured in Basilan Strait, Philippines by HMS CHELMER, she was taken to Hong Kong as war prize. **1915**: January 19: renamed BASILAN. February 3: registered in Hong Kong. July 22: renamed HUNSLET. Requisitioned by the Admiralty, she was used as a military hospital ship from July 1915 to February 1916. After that, she spent the rest of the war carrying troops as an Expeditionary Force Transport No. E1086. **1916**: Oceanic Steam Navigation Co. Ltd. (White Star Line) become managers and registered owners, as Crown nominees. **1917**: Transferred to the Shipping Controller ownership, and in May, management transferred to Union-Castle Mail S.S. Co. Ltd. **1921**: December: sold to Woermann-Linie A.G., Hamburg, and renamed WAGANDA. **1932**: December: sold to Hamburg breakers. **1933**: Broken up at Hamburg by Deutsche Werft A.G.

WESTERN AUSTRALIA Steel twin screw steamer (UC managed 1917-1919)
O.N. 161302 (from 1929)
Builders: Stabilimento Tecnico Triestino, Trieste (yard no: 334)
Tonnage: 2,937 gross 1,628 net 2,170 deadweight
Dimensions: 344 x 43 x 24.3 feet
Engines: Triple expansion by builder 712 h.p. 5,000 i.h.p. 16.5 knots
Passengers: 120

1901: Completed: August as MONGOLIA for the Chinese Eastern Railway Company Ltd., Vladivostok. She and her sister MANCHURIA were used on Vladivostok-Port Arthur-Shanghai express service. **1906**: After the Russo-Japanese War, sold to the A/S Det Østasiatiske Kompagni (East Asiatic Co.), Copenhagen but not registered in Denmark. July: ownership was transferred to the A/S Det Østasiatiske Kompagni's Russian subsidiary Russisk- Østasiatiske Dampskibsselskab, St.Petersburg for Far East service. Passenger capacity: 84 first, 16 second and 'tweendeck passengers in third. **1912**: May: sold to the Western Australian Government owned State Shipping Service, Fremantle as their first large coastal ship. Renamed WESTERN AUSTRALIA. **1915**: October 21: chartered by the British Government and converted into a 305-bed military hospital ship, under Royal Mail Steam Packet Co. management. **1917**: March 23: conversion completed. May: management transferred to Union-Castle Mail S.S. Co. Ltd. As Expeditionary Force Transport No. G16, was used as a cross Channel ambulance transport and later on prisoner-of-war service between Leith and Copenhagen. **1918**: January 28: collided with and sank the torpedo gunboat HMS HAZARD (1,070/1894) off Portland Bill. **1919**: June: sold to Rederi A/B Svenska Lloyd (Swedish Lloyd), Göteborg (Herbert Metcalfe, manager). Sent to Lindholmens Varv., Göteborg for a major refit (76 first and 226 second), she was renamed PATRICIA. **1920**: July 21: inaugurated new Göteborg-Newcastle emigrant service, and was later transferred to Göteborg-London route: 116 first, 434 second and 22 third. **1929**: May: sold to United Baltic Corporation Ltd., London and renamed BALTAVIA. Used on London-Baltic service: 18 first, 60 second and 372 third. **1935**: February: sold for scrap to John Cashmore Ltd., Newport, Monmouthshire.

PRINCE GEORGE Steel twin screw steamer (UC managed 1917-1919)
O.N. 110003
Builders: Earle's Shipbuilding & Engineering Co. Ltd., Hull (yard no: 438)
Tonnage: 2,194 gross 863 net 1,100 deadweight
Dimensions: 290.5 x 38 x 16.5 feet
Engines: Triple expansion by builder 718 h.p. 5,500 i.h.p. 16.5 knots
Passengers: not known

1898: Completed: November as a passenger ship for the Dominion Atlantic Railway Co. Ltd., London. Used on the Yarmouth, Nova Scotia-Boston service. Her sister was PRINCE ARTHUR. **1912**: August: following the lease of the Dominion Atlantic Railway to the Canadian Pacific Railway, PRINCE GEORGE and PRINCE ARTHUR were sold to the Eastern Steamship Corp., names unchanged. Both ships were registered at Yarmouth under the Boston & Yarmouth S.S. Co. Ltd. **1917**: June 5: chartered as Expeditionary Force Transport No. B80, and placed under Union-Castle Mail S.S. Co. Ltd. management. Used as a cross Channel troop transport and later on prisoner-of-war service between Hull and Rotterdam. **1919**: October: returned with PRINCE ARTHUR to owners. **1931**: September 25: arrived Baltimore, Maryland for demolition by the Boston Iron & Metal Company.

PRINCE ARTHUR Steel twin screw steamer (UC managed 1917-1919)
O.N. 110131
Builders: Earle's Shipbuilding & Engineering Co. Ltd., Hull (yard no: 439)
Tonnage: 2,041 gross 700 net
Dimensions: 290.5 x 38 x 16.5 feet
Engines: Triple expansion by builder 718 h.p. 5,500 i.h.p. 16.5 knots
Passengers: not known

1899: Completed: January as a passenger ship for the Dominion Atlantic Railway Co. Ltd., London. Used on the Yarmouth, Nova Scotia-Boston service. Her sister was PRINCE GEORGE. **1912**: August: following the lease of the Dominion Atlantic Railway to the Canadian Pacific Railway, PRINCE GEORGE and PRINCE ARTHUR were sold to the Eastern Steamship Corp., names unchanged. Both ships were registered at Yarmouth under the Boston & Yarmouth S.S. Co. Ltd. **1917**: October 11: chartered as Expeditionary Force Transport, and placed under Union-Castle Mail S.S. Co. Ltd. management. Used as a cross-Channel troop transport and later on prisoner-of-war service. **1919**: October: returned with PRINCE GEORGE to her owners. **1929**: January 14: arrived Baltimore, Maryland for demolition by the Boston Iron & Metal Company.

WAGANDA ex HUNSLET

WESTERN AUSTRALIA

PRINCE ARTHUR

VASCO DA GAMA Steel screw steam tug (UC managed 1917)
O.N. 108260
Builders: Carmichael MacLean & Co., Greenock (yard no: 6)
Tonnage: 107 gross
Dimensions: 80.7 x 17.9 x 8 feet
Engines: 2-cyl. compound by Campbell & Calderwood, Paisley
50 h.p. 300 i.h.p.

1897: Launched: September 8 for T. A. Compton & Co., London as tug to be based at Lourenço Marques. November: completed. **1899**: Sold to Transvaal Gold Fields Ltd. (A. R. Atkinson, manager), Lourenço Marques. **1912/3**: Sold to Premier Whaling Co. Ltd., Lourenço Marques, name unchanged. **1917**: October: came under the control of the Shipping Controller and management allocated to Union-Castle Mail S.S. Co. Ltd. November 6: foundered in Delagoa Bay (Lourenço Marques) in bad weather.

MAFIA Steel screw steamer (UC managed 1917-1921)
O.N. 139125
Builders: Soc. des Etabl. Bertin Frères, Bezons possibly for L. Levy, France
Tonnage: 531 gross 211 net
Dimensions: 161.8 x 24.9 x 11.2 feet
Engines: 2-cyl. compound by builder 39 h.p. 450 i.h.p. 9 knots

1910: Completed as OYAC. She and her sister ROBERT SUZANNE were not classed by Lloyds or Bureau Veritas. For some reason also, the engines were built in 1907 but the ships were only completed in 1910. **1913**: Sold to B. Bertucci, Victoria, Brazil and renamed RIO SÃO MATHEUS. **1916**: April: sold with RIO ITAPEMIRIM (PEMBA) to Sir J. R. Ellerman, A. B. T. Cayzer and Frank Ward (Frank Ward, managing owner), London and renamed MAFIA. Frank Ward was the manager of T. & J. Harrison's London office and the ships operated as East African feeder vessels between Beira and Chinde for the joint T. & J. Harrison, Hall and Clan Line service to East Africa. **1917**: Placed with PEMBA under Union-Castle Mail S.S. Co. Ltd. management by the Shipping Controller, presumably because Harrison was unable to provide the resources for ships based in East Africa. **1921**: July 5: sold with PEMBA to the British and South American Steam Nav. Co. Ltd. (Houston Lines), Liverpool for use on the South African coast. Remained on London register, with name unchanged. **1922**: December 5: ownership transferred to Thesen's Steamship Co. Ltd., Cape Town which was controlled by Houston Lines. Registered at Cape Town. **1927**: July: sold to Massinot & Thiery, Diego Suarez, Madagascar (French flag), same name. **1930**: March 22: on voyage Diego Suarez-Tamatave, with cargo of coffee and timber, stranded off Fenerive and was constructive total loss.

PEMBA Steel screw steamer (UC managed 1917-1921)
O.N. 139124
Builders: Soc. des Etabl. Bertin Frères, Bezons for L. Levy, France
Tonnage: 533 gross 212 net
Dimensions: 161.8 x 24.9 x 11.2 feet
Engines: 2-cyl. compound by builder 39 h.p. 450 i.h.p. 9 knots

1908: Completed as ROBERT SUZANNE. She and her sister OYAC were not classed by Lloyds or Bureau Veritas. For some reason also, the engines were built in 1907 but the ships were only completed in 1910. **1913**: Sold to B. Bertucci, Victoria, Brazil and renamed RIO ITAPEMIRIM. **1916**: April: sold with RIO SÃO MATHEUS (MAFIA) to Sir J. R. Ellerman, A. B. T. Cayzer and Frank Ward (Frank Ward, managing owner), London and renamed PEMBA. Frank Ward was the manager of T. & J. Harrison's London office and the ships operated as East African feeder vessels between Beira and Chinde for the joint T. & J. Harrison, Hall and Clan Line service to East Africa. **1917**: Placed with MAFIA under Union-Castle Mail S.S. Co. Ltd. management by the Shipping Controller, presumably because Harrison was unable to provide the resources for ships based in East Africa. **1921**: July 5: sold with MAFIA to the British and South American Steam Nav. Co. Ltd. (Houston Lines), Liverpool for use on the South African coast. Remained on London register, with name unchanged. **1922**: December 5: ownership transferred to Thesen's Steamship Co. Ltd., Cape Town which was controlled by Houston Lines. Registered at Cape Town. **1926**: August 6: on voyage Cape Town-Durban, with cargo of guano and empty drums, foundered off Port St. Johns in heavy weather with the loss of one life.

CHOW TAI Steel screw steamer (UC managed 1917-1920)
O.N. 105973
Builders: Fairfield S.B. & E. Co. Ltd., Glasgow (yard no: 387)
Tonnage: 1,777 gross 1,115 net
Dimensions: 289 x 37.8 x 21.5 feet
Engines: Triple expansion by builder 211 h.p. 1,500 i.h.p. 10 knots
Passengers: 6 first, 839 deck

1895: Launched: December 17 for the Scottish Oriental S.S. Co. Ltd. (Ferguson, Davidson & Co., managers), Edinburgh. **1896**: February: completed. Used Hong Kong-Bangkok service. **1900**: January: the company and the 14-ship fleet was bought by Norddeutscher Lloyd, Bremen. **1914**: August 3: taken as war prize in Singapore by the British Government and registered in Singapore. October 8: Management was awarded to Straits S.S. Co. Ltd., and she was used on the Borneo run and in the East Africa campaign. **1917**: Management transferred to Union-Castle Mail S.S. Co. Ltd. Used as an Expeditionary Force Transport No. B102 in East Africa and various other duties. **1920**: June management transferred to General Steam Navigation Co. Ltd. **1921**: August: sold to Luis Liaño S. en C., Santander, renamed JUAN ANTONIO. **1925**: Sold to Antonio Larrea, Bilbao, name unchanged. **1927**: Renamed ANA MARIA. **1930**: Sold Soc. Metalurgica Duro-Felguera, Gijon for scrap but continued to trade. **1931**: Renamed MOSQUITERA. **1935**: Sold to Cia. Nav. Amaya S.A., Bilbao. **1939**: Scrapped at Bilbao.

JUPITER Steel screw steamer (UC managed 1918)
O.N. 142419
Builders: Lindholmens M.V., Göteborg (yard no: 423)
Tonnage: 2,610 gross 1,222 net 1,750 deadweight
Dimensions: 305.7 x 41.7 x 18.8 feet
Engines: Triple expansion by builder 309 h.p. 2,750 i.h.p. 14 knots
Passengers: 225 first, 47 third

1915: Launched: September 11 for the Bergenske Dampskibsselskab (Bergen Line), Bergen. December: completed for Bergen Line's Bergen-Newcastle passenger service. **1917**: November: chartered by the Shipping Controller. Painted in dazzle, she operated a war time service between Bergen and Aberdeen. **1918**: Between April 24 to December 8 under Union-Castle Mail S.S. Co. management. **1919**: January: resumed Bergen-Newcastle service. **1938**: Placed on Bergen-Rotterdam route. **1940**: August: at Copenhagen, requisitioned by the German Government. **1946**: March returned to Bergen-Newcastle run. **1955**: Sold to Epirotiki Steamship Nav. Co. (George Potamianos, manager), Piraeus and converted into the cruise ship HERMES. **1960**: March 4: caught fire during refit at Piraeus. Towed out and beached at Sileniai Bay. March 9: refloated and later sold for demolition to Brodospas, Split.

MAFIA (ML)

JUPITER

VALDIVIA Steel twin screw steamer (UC managed 1918-1920)
O.N. 136743
Builders: Chantiers et Ateliers de Provence, Port de Bouc (yard no: 35)
Tonnage: 7,147 gross 4,335 net
Dimensions: 462.8 x 54.3 x 31.1 feet
Engines: Triple expansion by builder 726 h.p. 7,500 i.h.p. 16 knots
Passengers: 60 first, 80 second, 1,500 steerage

1911: Launched: August 27 as passenger liner for Soc. Générale de Transports Maritimes à Vapeur, Marseilles. Designed for S.G.T.M.'s Marseilles-South America service and near sister of SALTA. **1912**: March: completed. **1913**: January: chartered by Cie. de Nav. Sud Atlantique for nine months on Bordeaux-South America route as replacement for DIVONA (6,484/1886) which was being repaired following rudder problems. **1914**: November 29: chartered by the Admiralty and converted in a 551-bed Hospital Ship No. C126. **1917**: Between August 20, 1917 and August 15, 1918 described as "inefficient and off pay". **1918**: July: placed under Union-Castle Mail S.S. Co. Ltd. management. Ambulance transport between December 25, 1918 and December 22, 1919. **1919**: December 23: decommissioned as hospital ship. **1920**: March: returned to owners. **1933**: May 6: arrived for demolition at Savona.

PRINZESSIN Steel twin screw steamer (UC managed 1919-1921)
O.N. 143077
Builders: Blohm & Voss, Hamburg (yard no: 182) for Deutsche Ost-Afrika-Linie, Hamburg
Tonnage: 6,387 gross 3,697 net
Dimensions: 416 x 50.4 x 28
Engines: Triple expansion by builder 622 h.p. 4,000 i.h.p. 13.5 knots
Passengers: 112 first, 80 second, 106 third

1905: Launched: December 23 as passenger liner for Deutsche Ost-Afrika-Linie round Africa service. **1906**: April: completed. **1914-1918**: Spent the war laid up in Hamburg. **1919**: March: transferred to the Allies by the German Government and handed over to the Shipping Controller, she was managed by Shaw, Savill & Albion Co. Ltd., London. Name unchanged. December: management transferred to Union-Castle Mail S.S. Co. Ltd. **1921**: January: handed over to French Government as war reparation. Managed by Messageries Maritimes. **1923**: Sold to Soc. des Services Contractuels des Messageries Maritimes, Marseilles. Renamed GÉNÉRAL VOYRON, she operated on Madagascar-La Réunion service, with passenger capacity: 72 first, 99 second, 58 third. First voyage: August 26. **1934**: 1st quarter broken up at La Seyne by Soc. de Material Naval du Midi.

EDUARD WOERMANN Steel screw steamer (UC managed 1919-1920)
O.N. 143066
Builders: Bremer Vulkan, Vegesack (yard no: 452)
Tonnage: 5,609 gross 3,500 net
Dimensions: 403.4 x 49.2 x 27.1 feet
Engines: Triple expansion by builder 400 h.p. 2,500 i.h.p. 12.5 knots
Passengers: 37 first, 20 second, 39 third

1903: Launched: September 24 as cargo passenger liner ALABAMA for D.G. "Argo" A.G., Bremen. November: completed. **1904**: October: sold to Woermann-Linie K.G., Hamburg for use on their Hamburg-West Africa service. Renamed EDUARD WOERMANN. **1919**: March: transferred to the Allies by the German Government and handed over to the Shipping Controller. April: managed by Union-Castle Mail S.S. Co. Ltd., name unchanged. **1920**: September: management transferred to Valhalla Steamship Co. Ltd. (Watts, Watts & Co. Ltd., managers). **1921**: September: sold to A/S Sjøfart (T. H. Skogland & Søn A/S), Haugesund, Norway, and renamed HANNA SKOGLAND. **1929**: Transferred to A/S Skoglands Rederi (same manager). Sold to A/S Modesta (Johan Hvide, manager), Bergen as MODESTA. **1930**: Transferred to A/S Johan Hvide Rederei (same manager). **1933**: October: sold to Japanese breakers whilst lying in Shanghai. **1934**: 1st quarter broken up at Osaka.

CAP POLONIO Steel triple screw steamer (UC managed 1919)
O.N. 143188
Builders: Blohm & Voss, Hamburg (yard no: 221)
Tonnage: 20,597 gross 9,951 net
Dimensions: 637.7 x 72.3 x 39.5 feet
Engines: Triple expansion with low pressure turbine by builder 20,000 s.h.p. 17 knots
Passengers: 356 first, 250 second, 949 third

1914: Launched: March 25 as a passenger liner for Hamburg-Südamerikanische Dampfschifffahrts-Gesellschaft, Hamburg. August: fitting out temporarily suspended. December: converted into an armed merchant cruiser, and aft funnel was removed. **1915**: February 8: commissioned as VINETA but due to relatively slow speed, was rejected by the German Navy and returned to her builders. Renamed CAP POLONIO, work commenced on her completion as a passenger liner. **1916**: August: delivered but spent the rest of the war laid up at Hamburg. **1919**: April 15: surrendered to the Allied Shipping Commission and allocated initially to the United States and then to the Shipping Controller, London. May: the Union-Castle Mail S.S. Co. Ltd. was given the management contract. After one voyage to Cape Town during which time, she was unable to exceed 12 knots, she was refitted at the Devonport Dockyard and in September, the management was changed to Peninsular & Oriental Steam Nav. Co., London for one round voyage to Bombay. **1920**: July: laid up in Sandon Dock, Liverpool. **1921**: July: bought back by Hamburg Sud and refitted by Blohm & Voss. **1922**: February 16: first voyage from Hamburg to River Plate. **1931**: Reconditioned but laid up because of the Depression. **1933**: September: used as an exhibition ship at Hamburg. **1935**: June: sold for demolition to M. Stern AG, Essen. **1936**: 1st quarter broken up alongside the Technical Works of Norddeutscher Lloyd at Bremerhaven.

EDUARD WOERMANN (ML)

VALDIVIA (WSS)

Right - PRINZESSIN in Shaw Savill colours
Below - CAP POLONIO leaving Cape Town after
her only voyage for Union-Castle (ML)

WORLD WAR TWO

EMPIRE SUCCESS Steel screw steamer (UC managed 1940-1946/7)
O.N. 167430
Builders: A.G. "Vulkan", Hamburg (yard no: 636)
Tonnage: 6,009 gross 3,646 net 9,440 deadweight
Dimensions: 451.5 x 58.2 x 26.8 feet
Engines: Triple expansion by builder 820 h.p. 3,500 i.h.p. 11.5 knots

1921: Launched: February 21 as cargo ship HAGEN for for Deutsch-Australische Dampfschiffs-Gesellschaft (DADG), Hamburg. Completed: May. **1926**: DADG taken over by Hamburg-Amerikanische-Packetfahrt-Actien-Gesellschaft (HAPAG), Hamburg. **1928**: Low pressure geared turbine added to engine. **1939**: September 8: taken as prize in Durban by South African forces for the South African Government, and renamed IXIA. **1940**: January 30: transferred to Ministry of Shipping (Ministry of War Transport from May 1941) and renamed EMPIRE SUCCESS - management awarded to Union-Castle Mail S.S. Co. Ltd. September 30: damaged in air raid 5 miles east of Peterhead. **1946/7**: Union-Castle management ceased. **1948**: January: laid up at Liverpool with machinery and collision damage. August 22: scuttled in the Bay of Biscay with cargo of poison gas shells.

BOSKOOP Steel screw steamer (UC managed 1940-1945)
O.N. Not applicable
Builders: Van der Giessen & Zonen's Scheep. N.V., Krimpen (yard no: 575)
Tonnage: 5,538 gross 3,320 net 9,000 deadweight
Dimensions: 400.6 x 58.3 x 26.4 feet
Engines: Double compound by Rotterdam Dry Dock Co. 522 h.p.
2,500 i.h.p. 11.25 knots
Passengers: 48

1927: Completed: July as a cargo-passenger ship for Koninklijke Nederlandsche Stoomboot Maatschappij, Amsterdam. **1940**: July 22: chartered by the Ministry of Shipping (Ministry of War Transport from May 1941) and placed under Union-Castle Mail S.S. Co. Ltd. management. **1945**: July 3: returned to owners. **1960**: Sold to Spanish breakers Desguaces y Salvamentos S.A. Arrived Aviles: June 21.

EMPIRE ARUN Steel screw steamer (UC managed 1941-1946)
O.N. 159353
Builders: Stabilimento Tecnico Triestino, Trieste (yard no: 736)
Tonnage: 5,490 gross 3,417 net 8,599 deadweight
Dimensions: 391 x 54 x 29.6 feet
Engines: Geared steam turbines by Franco Tosi, Legnano 600 h.p.
3,500 i.h.p. 11 knots

1922: Completed: November as cargo ship SAVOIA for Navigazione Libera Triestina S.A., Trieste. **1936**: In the State reorganisation of Italian shipping, SAVOIA was allocated to Lloyd Triestino, name unchanged. **1941**: February 11: on voyage Kismayu-Diego Suarez, intercepted by HMS HAWKINS and taken as a war prize. March 6: requisitioned by the Ministry of War Transport and placed under Union-Castle Mail S.S. Co. Ltd. management. **1942**: Renamed EMPIRE ARUN. **1946**: August 26: Union-Castle management ceased. **1947**: Sold Ormos Shipping Co. Ltd. (Goulandris Bros.), London, renamed GRANLAKE. **1949**: Transferred to Cia. Maritima del Este, S.A., Panama - renamed DRYAD. **1951**: Sold Hikari Kisen K.K. & Others, Tokyo - renamed SHIRANESAN MARU. **1952**: Re-engined with a double compound (4 cyl.) engine with low pressure turbine built by Uraga Dock Co. **1954**: Sold to Mitsui Kinkai Kisen K.K. & Others, Tokyo. **1956**: Sold to Hokuyo Suisan K.K., Tokyo - subsequently converted into a crab cannery. **1962**: Sold Nichiro Gyogyo K.K., Tokyo, renamed TAINICHI MARU. **1969**: Broken up at Utsumi, Shodo-gun, Kagawa Pref. August 9: demolition commenced.

BOSKOOP at Cape Town (JM)

EMPIRE SUCCESS (HAN 1524/1617)

EMPIRE ARUN as SAVOIA (BS)

SONTAY Steel screw steamer (UC managed 1941-1946)
O.N. 168326
Builders: Bremer Vulkan, Vegesack (yard no: 596)
Tonnage: 8,917 gross 5,485 net 9,645 deadweight
Dimensions: 468.8 x 58.2 x 32.6 feet
Engines: Triple expansion by builder 3,700 i.h.p. 12 knots
Passengers: 17 first, 662 third

1921: Launched: June 2 as BAYERN for Hamburg-Amerikanische-Packetfahrt-Actien-Gesellschaft (HAPAG), Hamburg. The first new German passenger ship to be completed after World War I. August: completed and placed on the Hamburg-New York route. **1924**: Transferred to the River Plate service - passengers reduced to 568 third class. **1929**: Low pressure steam turbine added: 5,000 i.h.p. Service speed increased to 13 knots. **1936**: January: sold to Union Maritime Méditerranéenne an associate company of Messageries Maritimes and renamed SONTAY. Registered at Dunkerque, she was used to transport Légionnaires to Indo-China. Accommodation modified to 20 first, 25 second and 944 troops. **1939**: Requisitioned by French Government as a troop transport. **1941**: January 26: on voyage Tamatave-Dakar intercepted by British "Force T" 120 miles from Sainte Marie and taken to Durban. February 17: requisitioned by the Ministry of Shipping (Ministry of War Transport from May 1941) and placed under Union-Castle Mail S.S. Co. Ltd. management. **1946**: July 4: end of war service. Returned to owners. **1948**: Owners became Cie. des Messageries Maritimes, Dunkerque. **1955**: Sold at Kobe to Transp. Marit. Atlantida, (principals, Wheelock, Marden & Co. Ltd., Hong Kong) Panama, renamed SUNLOCK. **1959**: January: sold to Miyachi & Co., while laid up at Kasado. March: broken up at Sakai, Japan.

CHARLES L.D. Steel screw motorship (UC managed 1941-1942)
O.N. 135620
Builders: Götaverken A/B, Gothenburg (yard no: 475)
Tonnage: 5,267 gross 3,126 net
Dimensions: 428.2 x 56.6 x 25.7 feet
Engines: Oil 4S SA 8-cyl by builder 653 h.p. 3,600 b.h.p. 12.7 knots

1933: Completed: January as cargo ship CHARLES L.D. for Louis Dreyfus & Cie., Paris - registered at Dunkerque **1940**: Along with the rest of the Louis Dreyfus fleet, she was sequestered by the Vichy Government because the Dreyfus family was Jewish, and taken over by a specially formed company, Cie. Marseillaise de Navigation Coloniale (Soc. d' Arm. de Gérance & d' Etudes Techniques,

managers), Marseilles and renamed PROCYON. **1941**: March 24: intercepted by HMS LEANDER 200 miles off Mauritius and requisitioned for use by the Ministry of Shipping (Ministry of War Transport from May 1941). Placed under Union-Castle Mail S.S. Co. Ltd. management. Reverted to CHARLES L.D. **1942**: December 9: on voyage from Karachi and New York to the Clyde with general cargo, torpedoed and sunk by German submarine U 553, 500 miles east of Cape Farewell, Greenland (59.02N-30.45W). 36 lives were lost.

JEAN L.D. Steel screw motorship (UC managed 1941-1945)
O.N. 168690
Builders: Soc. des Ateliers et Chantiers de France, Dunkerque (yard no: 157)
Tonnage: 5,795 gross 3,333 net 9,130 deadweight
Dimensions: 446 x 57.1 x 25.8 feet
Engines: Oil 2S SA 8-cyl by Cie. de Construction Mecaniques Sulzer, St. Denis 912 h.p. 3,300 i.h.p. 14 knots

1935: Completed: March as cargo ship JEAN L.D. for Louis Dreyfus & Cie., Paris - registered at Dunkerque. **1940**: Along with the rest of the Louis Dreyfus fleet, she was sequestered by the Vichy Government because the Dreyfus family was Jewish, and taken over by a specially formed company, Cie. Marseillaise de Navigation Coloniale (Soc. d' Arm. de Gérance & d' Etudes Techniques, managers), Marseilles - renamed BÉTELGEUSE. **1941**: January 21: after slipping out of Dakar with a number of other Vichy ships, intercepted near Cape Town by Royal Navy. February 17: requisitioned by the Ministry of Shipping (Ministry of War Transport from May 1941) and placed under Union-Castle Mail S.S. Co. Ltd. management. Reverted to JEAN L.D. **1945**: March 16: end of war service. Returned to Cie. Marseillaise de Navigation Coloniale and renamed BÉTELGEUSE. Used to carry arms and tanks to Tonkin in French Indo-China - on arrival, she was attacked by the Vietnamese and a number of crew were killed and wounded. **1947**: After Cie. Marseillaise de Navigation Coloniale was wound up, she was returned to her original owners, Louis Dreyfus & Cie., and once again became JEAN L.D. **1954**: Transferred to the Louis Dreyfus British affiliate company, Buries Markes Ltd., London, and renamed LA LAGUNA. **1958**: Sold to Alma Shipping Co. S.A., Panama (Ceres Shipping Co. Ltd., London, managers) - Greek flag, renamed ACHAEAN. **1960**: Transferred to Transfruit Shipping Co. Ltd. - same managers. **1965**: Sold to Transropodi S.A., Geneva. Haitian flag, renamed TRANSRODOPI 1. **1966**: Transferred to Greek flag. **1968**: Sold to Navigation Maritime Bulgare, Varna, renamed ALPHECCA. Sold to Japanese breakers, Seibu Kogyo K.K. June 3: arrived Yawata for demolition.

CHARLES L.D. (LD)

JEAN L.D. (JM)

SONTAY (LD)

COMPIÈGNE Steel twin screw steamer (UC managed 1941-1945)
O.N. 168259
Builders: Ateliers & Chantiers de La Loire, Saint-Nazaire
Tonnage: 9,986 gross 5,959 net
Dimensions: 478.7 x 59.2 x 27.3 feet
Engines: Geared steam turbines by builder 966 h.p. 5,600 i.h.p. 13 knots
Passengers: 117 first, 84 second, 110 third, 526 steerage

1922: Launched: November 18 as JAMAÏQUE, one of a trio of passenger liners ordered from the yard by La Compagnie des Chargeurs Rèunis, Le Havre. **1923**: June: completed as COMPIÈGNE, she was taken over by the French Government and sold to Soc. des Services Contractuels des Messageries Maritimes - placed on the Marseilles-Indo-China line. **1941**: November 3: on voyage Indo-China-Madagascar-Marseilles, intercepted 350 miles from Port Elizabeth by a force led by HMS DEVONSHIRE and taken to East London. November 8: requisitioned by the Ministry of War Transport and placed under Union-Castle Mail S.S. Co. Ltd. management. **1944**: January: like TOUAREG, became a Merchant Navy training ship. Based at Gravesend, she remained in service until September 21, 1945. **1946**: Returned to her owners. February 25: left London for Rouen in tow of the tugs EMPIRE AID and EMPIRE MARY. Arrived Rouen three days later. July 27: at Fécamp, hit a mine and was beached. Refloated, she was towed to Dunkerque for repairs. **1948**: After a lengthy period of lay up and rebuilding, placed on the Indian Ocean service. **1949**: Title transferred to Min. de la Marine Marchande (Messageries Maritimes, managers). **1954**: April 13: arrived at La Seyne for demolition by Soc. de Material Naval du Midi.

VILLE DE STRASBOURG Steel screw steamer (UC managed 1941-1945)
O.N. 168236
Builders: The North of Ireland S.B. Co. Ltd., Londonderry (yard no: 95)
Tonnage: 7,159 gross 4,237 net
Dimensions: 411 x 53.8 x 28.3 feet
Engines: Triple expansion by J. G. Kincaid & Co. Ltd., Greenock 710 h.p. 3,750 i.h.p. 12 knots
Passengers: 36 first, 50 second

1920: Launched: August 20 as one of four passenger cargo ships ordered from the yard by Cie. Havraise Péninsulaire de Navigation á Vapeur, Le Havre. October: surplus to requirements on completion, she was chartered to Soc. des Services Contractuels des Messageries

Maritimes, Paris, and registered at Dunkerque. **1928**: Bought by Soc. des Services Contractuels des Messageries Maritimes and used on routes from North Europe to Australia via Suez and to New Caledonia via Panama. **1941**: March 2: intercepted by HMS SHROPSHIRE 100 miles south-east of Cape St. Mary, Madagascar and taken to Durban. March 24: requisitioned by the Ministry of Shipping (Ministry of War Transport from May 1941). November: placed under Union-Castle Mail S.S. Co. Ltd. management. **1943**: January 7: torpedoed by German submarine U 371 at Bougie. Towed to Algiers where she suffered further damage during an air raid. **1945**: April: end of war service. October: returned to owners. **1948**: Owners became Cie. des Messageries Maritimes, Dunkerque. **1952**: Sold to the British Iron & Steel Corporation (BISCO) for demolition by Metal Industries Ltd. December 6: arrived Faslane for demolition.

VILLE DE MAJUNGA Steel screw steamer (UC managed 1941-1945)
O.N. 168806
Builders: Ateliers et Chantiers de la Seine Maritime (Worms & Cie.), Le Trait (yard no: 60)
Tonnage: 4,972 gross 2,923 net 7,265 deadweight
Dimensions: 392.9 x 53.5 x 24.8 feet
Engines: Triple expansion by builder 370 h.p. 2,500 i.h.p. 11 knots
Passengers: 22

1931: Completed: July as a cargo ship for La Cie. Havraise Péninsulaire de Nav. à Vapeur, Le Havre. **1934**: Owners reorganised as Nouvelle Cie. Havraise Péninsulaire de Navigation. **1941**: March 1: intercepted by HMS CORNWALL 450 miles west of Cape Town. March 5: requisitioned by the Ministry of Shipping (Ministry of War Transport from May 1941). November: placed under Union-Castle Mail S.S. Co. Ltd. management. **1942**: December 6: loaded with munitions, went aground briefly at Oudekraal on the west side of the Cape Peninsula. Pulled off the rocks by the local tugs T. S. McEWAN and JOHN X. MERRIMAN, she was towed to Cape Town for repairs, which were only completed in July 1943. **1945**: April 18: end of war service. Returned to owners. **1957**: Sold to Wallem & Co. Ltd., Hong Kong and registered in the name of Pan Norse S.S. Co. S.A., Panama. Renamed CATHAY. **1959**: June 10: arrived for demolition in Hong Kong by Dah Chong Hong Ltd.

COMPIÈGNE at Gravesend in July 1945 (LD)

VILLE DE STRASBOURG (AM)

VILLE DE MAJUNGA

SAMSTEEL Steel screw steamer (UC managed 1943-1947)
O.N. 169643
Builders: California Shipbuilding Corporation, Los Angeles, California
(yard no: 233)
Tonnage: 7,219 gross 4,380 net 10,000 deadweight
Dimensions: 422.8 x 57 x 34.8 feet
Engines: Triple expansion by Iron Fireman Manufacturing Co., Portland, Oregon 2,500 i.h.p. 11 knots

1943: Launched: July 31 as U.S. standard dry-cargo Liberty ship JAMES H. ROBINSON for United States War Shipping Administration but delivered August 15 as SAMSTEEL on bareboat charter to Ministry of War Transport under Union-Castle Mail S.S. Co. Ltd. management. From keel laying to delivery took 35 days. August 29: sailed for Hobart, Tasmania with SAMPAN. **1945**: May 18: left Cardiff at the start of a 605 day voyage which ended at Liverpool January 13, 1947. **1947**: April 18: end of war service. September: returned to the USA - name reverted to JAMES H. ROBINSON. **1961**: November: sold to Union Minerals & Alloys Corp. for scrap at Panama City.

SAMPAN Steel screw steamer (UC managed 1943-1947)
O.N. 169802
Builders: California Shipbuilding Corporation, Los Angeles, California
(yard no: 234)
Tonnage: 7,219 gross 4,380 net 10,000 deadweight
Dimensions: 422.8 x 57 x 34.8 feet
Engines: Triple expansion by Iron Fireman Manufacturing Co., Portland, Oregon 2,500 i.h.p. 11 knots

1943: Launched: August 4 as U.S. standard dry-cargo Liberty ship WILLIAM I. KIP but delivered August 17 for United States War Shipping Administration as SAMPAN on bareboat charter to Ministry of War Transport under Union-Castle Mail S.S. Co. Ltd. management.

From keel laying to delivery took 36 days. August 29: sailed for Hobart, Tasmania with SAMSTEEL. **1947**: October 24: end of war service. Returned to the USA - name reverted to WILLIAM I. KIP. **1962**: Broken up at New Orleans by Southern Scrap Material Co.

SAMFLORA Steel screw steamer (UC managed 1943-1947)
O.N. 169677
Builders: Bethlehem-Fairfield Shipyard Inc., Baltimore, Maryland
(yard no: 2268)
Tonnage: 7,219 gross 4,380 net 10,000 deadweight
Dimensions: 422.8 x 57 x 34.8 feet
Engines: Triple expansion by General Machinery Corp., Hamilton, Ohio 2,500 i.h.p. 11 knots

1943: Launched: November 9 as U.S. standard dry-cargo Liberty ship ISRAEL J. MERRITT for United States War Shipping Administration but completed same month as SAMFLORA for bareboat charter to Ministry of War Transport under Union-Castle Mail S.S. Co. Ltd. management. December 1: left Baltimore for New York and Alexandria, Egypt, presumably with SAMTRENT. **1944**: November 4: left Manchester at the start of the longest voyage ever undertaken by a Union-Castle managed or owned ship. When she returned to Ellesmere Port on November 1, 1946, she had travelled for 747 days, 10 hours and 20 minutes and covered 75,207 miles. **1947**: April: sold to Putney Hill S.S. Co. Ltd. (Counties Ship Management Ltd., managers) and renamed PRIMROSE HILL. **1949**: February: transferred to London and Overseas Freighters Ltd. (Counties Ship Management Ltd., managers). **1950**: Renamed LONDON VENDOR. **1952**: January: sold to Arequipa Compania Naviera S.A. (Dimitrios L. Condylis), Panama and renamed CABANOS. **1963**: Sold to Compania Santa Helle SA (D. J. Papadimitriou' Sons), Panama and renamed THEBEAN. **1964**: Transferred to Compania Santa Roberta S.A., Greece. **1968**: Sold to Koshin Sangyo K.K., Japan for scrap. March 14: arrived at Onomichi for demolition.

SAMSTEEL

SAMFLORA (JC)

SAMPAN at Cape Town(JM)

SAMBUFF/FRANK A. VANDERLIP Steel screw steamer (UC managed 1943-1948)   **O.N.** 169700
Builders: Bethlehem-Fairfield Shipyard Inc., Baltimore, Maryland (yard no: 2269)
Tonnage: 7,219 gross 4,380 net 10,000 deadweight
Dimensions: 422.8 x 57 x 34.8 feet
Engines: Triple expansion by General Machinery Corp., Hamilton, Ohio 2,500 i.h.p. 11 knots

1943: Launched: November 13 as U.S. standard dry-cargo Liberty ship FRANK A. VANDERLIP for United States War Shipping Administration but delivered November 20 as SAMBUFF on bareboat charter to Ministry of War Transport under Union-Castle Mail S.S. Co. Ltd. management. From keel laying to delivery took 36 days. December 12: sailed Baltimore for Port Said. **1944**: Name reverted to FRANK A. VANDERLIP after complaint by his widow. **1948**: April 8: end of war service. Returned to the USA. **1967**: May: demolition commenced by Lipsett Division, Luria Bros. & Co. Inc., Kearny, New Jersey.

SAMTRENT Steel screw steamer (UC managed 1943-1947)
O.N. 169724
Builders: New England Shipbuilding Corp., South Portland, Maine (yard no: 2199)
Tonnage: 7,219 gross 4,380 net 10,000 deadweight
Dimensions: 422.8 x 57 x 34.8 feet
Engines: Triple expansion by General Machinery Corp., Hamilton, Ohio 2,500 i.h.p. 11 knots

1943: Launched: November 24 as U.S. standard dry-cargo Liberty ship PERCY D. HAUGHTON for United States War Shipping Administration but delivered November 30 as SAMTRENT on bareboat charter to Ministry of War Transport under Union-Castle Mail S.S. Co. Ltd. management. From keel laying to delivery took 50 days. December 1: left South Portland for New York and Suez, presumably with SAMFLORA. **1947**: October 10: end of war service. Returned to the USA. **1962**: April: scrapped Mobile by Pinto Island Metal Co.

TOUAREG Steel screw steamer (UC managed 1944-1945)
O.N. 168812
Builders: Soc. Anon. des Ateliers et Chantiers de Provence, Port de Bouc
Tonnage: 5,135 gross 3,123 net
Dimensions: 390.3 x 50.2 x 25.7 feet
Engines: Triple expansion by builder 376 h.p. 3,800 i.h.p. 13 knots
Passengers: 124 cabin, 580 deck

1924: Completed: June as a passenger-cargo ship for Cie. Marseillaise de Nav. à Vapeur (Cie. Fraissinet), Marseilles. Placed on Marseilles-North Africa service. **1936**: Owners restyled Cie. de Navigation Fraissinet. **1940**: September 16: on voyage Manioca-Port Bouet with deportees from the Congo and Cameroon, captured by HMS DRAGON and taken to Takoradi. **1942**: January 27: requisitioned by the Ministry of War Transport and placed under Elder Dempster Lines Ltd. management - registered at Liverpool. **1943**: April: management transferred to Moxey, Saxon & Co. Ltd. and again in December to Cie. Maritime Française, London. **1944**: January: like COMPIÈGNE, became a Merchant Navy training ship. February: management transferred to Union-Castle Mail S.S. Co. Ltd. Based on the River Thames, she remained in service until April 18, 1945. **1945**: October: returned to owners and sold to Belgian breakers Van Heyghen Frères, Ghent. **1946**: January 5: arrived at Ghent for demolition.

GERUSALEMME Steel twin screw steamer (UC managed 1945-1947)
O.N. not applicable
Builders: Cantiere San Rocco S.A., San Rocco (yard no: 29)
Tonnage: 8,052 gross 4,566 net 5,965 deadweight
Dimensions: 443.6 x 53.1 x 24.9 feet
Engines: Geared steam turbines by Stabilimento Tecnico Triestino, Trieste 5,500 s.h.p. 13 knots
Passengers: 73 first, 85 second, 408 third

1916: Launched as CRACOVIA, the last passenger ship ordered for Österreichischer Lloyd (Lloyd Austriaco), Trieste. Due to the war, construction work ceased. **1919**: January: with Trieste in Italian hands after the war, Lloyd Austriaco was converted from an Austrian to an Italian firm, Lloyd Triestino. **1920**: November: completed and placed on Lloyd Triestino's Trieste-Bombay route. **1924**: Converted to oil burning. **1933**: Transferred to Adriatic-Mediterranean service. **1934**: Renamed GERUSALEMME. **1937**: January: in the second State reorganisation of Italian shipping, she was allocated to "Adriatica" and continued to operate on Mediterranean routes. **1940**: May: undertook a voyage from Trieste to Durban. June 5: arrived Durban. June 10: Italy entered the war. June 11: after leaving Durban and to avoid capture by HMS RANCHI, she was run aground on the border with South Africa at Oro Point, Moçambique. Refloated, she was laid up in Lourenço Marques where she remained for four years. **1943**: October 10: taken over by the Portuguese authorities. **1944**: March 28: taken over by the Ministry of War Transport after the Italian Armistice, she was moved to Durban. **1945**: January: requisitioned by the Admiralty, she was converted at Durban into a 388-450 capacity hospital ship. April 16: sailed for Australia under Union-Castle Mail S.S. Co. Ltd. management. August 8 suffered a fire at Manus Anchorage, Admiralty Island. **1946**: On duty in Singapore and Hong Kong. **1947**: April 14: returned to owners at Venice. Chartered to Italia Soc. Anonima di Navigazione for use on Italia's South America and Central America routes. **1949**: Chartered to Lloyd Triestino for Genoa-East Africa-Durban route. **1952**: January 17: arrived Venice after final voyage. Sold for scrap. March 19 arrived at Savona for demolition.

SAMTRENT (AM)

FRANK A. VANDERLIP (WSS)

TOUAREG at Cape Town (JM)

GERUSALEMME at Singapore in Union-Castle colours

SAIL, CURRIE FAMILY & CHARTERED SHIPS

CURRIE SAILING SHIPS

STIRLING CASTLE (1) Iron full-rigged sailing ship (Castle 1863-1873)
O.N. 47454
Builders: Robert Napier & Sons, Glasgow (yard no: 108)
Tonnage: 1,165 gross
Dimensions: 209.1 x 34.2 x 22.4 feet

1863: Launched: April 4 as first Donald Currie Castle full-rigged sailing ship for Liverpool-Calcutta trade. Registered: June 26. **1865**: Transferred to London-Calcutta service. Still registered at Liverpool. **1873**: April: reported missing on voyage from New York to London.

WARWICK CASTLE (1) Iron full-rigged sailing ship (Castle 1863-1870)
O.N. 47486
Builders: Robert Napier & Sons, Glasgow (yard no: 109)
Tonnage: 1,166 gross
Dimensions: 209.4 x 34.2 x 22.4 feet

1863: Launched: May 20 as full-rigged sailing ship for Liverpool-Calcutta trade. Registered: July 29. **1865**: Transferred to London-Calcutta service. Still registered at Liverpool. **1870**: Sold to Robert Reid Paterson, Greenock but only transferred to Greenock register in April 1871. **1872**: June: sold to the Lancaster Shipowners' Co. Ltd. Registered at Lancaster - the first in the company (later known as the Lancashire Shipping Co. Ltd.) with a CASTLE name. **1880**: Reduced to barque rig. **1886**: Sold to Warwick Castle Co. Ltd. (W. J. Woodside & Robert Workman, managers), Belfast. **1890**: New managers: W. J. Woodside & Co. Sold to A/S Cimbria (O. C. Hirth, manager) Kolding, Denmark - renamed CIMBRIA. **1894**: A/S Cimbria (C. J. Haas, manager). **1897**: A/S Cimbria (S. W. Bruun, manager). **1905**: September: sold to Paola Luigia Schiaffino, Vedova (Cognato Schiaffino) Genoa, name unchanged. **1911**: January: sold for scrap to G. Pittaluga, Genoa. 4th quarter scrapped.

ROSLIN CASTLE (1) Iron full-rigged sailing ship (Castle 1863-1883)
O.N. 47536
Builders: Robert Napier & Sons, Glasgow (yard no: 111)
Tonnage: 1,170 gross
Dimensions: 208.1 x 33.9 x 22.5 feet

1863: Launched: July 30 as full-rigged sailing ship for Liverpool-Calcutta trade. Registered: September 22. **1865**: Transferred to London-Calcutta service but still registered at Liverpool. **1883**: April: sold to Charles Barrie, Dundee with ARUNDEL CASTLE, PEMBROKE CASTLE and TANTALLON CASTLE - reduced to barque rig and renamed LONDON. **1892**: December: 27: wrecked 10 miles north-east of the Rebecca Shoals Light on the Florida Keys whilst on voyage from Pensacola to Rio de Janeiro with cargo of deals.

PEMBROKE CASTLE (1) Iron full-rigged sailing ship (Castle 1863 – 1883)
O.N. 47575
Builders: Robert Napier & Sons, Glasgow (yard no: 112)
Tonnage: 1,171 gross
Dimensions: 208.2 x 33.9 x 22.5

1863: Launched: September 15 as full-rigged sailing ship for Liverpool-Calcutta trade. Registered: October 29. **1865**: Transferred to London-Calcutta service but still registered at Liverpool. **1883**: April: sold to Charles Barrie, Dundee with ARUNDEL CASTLE, ROSLIN CASTLE and TANTALLON CASTLE - reduced to barque rig and renamed GLASGOW. **1893**: December 25: Lost masts and abandoned in the Atlantic (47.04N-20.47W) whilst on voyage from Carrizal, Chile to Middlesbrough with cargo of manganese.

ARUNDEL CASTLE (1) Iron full-rigged sailing ship (Castle 1864-1883)
O.N. 51029
Builders: Robert Steele & Co., Greenock (yard no: 40)
Tonnage: 1,042 gross
Dimensions: 203 x 33.6 x 21.9 feet

1864: Launched: September 2 as full-rigged sailing ship for Liverpool-Calcutta trade. Registered: November 28. **1865**: Transferred to London-Calcutta service but still registered at Liverpool. **1883**: April: sold to Charles Barrie, Dundee with PEMBROKE CASTLE, ROSLIN CASTLE and TANTALLON CASTLE - reduced to barque rig - renamed CHITTAGONG. **1896**: October: sold to A/S Imperator (J. A. Henschien), Lillesand, Norway as IMPERATOR. **1901**: May: arrived East London, South Africa badly damaged after voyage Buenos Aires-East London with cargo of wheat. **1905**: September: sold to A. R. Watson, East London - became a coal hulk. **1917**: Bought by the South Africa Co. Ltd. (Mitchell Cotts & Co., managers). **1918**: Re-rigged as barque and reverted to CHITTAGONG, registered at East London. Owners restyled as British Africa Shipping & Coaling Co. Ltd. (Mitchell Cotts & Co.), Cape Town. **1920**: September: sold to C. E. Zalocostas, Piraeus - renamed ANNITSA ZALOCOSTA. **1922**: 4th quarter scrapped in Italy.

KENILWORTH CASTLE (1) Iron full-rigged sailing ship (Castle 1864-1871)
O.N. 51033
Builders: Robert Steele & Co., Greenock
Tonnage: 1,062 gross
Dimensions: 209 x 33.8 x 21.3 feet

1864: September: completed as full-rigged sailing ship for Liverpool-Calcutta trade. Registered: December 3. **1865**: Transferred to London-Calcutta service but still registered at Liverpool. **1871**: March: Missing on voyage from Calcutta to London.

TANTALLON CASTLE (1) Iron full-rigged sailing ship (Castle 1865-1883)
O.N. 51458
Builders: Robert Steele & Co., Greenock (yard no: 44)
Tonnage: 1,057 gross
Dimensions: 210.3 x 33.9 x 22 feet

1865: Launched March 9 as full-rigged sailing ship for London-Calcutta trade but registered at Liverpool: March 30. **1868**: Broke the London-Calcutta-London record: 80 days out and 78 days home. **1883**: April: sold to Charles Barrie, Dundee with ARUNDEL CASTLE, PEMBROKE CASTLE, and ROSLIN CASTLE - reduced to barque rig and renamed DACCA. **1898**: June: sold to A/S Macca (Martin Bruusgaard, manager) Drammen, Norway - renamed MACCA. **1911**: July: sold to Dutch breakers and scrapped at Dordrecht.

MACCA ex TANTALLON CASTLE (NOR)

CHITTAGONG ex ARUNDEL CASTLE (JN)

CARNARVON CASTLE (1) Iron full-rigged sailing ship (Castle 1867-1888)
O.N. 56826
Builders: Barclay, Curle & Co., Stobcross (yard no: 161)
Tonnage: 1,200 gross
Dimensions: 229 x 36.3 x 22.1 feet

1867: Launched: June 20 as full-rigged sailing ship for London-Calcutta trade. First Donald Currie sailing ship registered at London: July 31. **1888**: Sold to Carnarvon Castle Ship Co. Ltd. (Sinclair & Ellwood), London - name unchanged. Reduced to barque rig. **1895**: September: sold to Wakeham & Co., London. **1896**: New owner O. S. S. Piper, Port Talbot - still registered at London. **1897**: December: sold to Flügge, Johannsen & Lubinus, Hamburg - renamed NÜRNBERG. **1905**: Sold to A/S Nürnberg (Sven O. Stray, manager), Christiansand - name unchanged. **1910**: January 10: abandoned in the North Atlantic (35.30N-27.24W) after being dismasted in a gale on voyage from Isla Lobos de Tierra, Peru to Antwerp with a cargo of guano. Crew rescued by Scrutton & Sons' SALYBIA (3,352/1904).

CARISBROOKE CASTLE Iron full-rigged sailing ship (Castle 1868-1889)
O.N. 60879
Builders: Barclay, Curle & Co., Stobcross (yard no: 177)
Tonnage: 1,490 gross
Dimensions: 239.4 x 37.6 x 22.9 feet

1868: Launched: September 28 as full-rigged sailing ship for London-Calcutta trade. Also made several voyages to Australia & New Zealand. Registered at London: November 2. **1889**: June: sold to Charles Barrie, Dundee - renamed ERROL. **1900**: September: sold to A. P. Ulriksen med flere (with others), Mandal, Norway - reduced to barque - name unchanged. **1909**: June 18: On voyage in ballast from Chimbote, Peru to Newcastle, New South Wales wrecked on Middleton Reef, 415 miles east from Clarence River Heads, New South Wales. The first officer and two crewmen were swept overboard, fourteen others including the master, his wife and children subsequently died of exhaustion, exposure and dehydration. July 12: five survivors were picked up by Union S.S. Co. of New Zealand's TOFUA (4,345/1908).

CLUNY CASTLE (1) Iron full-rigged sailing ship (Castle 1883-1889)
O.N. 89500
Builders: Barclay, Curle & Co. Ltd., Whiteinch (yard no: 323)
Tonnage: 1,986 gross
Dimensions: 276.5 x 41.2 x 24 feet

1883: Launched: November 29. Last Donald Currie full-rigged sailing ship. Registered: December 19. **1889**: Sold to Rowena Ship Co. Ltd. (W. Letham, manager), Greenock - renamed ROWENA. **1892**: Same owners (Ferguson & Letham, managers). **1895**: Same owners (James Rae, manager). Some time between 1897 and 1900, reduced to a barque. **1889**: Sold to Ferguson & Letham Greenock. **1900**: Sold to Edenmount Sailing Ship Co. Ltd. (R. Ferguson & Co., managers), Greenock. **1906**: Sold to Ship Cambrian Hills Ltd. (W. Thomas Sons & Co. Ltd., managers), Liverpool. Remained on Greenock register. **1911**: County Shipping Co. Ltd. (W. Thomas Sons & Co. Ltd., managers). **1914**: February: sold to Rederi A/B Delfin (George Stenius manager) Helsingfors (Helsinki) - Russian flag - name unchanged. **1915**: February: lost rigging on voyage from Gulfport, Mississippi to Buenos Aires and arrived in Barbados in damaged condition. **1916**: October 17: sold by auction, still lying at Barbados in damaged condition, to Rederi A/B Finlandecia (V. Sundman, manager) Helsingfors. Subsequently towed to Mobile and rerigged with pitchpine masts. **1918**: Now under Finnish flag. **1921**: Same owner - new manager G. Takolander. Sold to Johan Frederik Gadd, Åbo, Finland. Remained registered at Helsingfors. **1924**: March: sold for demolition at Antwerp.

ERROL ex CARISBROOKE CASTLE (NOR)

CARNARVON CASTLE

ROWENA ex CLUNY CASTLE (JN)

CURRIE FAMILY SHIPS

ICELAND Iron screw steamer (Currie family transfer 1872-1873)
O.N. 65761
Builders: Built by J. & G. Thomson, Glasgow (yard no: 116)
Tonnage: 1,474 gross 946 net
Dimensions: 251.6 x 31.7 x 16.6 feet
Engines: 2-cyl. compound by builder 150 h.p. 900 i.h.p. 9.5 knots
 Trials: 11.5 knots
Passengers: 20 passengers

1871: Launched: February 22 as North Sea trader for Leith, Hull and Hamburg S.P. Co., Leith. Registered: May 15. **1872**: Chartered with GOTHLAND to George H. Payne's Cape & Natal Steam Navigation Co., London for two years. With the company unable to continue the charter, the service was taken over by Donald Currie. Arrived Cape Town: February 24. **1873**: May: transferred to Cape-Natal coastal run. October: replaced by FLORENCE and returned to North Sea trade. **1876**: December 18: ran ashore on Texel Island while on passage from Liverpool to Hamburg, and was a constructive total loss.

GOTHLAND Iron screw steamer (Currie family transfer 1872 - 1873)
O.N. 62298
Builders: Built by J. & G. Thomson, Glasgow (yard no: 115)
Tonnage: 1,469 gross 943 net
Dimensions: 251.6 x 32.0 x 16.6 feet
Engines: 2-cyl. compound by builder 150 h.p. 900 i.h.p. 9.5 knots
Passengers: not known

1871: Launched: January 10 as a North Sea trader for Leith, Hull and Hamburg S.P. Co., Leith. Registered: February 28. **1872**: Chartered with ICELAND to George H. Payne's Cape & Natal Steam Navigation Co., London for two years. With the company unable to continue the charter, the service was taken over by Donald Currie. Arrived Cape Town: March 10. **1873**: Back on North Sea run. **1874**: July 5: ran down and sank brig ANN POTTS of Blyth off the Lofoten Islands while on passage from Archangel to Dundee - five crew lost from sunken vessel. **1878**: May: transferred to Liverpool register. James Currie, managing owner. **1899**: New engine fitted: triple expansion by D. Rollo & Sons, Liverpool - 199 h.p. **1915**: January: sold to the Admiralty as a potential blockship but never used. **1919**: Sold to Claude Langdon Ltd. of London, name unchanged. **1922**: Sold to Dampfschiffs Reederei Friedrich Bremer, Rostock and renamed TRUDE BREMER. **1924**: 4th quarter broken up in the Netherlands.

WESTMORELAND Iron screw steamer (Currie family transfer 1872)
O.N. 63325
Builders: Built by J. & G. Thomson, Glasgow (yard no: 114)
Tonnage: 1,372 gross 878 net
Dimensions: 240.5 x 31.9 x 16 feet
Engines: 2-cyl. compound by builder 150 h.p. 900 i.h.p. 9.5 knots
Passengers: not known

1870: Launched: November 8 as North Sea trader for Liverpool and Hamburg Line (Donald Currie & Co.), Liverpool. **1871**: Registered: January 9. **1872**: April: transferred for one voyage to South Africa in place of the ill fated DOVER CASTLE which was sent on charter to South America for her maiden voyage. Arrived Cape Town: May 28.

1885: New engine fitted: 164 h.p. triple expansion by D. Rollo & Sons, Liverpool. **1912**: May: sold to E. Lemoigne, Marseilles and renamed MOGADOR. **1913**: May: sold to J. Perisini, Marseilles, name unchanged. **1915**: Sold to L. Castel, Cette, name unchanged. **1916**: November 4: attacked with gunfire by German submarine U 34 when 38 miles off Puerto de Soller, Majorca, captured and later sunk by explosives.

ELIZABETH MARTIN Iron screw steamer (Currie family transfer 1872-1882)
O.N. 67907
Builders: Robert Napier & Sons, Glasgow (yard no: 316)
Tonnage: 1,246 gross 809 net
Dimensions: 250.6 x 30.2 x 21.5 feet
Engines: 2-cyl. compound by builder 130 h.p. 500 i.h.p. 8.5 knots
Passengers: not known

1872: Launched: May 23 for Donald Currie's brother Alexander Currie & Co., Greenock and named in honour of their mother. Registered: September 24. Chartered to Donald Currie for Cape mail service. Arrived Cape Town: November 23. **1874**: Used as a transport during the Ashantee war. **1875**: September: inaugurated new service to Port Alfred (for Grahamstown) but unable to discharge cargo because of rough weather. **1879**: transferred to South African coastal run. July: was the first Castle ship on the new Durban-Mauritius route. **1882**: October: sold to Panhellenic S.S. Co., Piraeus and renamed ATHENS. **1891**: Renamed SAMOS, same owners. **1916**: October 3: captured, shelled and sunk by German submarine U 35, 70 miles south of Minorca (38.30N-04.05E) on voyage from Cette with a cargo of iron ore.

COURLAND Iron screw steamer (Currie family transfer 1872-1895)
O.N. 65777
Builders: Robert Napier & Sons, Glasgow (yard no: 317)
Tonnage: 1,241 gross 803 net
Dimensions: 250.4 x 30.2 x 21.5 feet
Engines: 2-cyl. compound by builder 130 h.p. 500 i.h.p. 8.5 knots
Passengers: not known

1872: Launched: July as North Sea trader for Leith, Hull and Hamburg S.P. Co., Leith. Registered: October 21 (Donald Currie, managing owner) and placed on Cape mail run. Arrived Cape Town: December 26. **1879**: Transferred to Cape-Natal coastal run. **1879**: Cape-Natal service extended to Mauritius. **1881**: March: transferred to London register. April: undertook a cruise to the Mediterranean with Donald Currie and party. **1884**: July 27 to October 9: chartered as a transport for the Egyptian Campaign. **1891**: September 22: ran ashore at Kosi River, 60 miles south of Delagoa Bay but refloated and taken to Cape Town for repair. **1895**: August: sold to Dada Abdullah & Co., Durban for service between Durban and Bombay, name unchanged. **1901**: February: sold to Hajee Ismail Hassum, Bombay, name unchanged. June - sold to Bombay Steam Navigation Co. Ltd., Bombay, name unchanged. Hajee Ismail Hassum was also the owner of the Bombay Steam Navigation Co. Ltd., the Indian coastal company which was established in 1845. **1916**: February 3: requisitioned as an Indian Expeditionary Force transport, apparently for service at Basra. **1918**: April 4: returned to owners. **1926**: February: broken up at Bombay.

ICELAND (AG)

GOTHLAND (AG)

ELIZABETH MARTIN (AG)

COURLAND (TH)

LAPLAND Iron screw steamer (Currie family transfer 1872-1880s)
O.N. 65778
Builders: Barclay, Curle & Co., Stobcross (yard no: 226)
Tonnage: 1,269 gross 822 net
Dimensions: 250.3 x 30.0 x 21.7 feet
Engines: 2-cyl. compound by builder 130 h.p. 500 i.h.p. 8.5 knots
Passengers: not known

1872: Launched: September 17 as North Sea trader for Leith, Hull and Hamburg S.P. Co., Leith. Registered: November 5 (Donald Currie, managing owner) and placed on Cape mail run. **1873**: Arrived Cape Town: 22.1. Later transferred to Cape-Natal coastal service and eventually returned to the North Sea trade. **1882**: August: carried 221 Norwegian emigrants to Natal. **1903**: March: sold to Glen & Co., Glasgow and renamed SHUNA. **1906**: December: transferred to Scandinavian Steamship Co. Ltd. (Glen & Co., managers), Glasgow. **1907**: March: sold to J. Philicas, Piraeus and renamed SOFIA M. **1908**: Sold to M. Vernicos & Co., Piraeus, name unchanged. **1911**: Sold to J. Cappolo, Constantinople and renamed SCUTARI. **1912**: Reverted to ownership of M. Vernicos & Co. and renamed VARVARA. **1913**: May 9: ran ashore in Sound of Mull, west of Scotland, while on passage from Glasgow to Gothenburg but later refloated. **1915**: Sold to D. Pavlatos & Co. Piraeus, name unchanged. **1917**: July 18: torpedoed and sunk by German submarine U 32 approximately 115 miles east of Capo Spartivento, Calabria, Italy while on passage from Patras to the United Kingdom with a cargo of currants.

FLORENCE Iron screw steamer (Currie family transfer 1873-1877: Castle 1877-1889)
O.N. 52609
Builders: Robert Napier & Sons, Glasgow (yard no: 116)
Tonnage: 497 gross 370 net
Dimensions: 189.4 x 25.5 x 14.5 feet
Engines: 2-cyl. simple by builder 80 h.p. 340 i.h.p. 8 knots **Trials**: 9.9 knots
Passengers: 10

1865: Launched: May 11 as North Sea trader for Leith, Hull and Hamburg S.P. Co., Leith. Registered: June 16 - Donald Currie, registered owner. **1873**: Transferred to Cape-Natal coastal service. Lengthened to 219.3 feet and given new engine: 70 h.p. 2-cyl compound by John Penn & Sons, London. New tonnage: 616 gross

382 net. Arrived Cape Town: October 9 and replaced ICELAND. **1877**: March: transferred to London register - the only clipper-stemmed steamer in the Donald Currie's South African fleet. **1889**: September: sold to Idare-i Mahsusa (Ottoman Steam Nav. Co.), Constantinople and renamed GIRIT (Crete) - the same company bought the former ROMAN (1) in 1895 and PEMBROKE CASTLE in 1906. **1910**: August: Idare-i Mahsusa was reorganised as Osmanli Seyrisefain Idaresi. **1919**: Broken up.

STETTIN Iron screw steamer (Currie family transfer 1876-1878)
O.N. 51068
Builders: Barclay, Curle & Co., Stobcross (yard no: 122)
Tonnage: 706 gross 558 net
Dimensions: 222.0 x 29.1 x 15 feet
Engines: 2-cyl. simple by builder 112 h.p.
Passengers: not known

1864: Launched: November 12 as North Sea trader for Leith, Hull and Hamburg S.P. Co., Leith. Registered: December 13. **1874**: Donald Currie, managing owner. **1876**: Transferred for two years to Cape mail service as a replacement for WINDSOR CASTLE. New engine fitted: 98 h.p. 2-cyl. compound by R. Napier & Sons, Glasgow. **1877**: Arrived Cape Town: January 5 - used mainly on Cape-Natal run. **1876**: James Currie, managing owner. **1878**: Returned to North Sea trade. **1885**: February 23: broke shaft off Firth of Tay while on passage from Dundee to Hamburg, and towed into Leith by company's BERLIN. **1889**: Engines tripled by Hawthorn & Co., Leith. **1924**: Laid up at Leith. **1933**: October: sold to Thomson & McGregor, Bo'ness for breaking up.

LAPLAND (TH)

FLORENCE (TH)

STETTIN at Durban (DUR)

EARLY CHARTERS

BOSPHORUS Iron screw steamer (Union charter 1858)
O.N. 25154
Builders: C. J. Mare & Co., Blackwall
Tonnage: 445 gross 330 net
Dimensions: 173.6 x 24.3 x 14.6 feet
Engines: 2-cyl. simple by Maudslay, Sons & Field 80 h.p.
Passengers: Few saloon

1849: Launched: July 7 for the London-Levant service of General Screw S.S. Co., London. Registered: July 17. **1850**: November 11: General Screw was awarded the England-Cape mail contract. BOSPHORUS took the first sailing in December. **1851**: Arrived Cape Town: January 27. **1854**: June: final General Screw sailing from the Cape. **1857**: August: sold to William Inman (trading as Inman Line), Liverpool. Sent to St. Vincent with coals for CITY OF MANCHESTER, which had been chartered to the East Indies Company as a troopship during the Indian Mutiny. **1858**: January: chartered to Union Line to carry mails to the Cape. Arrived Cape Town: February 13. June: after return to owners, placed on Liverpool-Antwerp cargo and passenger feeder service. **1882**: Converted into a barge - register closed November 14.

MARSDIN Iron screw steamer (Castle charter 1872)
O.N. 60205
Builders: Humphrys & Pearson, Hull (yard no: 9)
Tonnage: 1,424 gross 1,131 net
Dimensions: 258.0 x 34.3 x 18.2 feet
Engines: 2-cyl. compound by C. D. Holmes & Co., Hull 150 h.p. 9 knots

1870: Launched: February 19 for Brownslow, Lumsden & Co., Hull. Registered: May 20. **1872**: Chartered by Donald Currie for the Cape mail service. Arrived Cape Town: April 5. **1878**: Acquired by Thos. Wilson, Sons & Co., Hull. **1889**: March: renamed LIVORNO. **1901**: April: sold to Sambur S.S. Co. Ltd. (T. B. Stott & Co., managers), Liverpool - same name. **1907**: June 1: whilst on voyage from Piteå to Liverpool with cargo of wood, stranded at Valsörarna, Gulf of Bothnia. Refloated but constructive total loss and later scrapped at Wasa.

WARRIOR Iron screw steamer (Castle charter 1872)
O.N. 56837
Builders: Randolph Elder & Co., Glasgow (yard no: 39)
Tonnage: 1,502 gross 956 net
Dimensions: 264.7 x 32.2 x 21 feet
Engines: 2-cyl. simple by builder 200 h.p. 1,060 i.h.p. 10 knots
Passengers: 100 first

1867: Completed for London, Belgium, Brazil & River Plate Royal Mail S.S. Co. (Tait & Co.), London for London, Belgium, Brazil & River Plate Royal Mail S.S. Co. as CITY OF LIMERICK for London-South American mail and passenger service. Registered: August 15. **1870**: London, Belgium, Brazil & River Plate Royal Mail S.S. Co. went into liquidation. Sold to Thos. & Jas. Harrison, Liverpool and

renamed WARRIOR. **1871**: Messrs. N. Griffith and Tate & Co. founded the Cape & Natal Steam Nav Co. which offered a monthly service from London to South Africa via Dartmouth. In May, they chartered WARRIOR. Arrived Cape Town: June 3, having reduced southbound record to just under 27 days. **1872**: Chartered by Donald Currie for the Cape mail service. Arrived Cape Town: April 21. July: sold to Liverpool, Brazil & River Plate S. N. Co., Liverpool (Lamport & Holt). **1873**: Renamed VANDYCK. **1874**: Engines compounded by J. Jones & Sons, Liverpool. **1892**: Became a coal hulk at Rio de Janeiro. **1899**: Broken up in Brazil.

BLADWORTH Iron screw steamer (Castle charter 1872)
O.N. 65237
Builders: Richardson, Duck & Co., Stockton-on-Tees (yard no: 174)
Tonnage: 1,812 gross 1,375 net
Dimensions: 275.4 x 34.6 x 25.5 feet
Engines: 2-cyl. compound by C. D. Holmes & Co., Hull 170 h.p. 9 knots

1871: Launched: June 3 for H. Briggs, Hull who sold her on completion to Brownslow, Lumsden & Co., Hull. **1872**: Chartered by Donald Currie. Arrived Cape Town: August 22. **1873**: Sold to Royal Mail Steam Packet. Co., London. Renamed ESSEQUIBO. **1900**: Sold for scrap at Torre Annunziata.

CALDERA Iron screw steamer (Castle charter 1877)
O.N. 63294
Builders: William Denny & Bros., Dumbarton (yard no: 129)
Tonnage: 1,741 gross 1,051 net
Dimensions: 282.2 x 34.3 x 25 feet
Engines: 2-cyl. simple by builder 350 h.p. 1,571 i.h.p. 13 knots

1868: Launched: June 25. Completed as ASSAM on spec for Peninsular & Oriental S. N. Co., London but the company did not want the vessel. **1870**: Engines compounded by builder - the first by Denny. August: sold to Pacific Steam Navigation Co., Liverpool, and renamed CALDERA. **1874**: February: sold to J. Laird Jnr. Lengthened to 335.5 feet and given new compound engines by Laird & Co., Birkenhead. **1877**: Chartered for two Cape mail voyages to Donald Currie. Arrived Cape Town: April 18. **1879**: May: sold to Cie Générale Transatlantique (French Line) for their Marseilles-New York service - same name. **1886**: November: sold to F. Stumore & Co., London. Name unchanged. **1887**: July 15: lost in collision with British India's GOORKHA (4,104/1881) in the Red Sea (20.30N-38.32E) on voyage Pondichery-Marseille with cargo of groundnuts. AFRICAN (1) also owned by Stumore was lost nearby earlier that year.

SEATER WHITE (BIRD LINE) CHARTERS

PENGUIN Iron screw steamer (Castle charter 1872 & 1878)
O.N. 65765
Builders: Barclay, Curle & Co., Stobcross (yard no: 212)
Tonnage: 1,741 gross 1,123 net
Dimensions: 291.5 x 33.3 x 24.5 feet
Engines: 2-cyl. compound by builder 180 h.p. 9 knots
Passengers: not known

1871: Launched: May 18 for the London-Calcutta service of G. S. Seater & Co., Leith. **1872**: Chartered by Donald Currie for the Cape mail service. Reduced the southbound record to 24 days, 18 hours 15 minutes. Arrived Cape Town: May 2. **1878**: Chartered by Donald Currie as an "extra steamer." **1879**: November 20: ran ashore on Jibbel Zookur Island, Red Sea on voyage London-Calcutta with general cargo and one stowaway. Constructive total loss.

FLAMINGO Iron screw steamer (Castle charter 1876)
O.N. 70761
Builders: Barclay, Curle & Co. Ltd., Whiteinch (yard no: 248)
Tonnage: 1,828 gross 1,209 net
Dimensions: 310 x 33.3 x 25 feet
Engines: 2-cyl. compound by builder 190 h.p. 9 knots
Passengers: not known

1874: Launched: December 10 for the London-Calcutta service of Seater, White & Co., Leith. **1875**: Registered: February 8. **1876**: Chartered by Donald Currie for the Cape mail service. Arrived Cape Town: October 5. **1879**: July 30: collided with ALCAZAR (477/1873) of Liverpool, 14 miles north-west of Ushant during fog - the latter sank. **1881**: November 16: stranded in St. Margaret's Bay, Kent on voyage London-Calcutta with general cargo. Constructive total loss. December: broke in two.

GANNET Iron screw steamer (Castle charter 1878)
O.N. 70789
Builders: Barclay, Curle & Co. Ltd., Whiteinch (yard no: 282)
Tonnage: 1,824 gross 1,187 net
Dimensions: 301.6 x 33.2 x 25.1 feet
Engines: 2-cyl. compound by builder 220 h.p.
Passengers: not known

1878: Launched: February 20 for the London-Calcutta service of Seater, White & Co., Leith. Sister of DUART CASTLE. Registered: March 28. Chartered by Donald Currie as an "extra steamer." Arrived Cape Town: December. **1882**: February 14: ran ashore one mile west of Seaford Head, Sussex on voyage Calcutta-London with general cargo. Constructive total loss. March 1: broke in two.

SEA GULL Iron screw steamer (Castle charter 1879)
O.N. 62289
Builders: Barclay, Curle & Co., Stobcross (yard no: 200)
Tonnage: 1,564 gross 997 net
Dimensions: 272.6 x 33.0 x 24.5 feet
Engines: 2-cyl. compound by builder 150 h.p.
Passengers: not known

1870: Launched: June 16 for the London-Calcutta service of G. S. Seater & Co., Leith. Registered: August 18. **1879**: Chartered by Donald Currie for one southbound voyage on the Cape run. August 21: wrecked at Golfar, Maldive Islands on voyage Calcutta-London with general cargo and one passenger. Constructive total loss.

MAJOR CHARTERED CARGO SHIPS

LAMPORT & HOLT "M" CLASS

MILLAIS Steel screw steamship (UC chartered 1930-36)
O.N. 140536
Builders: Harland & Wolff Ltd., Glasgow (yard no: 460)
Tonnage: 7,224 gross 4,457 net 8,470 deadweight
Dimensions: 434.9 x 55.3 x 35.2 feet
Engines: Quadruple expansion by builder 808 h.p. 4,500 i.h.p. 13.5 knots
Refrigerated space: 349,102 cubic feet

1916: Launched: November 8 as refrigerated cargo ship for Liverpool, Brazil & River Plate S.N. Co., (Lamport & Holt Ltd., managers), Liverpool. **1917**: May: completed. Placed on Liverpool-River Plate service. **1930**: During the South African fruit season chartered by Union-Castle Mail S.S. Co. Ltd. This continued up to 1936. **1934**: Following the collapse of the Kylsant group, Lamport & Holt was placed in receivership and a new company was established as Lamport & Holt Ltd. **1938**: January: sold to Blue Star Line Ltd., London and renamed SCOTTISH STAR. **1942**: February 20: on voyage London-Buenos Aires with general cargo and whiskey, torpedoed and sunk in South Atlantic (13.24N-49.36W) by Italian submarine LUIGI TORELLI. Four lives were lost.

MOLIÈRE/ NELA Steel twin screw steamer (UC chartered 1930-37)
O.N. 137510
Builders: Russell & Co., Port Glasgow (yard no: 676)
Tonnage: 7,206 gross 4,427 net 8,280 deadweight
Dimensions: 440 x 56.2 x 35.6 feet
Engines: Quadruple expansion by David Rowan & Co. Ltd., Glasgow 885 h.p. 4,500 i.h.p. 12 knots
Refrigerated space: 322,958 cubic feet

1915: Launched: September 9 as refrigerated cargo ship for Liverpool, Brazil & River Plate S.N. Co., (Lamport & Holt Ltd., managers), Liverpool. **1916**: March: Placed on Liverpool-River Plate service. **1929**: Ownership transferred to Nelson Steam Navigation Co. Ltd. (H. & W. Nelson Ltd., managers), Liverpool. Name unchanged. **1930**: During the South African fruit season chartered by Union-Castle Mail S.S. Co. Ltd. This continued for most years up to 1937. **1932**: August: ownership transferred to Royal Mail Lines Ltd., London. **1933**: Renamed NELA. **1945**: November: sold to Van Heyghen Frères, Ghent for demolition.

MURILLO/ NALON Steel twin screw steamer (UC chartered 1930-37)
O.N. 137478
Builders: Russell & Co., Port Glasgow (yard no: 674)
Tonnage: 7,206 gross 4,432 net 8,280 deadweight
Dimensions: 440 x 56.2 x 35.6 feet
Engines: Quadruple expansion by Harland & Wolf Ltd., Belfast 887 h.p. 4,500 i.h.p. 12 knots
Refrigerated space: 316,307 cubic feet

1915: Launched: March 19 as refrigerated cargo ship for Liverpool, Brazil & River Plate S.N. Co., (Lamport & Holt Ltd., managers), Liverpool. September: completed. Placed on Liverpool-River Plate service. **1930**: Ownership transferred to Nelson Steam Navigation Co. Ltd. (H. & W. Nelson Ltd., managers), Liverpool. Name unchanged. During the South African fruit season chartered by Union-Castle Mail S.S. Co. Ltd. This continued for most years up to 1937. **1932**: Ownership transferred to Royal Mail Lines Ltd., London. Renamed NALON. **1940**: November 6: bombed by enemy aircraft and sunk off the west coast of Ireland (53.57N-15.03W) on voyage from Beira, via Cape Town to Clyde, with general cargo and copper.

MEISSONIER/ NASINA Steel twin screw steamer (UC chartered 1930-35)
O.N. 137456
Builders: Russell & Co., Port Glasgow (yard no: 673)
Tonnage: 7,206 gross 4,432 net 8,250 deadweight
Dimensions: 440 x 56.2 x 35.6 feet
Engines: Quadruple expansion by Harland & Wolf Ltd., Belfast 887 h.p. 4,500 i.h.p. 12 knots
Refrigerated space: 316,307 cubic feet

1914: Launched: December 21 as refrigerated cargo ship for Liverpool, Brazil & River Plate S.N. Co., (Lamport & Holt Ltd., managers), Liverpool. **1915**: June: completed. Placed on Liverpool-River Plate service. **1930**: Ownership transferred to Nelson Steam Navigation Co. Ltd. (H. & W. Nelson Ltd., managers), Liverpool. Name unchanged. During the South African fruit season chartered by Union-Castle Mail S.S. Co. Ltd. This continued up to 1935. **1932**: August: ownership transferred to Royal Mail Lines Ltd., London. **1933**: Renamed NASINA. **1935**: Sold to Soc. Anon. Cooperativa di Nav. Garibaldi, Genoa. Renamed ASMARA. **1937**: Transferred to Italian Navy as transport with Garibaldi remaining as managers. **1943**: August 11: torpedoed and sunk by submarine HMS UNSHAKEN two miles east of Petagne Island, near Brindisi.

MARCONI Steel twin screw steamer (UC chartered 1930-37)
O.N. 137532
Builders: Harland & Wolff Ltd., Glasgow (yard no: 462)
Tonnage: 7,402 gross 4,519 net 8,270 deadweight
Dimensions: 440.8 x 56.2 x 35.6 feet
Engines: Quadruple expansion by Harland & Wolf Ltd., Belfast 887 h.p. 4,500 i.h.p. 13.5 knots
Refrigerated space: 328,043 cubic feet

1916: Launched: April 19 as refrigerated cargo ship for Liverpool, Brazil & River Plate S.N. Co., (Lamport & Holt Ltd., managers), Liverpool. **1917**: February: completed. Placed on Liverpool-River Plate service. **1918**: February 27: torpedoed east of Gibraltar (36.3N-4.17W) by German submarine U 35 whilst on voyage Marseilles-River Plate in ballast. Two lives were lost and she was towed to Gibraltar for repairs. **1930**: During the South African fruit season chartered by Union-Castle Mail S.S. Co. Ltd. This continued up to 1937. **1934**: Following the collapse of the Kylsant group, Lamport & Holt was placed in receivership and a new company was established as Lamport & Holt Ltd. **1937**: Sold to Marconi Steamship Co. Ltd. (Kaye, Son & Co. Ltd., managers), Liverpool. **1941**: May 21: on voyage Manchester-Rio Grande in ballast (part of Convoy HX.126), torpedoed and sunk in North Atlantic (58N-41W) by German submarine U 109. Twenty two lives were lost.

NALON (JC)

Left - MOLIÈRE (AD) and MARCONI (FH) - below - in Union-Castle livery during the fruit season

FORT CARILLON Steel screw steamer (UC chartered 1946-1949)
O.N. 168482
Builders: Davie Shipbuilding & Repairing Co. Ltd., Lauzon, Quebec
(yard no: 542)
Tonnage: 7,129 gross 4,244 net 10,000 deadweight
Dimensions: 424.6 x 57.2 x 34.9 feet
Engines: Triple expansion by Dominion Engineering Works Ltd., Montreal
2,500 i.h.p. 10 knots

1943: Completed: May as Canadian built "North Sands" type standard
dry-cargo ship FORT CARILLON for the Dominion of Canada.
Bareboat charter to Ministry of War Transport, Dodd, Thomson &
Co. Ltd. managers. **1946**: September: chartered to Union-Castle Mail
S.S. Co. Ltd. as a supplementary cargo vessel. **1949**: Management
transferred to Maclay & McIntyre Ltd., Glasgow. **1950**: Sold to Fort
Carillon Shipping Co. Ltd. (J. P. Hadoulis Ltd., managers), London
and renamed MOUNT ROYAL. **1956**: Sold to Callao Cia Nav. S.A.
(Giannis A. Kairis), Monrovia and renamed MONTE RICO. **1960**:
Transferred to Greek registry, same owner, Andros, and renamed
LAMYRIS. **1963**: Sold to Stamle Cia Nav. S.A. (Franco Shipping
Co.), Andros and renamed BARBARINO. **1968**: January 7: wrecked
during severe weather whilst at anchor in ballast outside the port of
Novorissisk in the Black Sea. Abandoned as constructive total loss.

ANDALUCIA STAR Steel screw motorship (UC chartered 1976-1977)
O.N. 365848
Builders: Smiths Dock Co. Ltd., Middlesbrough (yard no: 1329)
Tonnage: 9,784 gross 5,428 net 11,092 deadweight
Dimensions: 471.4 x 69.9 x 41.6 feet
Engines: Burmeister & Wain design oil 2S SA 9-cyl. by J. G. Kincaid & Co.
Ltd., Greenock 17,400 b.h.p. 23 knots
Refrigerated space: 466,226 cubic feet

1975: Launched: January 14 as fast-refrigerated cargo ship for Blue
Star Line Ltd., (Blue Star Ship Management Ltd., managers), London.
October: completed. **1976**: June: chartered to Union-Castle Mail S.S.
Co. Ltd. (Cayzer, Irvine, managers) for mail service in place of
PENDENNIS CASTLE and painted in Union-Castle colours. **1977**:
August: returned to owners. **1982**: Chartered by the British
Government as supply ship during the Falklands War, with helicopter
pad fitted aft. **1984**: September: sold to Highvale Ltd. (Wallem Ship
Management (Hong Kong) Ltd., managers), Hong Kong, and renamed
FIFE. **1986**: September: sold to Adriatic Reefer Corp. Inc. (Atlanship
S.A., managers), Monrovia, renamed ORANGE STAR and converted
into a refrigerated orange juice concentrate tanker. **1999**: Still in
service.

FORT CARILLON (HAN 1788/1872)

ANDALUCIA STAR (IS)

LOCATION OF CASTLES

The names of the castles usually reflected the interests of whoever was in charge of the company at the time. Donald Currie often chose names of places close to his Garth estate in Scotland, whilst during the Owen Philipps era, Welsh names were given. Cornish castles i.e. Pendennis Castle featured during the brief chairmanship of the Cornishman George Christopher whilst other Scottish names appeared when the Cayzer family took charge.

Currie also used names when seeking to gain political favour - Hawarden Castle, for example, was the home of Prime Minister Gladstone.

ALNWICK CASTLE Northumberland
Seat of the Dukes of Northumberland (Percy family) since 1309, this 12th century castle stands above the town on the south bank of the River Alne.

ARMADALE CASTLE Isle of Skye
Gothic style castle built in 1815 at Sleat, the southern arm of Skye. Seat of the Lord Macdonald of Sleat, the hereditary chiefs of Skye with the Macleods of Dunvegan.

(AMROTH CASTLE) Dyfed
Late 18th century castillated house 5 miles from Tenby. Grounds now a caravan park.

(ARDTORNISH CASTLE) Highlands
The 14th century ruin overhangs the sea near Loch Aline and commanded the Sound of Mull by signalling Duart and Aros Castles. The ancient domain of the Lord of the Isles

AROS CASTLE Isle of Mull
The ruins of the 13th century castle stands facing Ardtornish across the Sound of Mullany. After many owners, it was last garrisoned in 1690 by the Campbells.

ARUNDEL CASTLE Sussex
The residence of the Dukes of Norfolk for over 500 years. 11th century castle built by Roger Montgomery overlooks the River Arun.

ATHLONE CASTLE Westmeath, Eire
Standing on the River Shannon, the castle has drum-shaped towers and curtain walls. It was built by John de Grey, Bishop of Norwich in 1210.

AVONDALE CASTLE Strathclyde
The ancient ruins of the castle are situated in the town of Strathaven.

BALMORAL CASTLE Grampian
6 miles north-east of Braemar on the right bank of the River Dee. Bought by Queen Victoria and Prince Albert and rebuilt as a castle mansion in the baronial style.

BAMPTON CASTLE Oxfordshire
Part of the castle (now a private home) exists west of the church. Built by the Earl of Pembroke who obtained license to crenellate in 1325.

BANBURY CASTLE Oxfordshire
Built in the 12th century by the Bishop of Lincoln. Completely demolished in 1648 after damage in the Civil War.

BERWICK CASTLE Northumberland
At the mouth of the Tweed are slight remains of a 12th century castle.

BLOEMFONTEIN CASTLE South Africa
The judicial capital of South Africa and the former provincial capital of the Orange Free State.

BRAEMAR CASTLE Grampian
The castle was built on a bluff overlooking the River Dee by the 2nd Earl of Mar in 1628.

HARLECH CASTLE, WALES
List of Passengers
R.M.S. "Windsor Castle"
leaving CAPETOWN 16th April, 1937.

BRATTON CASTLE Wiltshire
An iron-age hill fort on the north-west edge of Salisbury Plain.

CAPETOWN CASTLE South Africa
The oldest building in South Africa, the castle was started in 1666 and completed in 1679. Much of the brick was brought out from Holland.

CARISBROOKE CASTLE Isle of Wight
South-west of Newport stands the remains of a mighty 12th century castle built on the site of a Roman fort. Charles I was imprisoned her in 1647.

CARLISLE CASTLE Cumberland
Sited on the highest point along the River Eden, the castle was begun by William II and completed by David I of Scotland. Apart from the Norman keep, it has been remodelled many times.

CARLOW CASTLE Co. Leinster, Eire
Only a few fragments remain of the late 12th century motte and bailey castle built by Hugh de Lacey overlooking the River Barrow.

CARNARVON CASTLE Gwynedd
Situated at the south-west end of the Menai Straits, this impressive castle was begun in 1283-4 as part of Edward I's plan for control of Wales.

CAWDOR CASTLE Highlands
5 miles from Nairn is the picturesque mediaeval castle with central tower dating from the late 14th century. The moat is still crossed by drawbridge.

CHEPSTOW CASTLE Gwent
A Norman fortress built in the late 11th century stands on a cliff above the River Wye. 15 miles north-east of Newport, it was built as a defence for the Roman road to South Wales.

CLUNY CASTLE Highlands
2 miles east of Laggan, the present castle was built by MacPherson of Cluny in the early 19th century to replace an earlier castle destroyed by fire in 1746.

COMRIE CASTLE Tayside
The diminutive castle was built by the Menzies family in the 13th century. 4 miles west of Aberfeldy, beside the River Lyon, the ruin stands in an orchard.

CONWAY CASTLE Gwynedd
Built between 1283 and 1287 the castle has eight identical towers built round two wards. The stonework is virtually complete.

CORFE CASTLE Dorset
A majestic Norman ruin situated at a cleft in the spine of the Purbeck Hills.

CRAWFORD CASTLE Strathclyde
On the bank of the Clyde, built to dominate the river valley. Held in the 13th century by the Lindsays who later became the Earls of Crawford.

DOUNE CASTLE Central
North-west of Stirling on the River Teith, the castle is believed to have been built by Murdock, 2nd Duke of Albany in the 14th century.

DOVER CASTLE Kent
Built in the late 12th and early 13th centuries, it commands an important harbour and the shortest sea route to the continent.

DRAKENSBERG CASTLE Natal, South Africa
The highest portion of the great eastern escarpment of the South African plateau.

DROMORE CASTLE Co. Down, Northern Ireland
Remains of this motte and bailey castle can still be seen on the Upper Lagan River.

DRUMMOND CASTLE Tayside
Near Crief, built by Sir John Drummond in the last 15th century. Mostly rebuilt after the Civil War and added to in Victorian times. Home of the Earls of Ancaster.

DUART CASTLE Isle of Mull
Standing on a rocky site at the entrance to the Sound of Mull, the castle was built in the 13th century with additions in the 16th and 17th centuries and completely restored in the 1930s.

DUBLIN CASTLE Eire
The castle stands on high ground west of Dame Street and was built between 1208 and 1220 and has been altered many times over the years.

DUNBAR CASTLE East Lothian
Built on the cliffs as early as 856. Partially dismantled in 1568, the ruins still stand above the harbour.

DUNDRUM CASTLE Co. Down, Northern Ireland
Situated on the almost landlocked Dundrum Bay, to the north-east of the Mourne Mountains stands the ruin of the Norman keep.

DUNLUCE CASTLE Co. Antrim, Northern Ireland
Built in the 13th century by the Earls of Ulster, this Anglo-Norman ruin stands on top of a basaltic rock separated from the mainland by a 20 foot wide chasm.

DUNNOTTAR CASTLE Grampian
One mile south of Stonehaven stands this spectacular castle overlooking the sea. It was partially dismantled after the Jacobite rebellion of 1715. The ruin of tower and chapel date from the 14th century.

DUNOLLY CASTLE Strathclyde
The remains of an 11th century keep crown an 80 foot rock surrounded by sea on three sides overlooking Loch Linnhe.

DUNROBIN CASTLE Highlands
The castle overlooks the Moray Firth and has parts dating back to the early 14th century. The historic home of the Sutherland family.

DUNVEGAN CASTLE Isle of Skye
Erected in the 9th century, the home of the Chiefs of Macleod for over 500 years.

DURBAN CASTLE South Africa
A seaport on the coast of Natal

DURHAM CASTLE Durham
The castle lies to the north of the cathedral. Existing buildings date from 1070 but much renewed at later dates. Now used by Durham University.

EDINBURGH CASTLE Lothian
Dominating the city, the building may have started as early as the 11th century with many alterations over the years.

GALWAY CASTLE Co. Galway, Eire
Anglo-Norman castle built in the 13th century by Richard de Burgo. The de Burgo's became the Earls of Ulster.

GARTH CASTLE Tayside
Garth was Sir Donald Currie's Estate near Fortingall.

GLENART CASTLE
No castle can be found for this World War I renaming of GALICIAN

GLENGORM CASTLE Isle of Mull
Standing at the north end of the island, the castle was built in the Scottish baronial style, with a square tower, for James Forsyth of Quinish in 1860.

GLOUCESTER CASTLE Gloucestershire
H.M. Prison was built on the site of the castle, which had been added to from the time of Henry II to Edward IV. By the end of the 17th century the last remains were demolished.

GOOD HOPE CASTLE Cape Town, South Africa
Another name for the castle at Cape Town.

GORDON CASTLE Highlands
The castle was the property of the Gordons of Huntley from the late 15th century. The once 568 foot castle is now much diminished.

GRANTULLY CASTLE Perthshire
2 miles south-west of the village on the Tay River, the castle is mainly 16th century but altered over the years. Also called Grandtully Castle.

GUILDFORD CASTLE Surrey
Well preserved ruins of a 12th century castle built by Henry II stand above the town.

HARLECH CASTLE Gwynedd
25 miles south-east of Carnarvon stands one of Edward I's Welsh Castles. Built of local grey sandstone in 1283-90.

HAWARDEN CASTLE Clwyd
The home of Prime Minister Gladstone, the castle is 7 miles from Chester. Built in 1752 on the original mediaeval site.

KENILWORTH CASTLE Warwickshire
The dramatic ruins of this great castle were built in the early 12th century for Henry II, and turned into a palace in the 16th century for Robert Dudley.

KENYA CASTLE Kenya
A country in East Africa.

KILDONAN CASTLE Isle of Arran
Overlooking Lamlash Bay, the castle now a ruin, was used as a hunting seat by the Scottish Kings when Arran was crown property.

KINFAUNS CASTLE Tayside
Now a hotel, the castle was a castlellated folly built for Lord Gray in 1822 on the site of an earlier house.

KINNAIRD CASTLE Tayside
Overlooking the Carse of Gowrie, the River Tay and the Orchil Hills, the castle dates from the 12th century. Restored in 1855, it is now a private home.

KINPURNIE CASTLE Tayside
The Scottish baronial style house built for Sir Charles Cayzer between 1902 and 1908 on his estate at Newtyle.
LEASOWE CASTLE Cheshire
Two miles west of Wallasey, it started life as an octagonal tower built in 1593 for the Earl of Derby as a stand for watching races. Much altered over the years, the house became the Railwayman's convalescent home.
LISMORE CASTLE Co. Waterford, Eire
Situated on the River Blackwater at the foot of Knockmealdown Mountain, the castle was built in the 12th century. It passed into the hands of Sir Walter Raleigh and later the Dukes of Devonshire.
LLANDAFF CASTLE South Glamorgan
At the east end of the Cathedral Green stands the ruin of the 13th century gate house of this fortified mansion, sometimes known as Bishops Castle.
LLANDOVERY CASTLE Dyfed
On the Towey, 35 miles from its mouth stands the ruins and the keep of this 12th century castle.
LLANGIBBY CASTLE Gwent
2¾ miles south of Usk, on a hilltop stands a fairly small 14th century castle. Also known as Tregrug Castle, it was never completed.
LLANSTEPHAN CASTLE Dyfed
Situated on the peninsula between the River Taf and Tywi, stands the ruin of this Norman Castle. Lord Kylsant was lord of the manor.
METHVEN CASTLE Tayside
About 8 miles west of Perth, the present castle was finished in 1680, and is said to be built on the site of the battle of 1306 when Robert Bruce was defeated soon after his coronation.
NEWARK CASTLE Nottingham
Built on the riverbank of the River Trent, the castle was erected by Bishop Alexander in 1123 and was destroyed by the parliamentarians during the Civil War.
NORHAM CASTLE Northumberland
The great keep of the Norman castle stands high above the River Tweed.
PEMBROKE CASTLE Dyfed
The castle founded in 1097 stands on a promontory almost surrounded by the Pembroke River. The great circular keep dates from 1200 and is 75 feet high. Henry VII was born here in 1457.
PENDENNIS CASTLE Cornwall
Built in 1540 by Henry VIII on the knoll guarding the harbour entrance of Falmouth Bay.
POLGLASS CASTLE Highlands
There is a Polglass village in the Highlands but no evidence of a castle.
PRETORIA CASTLE South Africa
In 1855 the town was named and became a city in 1931. The capital of South Africa.
RAGLAN CASTLE Gwent
Built in the 15th century, this fortified house was much destroyed in the Civil War.
RHODESIA CASTLE Rhodesia
A country in Southern Africa – now Zimbabwe.
RICHMOND CASTLE North Yorkshire
The hill top ruin of the 11th century castle overlooks the River Swale. The 12th century keep is 100 feet high.
RIEBEECK CASTLE Cape Town, South Africa
Jan Van Riebeeck founded Cape Town in 1652 and built the first castle.
RIPLEY CASTLE North Yorkshire
The crenellated house is the home of the Ingilby family since 1350. It has a 15th century gate house and was much altered in the 18th century.
ROCHESTER CASTLE Kent
Standing high above the town and the River Medway to defend the crossing. The keep is one of the best preserved in England.
ROSLIN CASTLE Lothian
Above the village on the Esk stands the ruin of the 14th century stronghold of the 3rd Earl of Orkney.

ROSYTH CASTLE Lothian
On the Firth of Forth, the lands of Rosyth with what remains of the castle were acquired by the government inn1903 to construct a naval base. The castle tower, reachable only at low tide is now surrounded by naval top security.
ROTHERWICK CASTLE Hampshire
Tylney Hall, home of Lord Rotherwick.
ROTHESAY CASTLE Isle of Bute
Sitting at the foot of the Cowal peninsula, the remains of the 13th century castle are surrounded by a deep moat. The castle is still a royal possession.
ROWALLAN CASTLE Strathclyde
Near Killmaurs, the castle dates from 1562 and has twin circular towers flanking the first floor entrance. Home of the Mures of Rowallan.
ROXBURGH CASTLE Borders
Of the 12th century castle, there are scant remains on a grassy mound between the Rivers Tweed and Teviot. In 1460 during a siege James II of Scotland was killed by an exploding cannon.
RUSTENBURG CASTLE Transvaal, South Africa
A fruit-growing town established in 1851.
SANDGATE CASTLE Kent
Built by Henry VIII in 1539 as one of his coastal forts. In 1806 it was so changed it looked more like a Martello Tower.
SANDOWN CASTLE Kent
Just beyond the north end of Deal town are fragments on the shore of the 16th century castle.
SOUTHAMPTON CASTLE Hampshire
Standing near the head of Southampton Water is the site of the castle originally a Saxon fortress. It was partially demolished in 1650.
STIRLING CASTLE Central
The present 15th century castle stands on a sheer 250-foot crag overlooking the Forth River. The origins are unknown but Alexander I of Scotland died within its walls in 1124.
TANTALLON CASTLE Lothian
3 miles east of North Berwick stands the remains of the castle built in 1375 on a headland with 100-foot cliffs on three sides. The stronghold of the Douglas family.
TAYMOUTH CASTLE Tayside
At the eastern end of Loch Tay, 1 mile from Kenmore, it was built in the 19th century on the site of a 16th century castle.
TINTAGEL CASTLE Cornwall
Standing on the north-west coast of Cornwall, the 12th century castle, a ruin for 500 years will always be associated with the Arthurian legend.
TRANSVAAL CASTLE South Africa
A province of South Africa now called Gauteng.
WALMER CASTLE Kent
One of the coastal forts erected by Henry VIII. In the 18th century it was adapted as the official residence of the Lord Warden of the Cinque Ports. The Duke of Wellington died here in1852.
WARWICK CASTLE Warwickshire
8 miles from Stratford the castle is perched on a crag above the River Avon. A fine example of 14th century fortification.
WINCHESTER CASTLE Hampshire
The remains of the Norman castle stand at the western end of the city. The great hall of 1235 is the finest and largest in Britain after Westminster.
WINDSOR CASTLE Berkshire
21 miles from London, the largest castle in England established by William the Conqueror has been changed and added to over the years and is one of the homes of the present royal family.
YORK CASTLE Yorkshire
The castle was built by William the Conqueror in the angle between the River Ouse and Foss.

PASSENGERSHIP INTERIORS

The next section gives a flavour of the interiors on the Union-Castle mailships from the Edwardian era until the final mailships of the 1960s. As taste is a very personal subject the photographs speak for themselves.

BALMORAL CASTLE 1910

Right - the first class dining saloon on the upper deck was overlooked by the lounge balcony (above), whilst the smoking room (bottom) was situated on the boat deck

WINCHESTER CASTLE 1930

Left - first class writing room (TH)
Below - first class cabin-de-luxe (TH)

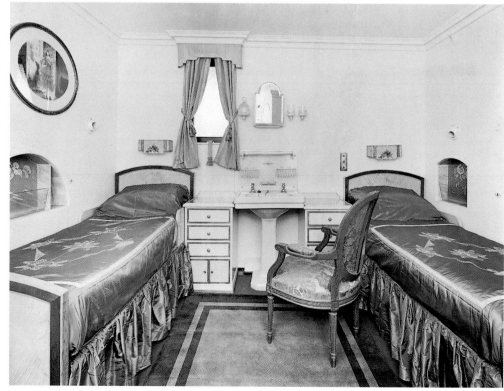

Left - first class dining saloon (TH)
Below - second class lounge (TH)

STIRLING CASTLE 1936

First class: top - long gallery
below - lounge
opposite top - dining saloon
opposite below - cabin-de-luxe

WINDSOR CASTLE 1960

First class lounge

First class drawing room

TRANSVAAL CASTLE 1962

Golden Room

Assembly Room

BIBLIOGRAPHY

Numerous sources, too many to mention, have been used in preparing this book. Of the books on Union-Castle Line, the most outstanding are those written by Marischal Murray and Brian Ingpen. For background on Donald Currie and his method of operation, Andrew Porter's volume on the subject is highly recommended.

The primary sources, key journals and books are listed below:

Primary Sources:
Bureau Veritas
Lloyd's Register
Lloyd's Register Wreck Books
Lloyd's War Losses - World War One
Lloyd's War Losses - World War Two
Lloyd's List
Lloyd's Shipping Index
Lloyd's Confidential Index
Lloyds Weekly Casualty Reports
Mercantile Navy List
World War One Service List
World War Two Ministry of War Transport Service List
Public Record Office, Kew: BT108-110 Ship registers
White papers on Boer War Transport movements
Rhodes Directory of Passenger Steamers

Journals:
Southampton Times & Hampshire Express
The Hampshire Independent
Sea Breezes
Marine News
Ships Monthly
Flotsam & Jetsam
Illustrated London News
The Ship Builder
The South African Shipping News & Fishing Review

Key Books:

BARNICHON, G. French Hospital Ships during the XXᵗʰ Century, Editions Marcel-Didier Vrac, 1998
BELL, A. & MALLETT, A. S. The Pirrie-Kysant Motorships 1915-1932, Mallett & Bell Publications, 1984
BOIS, P. Armements Marseillais, Chambre de Commerce et d'Industrie de Marseille, 1988
BONSOR, N. R. P. North Atlantic Seaway, Brookside Publications, 5 vols. 1980 South Atlantic Seaway, Brookside Publications, 1983
CRUTCHLEY, W. C. My Life at Sea, Chapman & Hall, 1912
DUNN, L. Ships of the Union Castle Line, Adlard Coles, 1954;
Passenger Liners, Adlard Coles, 1961;
Famous Liners of the Past - Belfast Built, Adlard Coles, 1964
GIBBS, C. R. Vernon, British Passenger Liners of the Five Oceans, Putnam, 1963
GREEN, E. & MOSS, M. A Business of National Importance - the Royal Mail Shipping Group, 1902-1937, Methuen, 1982
HAWS, D. Merchant Fleets Vol.18 Union, Castle & Union-Castle Lines, Duncan Haws, 1990; Clan, Houston, Turnbull Martin & Scottish Tankers, Duncan Haws, 1997

INGPEN, B. D. South African Merchant Ships, A. A. Balkema, 1979;
Mailships of the Union-Castle Line, Fernwood Press, 1994;
Safmarine 50, Safmarine & Fernwood Press, 1996
KLUDAS, A. Great Passenger Ships of the World, Patrick Stephens, 6 vols. 1975 to 1992;
Die Schiffe der deutsche Afrika-Linien 1880-1945, Stalling, 1975;
Die Schiffe der Hamburg-Amerika Linie 1847-1970 (with Herbert Bischoff), Koehlers, 1979;
Die Seeschiffe des Norddeutschen Lloyd 1920-1970, Koehlers, 1992
KNIGHT, E. Union-Castle at War 1914-1918, Union-Castle, 1920
KNOX-JOHNSON, R. The Cape of Good Hope: a maritime history, Hodder & Stoughton, 1989
LANFANT, Commandant Historique de la Flotte Des Messageries Maritimes 1851-1975, 1979
LANGENSIEPEN B. & GÜLERYÜZ, The Ottoman Steam Navy, Conway Maritime Press, 1995
LYON, D. J. The Denny List, National Maritime Museum, 1976
MABER, J. M. North Star to Southern Cross, T. Stephenson & Sons, 1967
MALLETT, A. S. The Union-Castle Line - a celebration in photographs and company postcards, Ship Pictorial Publications, 1990;
Idyll of the Kings, World Ship Society, 1980
MITCHELL, W. H. & Sawyer, L.A. The Cape Run, Terence Dalton, 1987;
Empire Ships, Lloyds of London Press, 1990;
British Standard Ships of World War 1, Sea Breezes, 1968;
Liberty Ships, Lloyds of London Press, 1985
MOSS, M. & HUME, J. R. Shipbuilders to the World – 125 years of Harland & Wolff, The Blackstaff Press, 1986
MURRAY, M. Ships and South Africa, Oxford University Press, 1935
The Union-Castle Chronicle, Longmans, 1953
NEWALL, P. Cape Town Harbour 1652 to the present, Portnet, 1993
PABST, R. & INGPEN, B. D. Maritime South Africa: a pictorial history, Janes, 1985
PORTER, A. Victorian Shipping Business & Imperial Policy - Donald Currie, the Castle Line & Southern Africa, Royal Historical Society, 1986
RABSON, S. & O'DONOGHUE, K., P & O, A Fleet History, World Ship Society, 1989
RANCE, A. B. Shipbuilding in Victorian Southampton, Southampton University, 1981
RANKIN, S. Shipbuilding in Rotherhithe - Greenland Dock & Barnard's Wharf, Dockside Studio, 1999
SPINDLER, Rear Adm. Der Kneg zur See: Der Handelskrieg mit U-booten, Volumes 1 to 5, Mittler & Sons, 1932-1966
TENNANT, A. J. British Merchant Ships sunk by U-boats in the 1914-1918 War, The Starling Press Ltd., 1990
TURNER, M. Shipwrecks & Salvage in South Africa - 1505 to the present, C. Struik, 1988
UNIBASO, F. G. Correos Maritimos Españoles, Volumes III & IV, Mensajero 1991 & 1996
WALKER, F. M. Song of the Clyde - a history of Clyde Shipbuilding, Patrick Stephens, 1984
YOUNG, G. Salt in my Blood, Midgley, 1975

INDEX OF SHIP NAMES

This index has been designed for easy access to the histories of individual ships featured in the fleet history. The names of ships in bold capitals are those used during their time in the fleet - the period of service is in brackets. Lower case names are those before or after they were in company service. BBC = Beira Boating Company; ABC = African Boating Company; B&C = British & Commonwealth; MBCS = Messina Bros., Coles & Searle; and UC = Union-Castle.

TROJAN (Union 1880-1900)	46
Trude Bremer	230
Tyne Breeze	150
TYRIAN (Union 1890-94)	170
ULUNDI (2) (MBCS 1922-27)	188
ULUNDI (3) (MBCS 1927-35)	190
Umkuzi	104
Umlazi	138
Umvoti	104
Umzinto	130
UNION (1) (Union 1854-58)	24
UNION (2) (Union 1878-94)	196
VALDIVIA (UC managed 1918-20)	214
Valencia	38
Vandyck	234
Varvara	232
VASCO DA GAMA (UC managed 1917)	212
Vasco Nuñez de Balboa	58
Vasilissa Sophia	208
VENICE (Castle 1878-98)	168
Veronique	88
Victoria W. Kunstmann	134
Victoria	118
VILLE DE MAJUNGA (UC managed 1941-45)	220
VILLE DE STRASBOURG (UC managed 1941-45)	220
Vineta	214
Waganda	210
WALMER CASTLE (1) (Castle 1872-80)	38
WALMER CASTLE (2) (UC 1901-32)	60
WALMER CASTLE (3) (UC 1936-41)	174
War Climax	140
War Duty	138
War Earl	138
War Fervour	138
War Oak	136
War Poplar	136
War Soldier	136
WARRIOR (Castle charter 1872)	234
WARWICK CASTLE (1) (Castle 1863-70)	226
WARWICK CASTLE (2) (Castle 1877-97)	42
WARWICK CASTLE (3) (UC 1931-42)	70
WARWICK CASTLE (4) (UC1946-62)	120
Wassau	46
WESTERN AUSTRALIA (UC managed 1917-19)	210
WESTMORELAND (Currie family transfer 1872)	230
Westmount	88
WHELP (ABC 1902-?)	200
Wilbo	98
William I. Kip	222
WILLIAM MESSINA (MBCS 1925-41)	190
WILLIAM MILLER (Castle 1872)	38
WINCHESTER CASTLE (1) (UC 1930-60)	70
WINCHESTER CASTLE (2) (UC 1965-80)	158
WINCHESTER UNIVERSAL (UC 1965-80)	158
WINDSOR CASTLE (1) (Castle 1872-76)	38
WINDSOR CASTLE (2) (UC 1922-41)	66
WINDSOR CASTLE (3) (UC 1960-77)	78
YORK CASTLE (UC 1901-24)	132
Yungning	24
ZANZIBAR/ZULU (Union 1872-77)	166
Zeta	170

UNION-CASTLE
ROUTES ROUND
AFRICA